faith alone

A Mother and Son's Story
Of Hope and Love

The sun is shining brightly in your life

By
Joy L. Carlson

Joy Carlson

Joy Publishing LLC Minnesota

joypublishingllc.com

ISBN: 979-8-9854004-0-3

Library of Congress Number: Pending

Front cover design by Patty Butkowski
Book design by Katie Lano

First printing edition 2022

Joy L. Carlson
Faith Alone

Joy Publishing LLC
3495 Iresfeld Avenue NW
Maple Lake, MN 55358

joypublishingllc.com

This book is dedicated to my son, Sgt. Kevin Ash, and to all the service men and women who served our country and returned home with the invisible wounds of war. It is dedicated to the mothers, fathers, spouses, siblings, and friends of our service members who have found themselves becoming the caregivers to those who served and can no longer care for themselves.

"The world of books is the most remarkable creation of man. Nothing else that he builds ever lasts. Monuments fall; nations perish; civilizations grow old and die out; and, after an era of darkness, new races build others. But in the world of books are volumes that have seen this happen again and again, and yet live on, still young, still as fresh as the day they were written, still telling men's hearts of the hearts of men centuries dead." –Clarence Shepard Day

Prologue

People often say, "Your life can change in the blink of an eye." While that statement is true, it is also so innocent and naïve. To those of us who have suffered catastrophic changes, it is glib. To those of us who get that call, that unexpected knock on the door, change can seem to come out of nowhere. When I think about how I got to that simple moment, it was not simple or easy. It was not a random moment that brought me to that horrific and climactic event. My life followed a path laced with great happiness, mundane moments, periods of monotony, all woven together to reach that single final moment. To say "your life can change in the blink of an eye" does little to acknowledge all the things that led up to that quiet, dark, and agonizing night. This story is a tapestry. It is filled with love, wonder, happiness, and immense sadness. The pain and agony are beyond our comprehension, but I have lived this life. It is my story.

Chapter 1

I love early mornings. The sun slowly rises above the horizon until it explodes into brilliant yellows, oranges, and reds. I walk on the road as it gradually leads me up the hill and into the dawn. The sun is just beginning to peek above the horizon. The crickets chirp as I walk by their hiding places, awakening them to the morning. Their chirps become a percussion rhythm to the rising sun. The elm trees canopy over the road and the gentle breeze moves the leaves so the shadows dance in and out of the light. My footsteps are a counterpoint to the crickets and the breeze. Two mourning doves coo to each other. One is behind me, and one is in front of me. My steps quicken and become a staccato that adds to the early morning wakening. As I start running, he emerges at the top of the hill just as the first rays of the morning sun pull me onward. He is a shadow figure, and I don't recognize him. I know that I know him, but I don't know who he is. He is in his desert fatigues and his M16 is strapped across his shoulder. His bucket hat is pulled down low over his forehead. His mouth is covered to keep out the sand of the desert. He sees me and his heavier steps begin to match mine. Our heart beats match each other. His heavier steps match mine now as the sun charges into the sky, a blazing ball of red, orange, and yellow. He reaches me as I reach him. Our hearts beat as one as we embrace. He whispers words I don't understand. And I wake up.

When I first started to have this dream, I tried to make sense of it. I was what, 15? Some nights I went to bed wondering if I would have The Dream again. I never told anyone about it. I knew the soldier was someone in my life, but who was he? Then, one day, when I was about 20 years old, I realized I wasn't dreaming about him anymore. I forgot about that soldier who ran to embrace me. I forgot about that soldier in his desert fatigues whose heartbeat with mine as we embraced, and he started to whisper something to me.

I was 25 years old when my beautiful son was born with dark hair, blonde eyelashes, and bright blue eyes. He came into the world almost three weeks beyond his due date. I remember doing everything I could to encourage him to join this world. It seemed like he had no interest in doing so. He was comfortable, and my doctor wasn't worried. "He'll come when he's ready," the doctor told me.

It was a snowy, cold winter in 1982. Surely shoveling the snow would bring on labor. It didn't. Perhaps riding in our old faded red pick-up truck would bring on labor. It didn't. Finally, as we were watching the Super Bowl between the San Francisco 49ers and the Cincinnati Bengals that was being played in Pontiac, Michigan. I just knew that this winter was special–my baby would be born. Then the labor pains started. We made it to the end of the game but headed out in a blizzard to drive to the hospital. My baby boy would be born in a snowstorm.

We made it to the hospital, but the doctor did not. I asked the nurse who was with me how many babies she had delivered. "Just one," she said. "But don't worry. We learned how to deliver babies in school." By then, I wasn't even concerned. Each time a labor pain shot through my body; I knew that the baby was coming. It was a quick 5 hours of labor, and it had my full attention. After I held my sweet baby boy, I had to ask one of the nurses who won the Super Bowl. Looking at my little baby boy, I couldn't remember!

As an infant, Kevin looked at me with a wisdom beyond his years. He had a solemn expression. It was as if he was assessing everything around him. He was attentive to everything.

Each time our eyes met, I felt like he could see into my soul. I loved it when that gaze would break with his beautiful smile parenthesized by his dimples. I didn't see that as often as I would have liked. He and I had a bond that neither one of us could explain. He grew up a strong and quiet child who wanted to please others. His childhood was not without trials, but that isn't what this story is about. He was athletic and intelligent, but school was difficult for him. But that isn't what this story is about either.

It is a beautiful fall day. I love the smell of the drying leaves that cluster along the quiet city street as I walk to the café downtown. "Hey, catch," a high school age boy yells to his buddy as they toss a football in the courthouse lawn. Laughter, fall leaves, and the sound of people having fun under the sapphire blue sky brings a smile to my face.

"What a perfect day," I think to myself. I stop to pick up a perfect red maple leaf. It is deep red, almost burgundy, that merges into a burnt orange color. I smile as I run my hand along the stem. "I'll press it when I get home on Sunday," I think to myself. I pause as I pass by a bench near the sidewalk. I check my watch. It is still two hours before the hockey game. Just enough time to get a bite to eat and get to the hockey arena. Hockey arenas–our home away from home once the season starts.

I pause, taking in the scene. The trees are in full fall color; kids are laughing and playing without a worry on their minds. I pick up the pace and walk quickly to the café, pull the door open and order a cheese plate, and treat myself to a glass of cabernet. I set my snack on the open table by the window and pick up a piece of aged cheddar cheese. Yummy.

Kevin should be done with his rugby game soon. He said he would meet me at the hockey arena after his game to watch his brother start his senior hockey season. Kevin was on full combat duty for his third tour, which ended ten months ago. Even though he enlisted in the National Guard, he was deployed right out of boot camp. He spent one year in Kosovo and then was deployed again for his first tour to Iraq. He came home, and a few years later, he was deployed for the third time, again to Iraq, this time as a sergeant. This third deployment was rough on him, and since he got back, he spends most of his time working third shift. He tells me wants to be alone. I see the pain in his eyes, and I don't know what to do.

Two weeks ago, Kevin called me. "Hey mom, come watch me play rugby. The game is only 30 miles away from you."

I was elated that he reached out to me. I thought, "He's finally coming around." The rugby team is his new band of brothers. Of course, I would watch the game! We had a great time that weekend.

Sitting in the café, I think about my three children. My daughter lives in Kentucky with her family. Kevin is a soldier and has been all over the world. Connor, my youngest son, plays hockey for Shattuck-St. Mary's school in Minnesota. He moved there to go to school and to play hockey. Now he only comes home a few times a month.

My children have all made their own way in the world. Still, I cherish the times we can get together, especially since Kevin was discharged from duty. Kevin took his duties seriously. He enlisted after 9/11 and the attack on the Twin Towers in New York City. Like for other families, 9/11 exploded into our lives on a fall day in 2001. It shook our innocence out like dust from a spare room–ignored for so long. And on that beautiful September day in 2013, just a dozen years after that first blast that shook us to our cores, our lives would change again.

I was looking forward to a typical and enjoyable fall weekend watching my sons' sporting events. I planned a mother and son weekend with both of my sons. Kevin, the older son, was playing rugby, and Connor was playing hockey. We planned to meet Saturday evening for sushi and conversation after the games were finished.

I was sitting in the café waiting to head to the hockey game, reading a book and sipping my wine when my cell phone rang. Odd, I thought. I recognized the number–not a person who usually calls me. I answered the phone with, "Hey, what's up?"

"Kevin had an accident. The team didn't have your phone number, so they wanted me to call you. He gave me a phone number. Call this number back right away. It's urgent," the disembodied voice said.

With shaking hands, I headed out to the street to make the call. "What's up?" I asked, my voice shaking.

"Kevin went down," the captain of the team told me frantically. "We don't know what happened. It was a simple play. The game was almost over."

"He went down? What? What's going on?" I asked in a deadly quiet voice.

"The EMTs are with him. They are trying to decide if they will send him by ambulance or helicopter. We're waiting to find out where they are taking him. He's unconscious. We think he may have stopped breathing. Wait. They're taking him to Regions Hospital in St. Paul."

"What- what- what? I'll be there as fast as I can but I'm a couple of hours away." I felt like I was in a dream as I rummaged in my purse, as I looked for the keys to my Jeep.

"They're going by ambulance. I'll follow it and meet you there."

We ended the call, and I ran into the café. "My son has been in an accident. They are taking him to the hospital right now. He's unconscious. I have to go now," as I tossed my debit card to the young man who was managing the cash register. He looked at me like I was crazy.

After I paid, I snatched my debit card, dropped it into my

purse, and dashed out onto the street. It was still a beautiful fall day. Yet, I couldn't see it anymore. I put the key into the ignition, buckled my seat belt, tossed my purse onto the passenger seat, and put my Jeep into gear. I knew I'd better take a deep breath and drive carefully.

"It will be okay," I wished to myself. "People lose consciousness. People recover, don't they?" But somehow, I wasn't sure I believed it. My thoughts were racing. This couldn't be happening. He came back from three tours of duty without a scratch on him. He couldn't be unconscious. He had to be okay. I had to get there. I backed out of my parking spot as I looked in the rearview mirror. I gripped the steering wheel and prayed. I put my Jeep into drive and pulled onto the street and headed toward the interstate. Of course, it was under construction. It was fall in Minnesota. I drove while my hands were sweating, and my heart was pounding in my chest.

By the time I got to the hospital Kevin had already been taken to the Surgical Intensive Care Unit. My beautiful boy who survived three combat tours of duty was silent and unresponsive. He was so very, very still. The medical team assured me that he would likely awaken in a few hours. But he didn't. He didn't awaken for many weeks.

That is where this story begins.

Posted for family and friends: Week 1–Surgical Intensive Care Unit

September 23, 2013

Kevin had some brain swelling overnight, as well as an increase in blood pressure, and a fever. Fortunately, the trauma team is monitoring his brain very closely. He was placed on a medication that induces a coma so that his brain can rest. The goal today is to keep him cool and quiet. Please keep him in your prayers and share with his soul that he is so loved.

The neurologist has ordered a port to be placed for administration of medications. They are going to begin a stronger saline solution to help reduce fluid in his brain. They have also decided to reduce his body temperature with a hypothermic process.

September 24, 2013

Kevin remains completely sedated with the goal to keep his brain pressure down. The good news is that all is well on that front. We are hoping for a medically uneventful day. The trauma team is exceptional. I know Kevin is receiving every possible medical advantage. The power of God and the prayers of his people is undeniable. Please keep Kevin and all the other trauma patients in your prayers.

September 24, 2013

Kevin has a feeding tube through his throat as of this afternoon. The purpose is to keep his intestines working. He is still in a medical coma, and on a ventilator. They are now monitoring for blood clots. He is really a very sick young man. Please keep your prayers coming. With that being said, the medical team is happy that they are meeting their goals today. The medical team is very, very good and I am grateful for their wonderful care.

September 24, 2013

Thank you to the amazing nurses and doctors. Keep them in your prayers with Kevin and all the other trauma patients. The night shift has just started. Kevin has been stable all day, under the watchful care of his nurses. "We have many miles to go" as Robert Frost once wrote. Thankfully, our journey is not one that we must travel alone. I know Kevin feels the prayers lifting him up. I feel them too. Thank you all. Tomorrow is another day.

September 25, 2013

Kevin has had stable vitals for 24 hours now. Most importantly his pressure in his brain is where it should be. As a part of this medical coma, his brain is operating 20-30%. The neurologist described this state as being "turned off." Kevin will remain in this state for the next four days. He will then be phased off the drug. The neurologist said he is cautiously optimistic about Kevin's prognosis. We'll take that! He also said to keep the prayers coming as prayers do amazing things. Keep Kevin and the other patients, the doctors, nurses, and staff surrounded by prayers.

September 26, 2013

Kevin has had another uneventful night. His intracranial pressure numbers are holding steady at around 9. Kevin's intestines are working properly, which means we have one less thing to worry about. I have never seen so many grown adults excited about poo! When Kevin wakes up and reads about his journey, he can blame his sister Erica for this post. Keep the prayers coming.

September 27, 2013

Steady as it goes. In John 16:33 we see these words: In this world you will have trouble, but fear not. I have overcome the world. *Kevin continues to maintain his numbers although his intracranial pressure is of concern to the medical team. I learned that a burst-suppression level is an electroencephalographic pattern where high amplitude bursts alternate with periods of low or even flat line suppression. In a medically induced coma, the intent is to greatly reduce brain activity. Each time the brain waves burst above the suppressed level more medication is required to reduce the brain activity. Kevin's pattern seems to fluctuate a lot and the team works diligently to keep these steady. I learned that a fluctuating pattern can predict a poor prognosis. We are acutely aware of every little change in his numbers. The medical team assures us that he is doing well in this phase. So, please keep your prayers going. Not only for Kevin, but for the medical team and all the patients and their families at the SICU at the hospital.*

September 27, 2013

I just want all of you to know how grateful we are for your thoughts and prayers. To the brotherhoods of the Masons, the rugby players, the military, and all of you who are praying for Kevin–you are making a difference. Please do not stop your efforts even though we are in this space where we can't see immediate results. Kevin needs you now more than ever.

We are getting ready for the shift change and the end of week #1. This is a marathon and that is what Kevin has been training for (pray that he will run that race in due time.)

How does a simple tackle, something Kevin did hundreds of times over the years when he played football and then rugby result in such devastation? People survive massive car accidents and falls, and they recover quicker than he is recovering. The players from both teams assured me that the tackle was perfectly normal. Kevin's tackling technique was superb. This was the only time that Kevin had been knocked out. He returned from his three deployments unscathed–he had never been wounded. He survived many IED blasts without injury. Sure, he had dizziness, and headaches. But he never really complained. How can this be happening to him?

The nurses attempted to evoke responses to stimulation. They pinched him and ran their fingers across the soles of his feet. I saw bruises on his chest. "What are those bruises from," I asked one of the nurses.

"You don't want to know," he responded.

"Were they from the accident," I asked, fully expecting the answer to be affirmative.

"That is from pinching him to get a response," was the response.

"You have to pinch him that hard?" I was shocked by that. I was afraid for him. How can that be? He was in perfect physical shape. He was working out for hours every day. He was going to compete in a triathlon. He was a black belt in Taekwondo. People aren't involved in a simple tackle and become comatose. Even if they are knocked out, they wake up and they go on with their lives. It can't be happening. I don't understand why this is happening. The doctors had no explanation other than, "Sometimes these things happen. We don't know why."

Posted for family and friends: Week 2–Surgical Intensive Care Unit

September 28, 2013

The plan is to cut the Pentobarbital in half at 8:00 p.m. tonight. This is the drug that produces the medical coma, and it results in a suppression level. Kevin is currently at 90+ suppression level. If a person were to have a medical procedure one would expect to have a 50% suppression level. The good thing about this is that all of Kevin's energy is going into healing. Thank you for your continuing prayers.

September 28, 2013

I think of all the moments that make up this past week. It has been excruciatingly painful at times, but also, so filled with prayers for Kevin. I walk into his room at the hospital, and it is a sacred space where I do feel the prayers enfolding him in God's love. This love has been magnified by the prayers of so many. As we go through these next few days, I pray that we see the glimmers of Kevin come through the darkness. As he awakens, I know he will need more people to help him regain his place. He is so lucky to have the brotherhoods of so many–the army, the Masons, the rugby community, his families, and the people in many churches. I am so thankful for all of you–both old and new. Thank you for your prayers and your faith.

September 29, 2013

We met with the team on their rounds this morning. The Pentobarbital

is being reduced again tonight at 8 p.m. All we as family and friends can do is continue to pray and wait. There is no way to tell how long it will take for his body to burn through the medicine, all we can do is wait. Kevin continues to look healthy in his bed and I am constantly reminding myself that this isn't a movie where he will open his eyes in an hour and a half and say, "What's going on, why are you all looking at me." Give prayers to the doctors and nurses as well as all the support staff. They have been trying to help us through all of this as well.

September 29, 2013

Everything is quiet in Kevin's room. In a few hours the sedation medication will be cut in half again. He continues to have good numbers across the board. We are so grateful for all your prayers. The night nurses are beginning to arrive for the shift change. May God provide us all with His peace tonight.

September 30, 2013

Today has been a day of waiting. Kevin is almost off the Pentobarbital coma medications. All numbers seem to be running where they are supposed to be. We thought he might like to hear a hockey game as he lay in his bed, but we think his team was losing because his blood pressure started to go up. Kevin has always enjoyed sports. Still waiting for Wednesday to arrive: the D-day of sorts, which most doctors say is the first day he may possibly wake up from the coma medications. Prayers, prayers, prayers!

October 1, 2013

Today, Kevin coughed and opened his eyes. He also wiggled his big toe when we lightly brushed the bottom of his foot. We all felt such a relief.

He's not out of the woods, as we all know. In the movie I am making in my head I hear him ask me, "What's going on? When can I get out of here?" I can't tell you how much your prayers mean. We can all feel God's presence in this place. Thank you and keep those prayers coming for Kevin, the hospital staff, the other patients, and their families. I believe in miracles.

I hold onto the stories I read about those who have terrible accidents and come through it. I talk with the other parents and families whose loved ones are also in the SICU. The conversations all follow the same pattern. What happened? How is it going? How long did it take? What is the prognosis? In some cases, families move to a different waiting area. I hear the wailing and watch as a minister enters the hallway. I hear the bustle of the nurses and the silence in the rooms. The doors are shut, curtains are closed. There is an unnaturalness, an otherworldliness to the quiet by those rooms. There is unbearable sadness. That is not where I want to be.

Some people don't make it, either. That is why I hold onto the stories of those who do–the ones who survived terrible car accidents and are now being moved into the rehab wing and the ones who had strokes and are now asking for something to drink. We share stories, and hugs, and hopes and dreams.

It was a terrible day when the doctors brought us together and told me that they wanted to insert tubes to help Kevin breathe and to feed him. I tried so hard to suppress my tears.

"Is he brain dead?" I asked. I was grateful to hear that he

was not. Yet, a trach through his throat to breathe and being fed through a tube through his abdomen sounds so horrible. "What are our options?" I asked through my tears.

"Well, he needs to have the tube taken out of his throat. He is at the limit of time that we can keep it there without it damaging his throat. He must eat, and IV fluids aren't enough. If he can't breathe on his own or eat, he will die," one of the doctors answered.

I wanted time to think about it. What would Kevin want? It was evening, and the hospital was quiet as those who could were in the dining room or heading home. I didn't want to have to make the decision–extreme measures to keep him alive. I didn't want to. It was so unfair to have to decide between life and death for someone you love. I went into his room and prayed Psalm 23.

The Lord is my shepherd; I shall not want. He makes me lie down in green pastures, he leads me beside quiet waters, he refreshes my soul. He guides me along the right paths for his name's sake. Even though I walk through the valley of death, I will fear no evil, for you are with me; your rod and your staff, they comfort me.

You prepare a table before me in the presence of my enemies. You anoint my head with oil; my cup overflows. Surely goodness and mercy will follow me all the days of my life, and I will dwell in the house of the Lord forever.

I swear, it is true, I looked at my beautiful boy and he moved his lips, "Don't. Give. Up." He mouthed the words.

Later, people would say out of kindness, "Do you think you were just wishing he said that?"

"No, I saw it. I know that is what he wanted. I wouldn't give up, ever."

Posted for family and friends: Week 3–Surgical Intensive Care Unit

October 2, 2013

Kevin is enveloped in your prayers! He continues to get stronger and stronger. He has been taking a few breaths over the ventilator each minute. He is still coughing and trying to figure out what the tubes are doing in mouth. But the most exciting thing to me was when I told him his rent is now paid for October AND when he gets out of this place, I am getting him the dog he has been wanting. Guess what? He opened his eyes and looked directly at me! I swear it is true so does anyone know where I can get a Shaba Innu?

The doctors say it will probably be a few more days before the sedation drugs are out of his system. Let's keep the prayers going!

October 3, 2013

Kevin has had some setbacks today and two new medications have been added to his menu. I had hoped to hear talk about removing the breathing tube. That discussion will not occur today. We are praying that this will be a short setback and that Kevin will have a better day tomorrow. I know that he is surrounded by prayers. We are thankful for each and every one of you.

October 4, 2013

Yesterday Kevin developed seizure activity and the medical team got that under control around 1:30 a.m. With the new medications, he has had

minimal seizures today. So, the plan for the weekend is to keep him seizure free and continue to attempt to wake him up. He is still on a breathing tube, and he continued to take a few breaths over the vent. It is so hard to see him like this. Please pray for all of us. We know that God is good, and his love is endless.

October 6, 2013

They ran the Twin Cities Marathon today. It ended just blocks away at the state capital building. I hope for Kevin to recover and fulfill that dream. He is ever so slowly waking up. Every word I speak to him he hears, and I imagine how hard it must be to put all these sounds together and to make sense out of his situation. When I talk, he does open his eyes. I try to share the love and hope and prayers with him by looking into his eyes. Eyes are the windows to our souls... Thank you for your comments and prayers. I read the guest book to him each day. Hope and pray...

October 7, 2013

I always knew Kevin was unique–all people are unique, and Kevin seems to be in that small percent of people who are on the edges. The doctors are surprised that he metabolizes medicines very quickly. That means the doctors are expecting the residual effect of the seizure medications to stay in his body. Not so–when they checked his levels in his liver, there was only the smallest trace. So, he has been experiencing seizures again and he is back on continuous monitoring with an EEG. They have increased the two current seizure meds and added a third one. He will be sedated again today as he will also have the tracheotomy today. I know his soul knows you are praying for him. Help him shine his light through this nightmare.

October 8, 2013

I am sitting with Kevin and waiting for the team to arrive to put the PEG feeding tube in his abdomen. His neurologist saw Kevin give a "thumbs up" sign this morning. Praise to God for giving us this sign. While he did not have seizures last night, he is metabolizing the medications very quickly and therefore he continues to get "load" doses so that he is at a therapeutic level. I am going to be talking with the interventionist later today. Say prayers of praise and hope today. The power of God is in this place.

Why is this Kevin's journey? How is it fair to him? How can he have survived the nightmare of war, not just once but three times, to have this happen? What is going on in his head?

I received a phone call from yet another insurance company. Oh, I thought to myself, this is yet another checklist.

"Hello. Do you have a few minutes to answer some questions about your son's condition?" the insurance woman asked in an annoyingly cheerful tone. "He had an accident on September 21?"

"Yes," I responded wondering how many times I would have to go through this.

"How many bones did he break? Did he lose blood? How many surgeries did he require?" she continued.

Frustrated, I answered, "No broken bones. No loss of blood. One surgery to relieve the pressure on his brain. Oh, yeah, and a tracheotomy."

In an amazingly happy voice, she responded, "So it was only his head."

Unbelievable. "I think that is pretty important–like the most important thing," I said. It was all I could do to speak without screaming. I wiped the tears from my eyes as I abruptly ended the call. She never called back.

As a teenager, Kevin loved to play football. He was tenacious and had grit, even back then. When he was in middle school, he weighed 90 pounds. I remember that the football coaches asked if we would let him move up to the "heavy weight" team even though he technically was too small for that division. However, he was a solid player, and could tackle any size player. He was thrilled. He wanted to play football, and he loved that his skills were recognized. He worked even harder on his skills.

Kevin worked out in the weight room at the high school every morning in the summer. He was thrilled and honored when he was awarded the "most improved" in strength gains the summer before his junior year. He worked hard for the proverbial "six pack" that was his abdomen. He would laugh, and say, "I guess I just have a four pack." He loved physical challenges, and it seemed like he could overcome all physical obstacles.

Between 8th and 9th grade, Kevin decided to run a 5K race during the local summer festival. "Hey, Mom," he said one morning. "Can I have twenty bucks?"

"What do you need that for?" I asked. As usual, he asked questions like this at the most inopportune time. I was busy doing laundry to the banging noise of the dryer. He told me it was the entry fee for an upcoming race, and he would get a cool t-shirt. "Go get my purse," and I gave him two tens. He stuffed the money into a pocket of his shorts.

"I'm going to run to give them my entry fee," he said as he dashed out of the house.

As the date of the race approached, I asked him, "Have you been practicing enough? It is a 5K."

"Don't worry Mom," Kevin said. "I'm fine."

And fine he was. He finished second in the race. He might have finished first if he had ever practiced. He told me later that it was the first time he had ever actually run a 5K. That was my boy. Things were always "fine." And up until now, that was the truth.

Posted for family and friends: Week 3–Surgical Intensive Care Unit

October 9, 2013

Up and down, two steps forward one step back. Kevin's seizures are somewhat under control. He had a medication increase today. He is opening his eyes more than yesterday and the seizure activity is less than yesterday. He was not as responsive, though. Of course, we want him to respond and make improvements by leaps and bounds. I am grateful that he is beginning to breathe on his own. He is taking deeper breaths when we talk to him. Please continue the strong prayers. This is a long, long journey.

October 10, 2013

Kevin is exhausted. He is trying to wean off the ventilator, adjust to

seizure medications, and pull together cognitive functioning. The team is changing his seizure medication doses and dropping one of the three. He is not at therapeutic level again, so he will be getting a load dose once again, later this afternoon. I know I keep asking for your prayers. I know he is in God's hands. This journey is so hard...

October 11, 2013

Today, we continue the agonizingly slow journey toward recovery. Off one of the three seizure medications because it was interacting with one of the remaining two drugs. Are the seizures related to the traumatic brain injury? The doctors say probably that they are. The goal is to maintain therapeutic levels for 48 hours. His level was still low, so the doctors increased medication again. Breathing for him is hard work, while we take breathing for granted. Kevin works hard to breathe without the vent. Praise to God for each small improvement. Only God knows the plan.

October 12, 2013

The doctors' report that Kevin is slowly becoming more medically stable. He still has an infection, a superficial blood clot, and he is having trouble maintaining his therapeutic level for the anti-seizure medication, but he is making forward progress from the medical perspective. He is still not responding to commands. I tell myself every day that Kevin is in God's hands. Thank you for your continuing prayers, your love, and your hope.

October 14, 2013

It has been an emotional day. Kevin is medically stable–praise be to God for that. He will be transferred to a long-term care hospital as early as tomorrow afternoon depending on paperwork. It will be a good transition, as the hospital is specifically set up for people who have the challenges that Kevin faces. I continue to hear that Kevin will have better outcomes if he is surrounded by people who love and care for him. And we (his family) need all of you to care for him and us. God bless all of you.

October 15, 2013

Kevin is breathing better today. His breaths are slower and deeper. He opened his eyes several times while I was talking to him. I know these are small steps, and we often take them for granted. We continue to wait for the word that he will transfer to his new hospital. Over three weeks in SICU.

Kevin graduated from high school and decided to attend the local community college. "Why community college?" I asked him.

"They don't require that I take the ACT," Kevin told me. "I am not going to take one more test just to get into college. I can always transfer to a 4-year college after I get my Associates degree." Kevin had researched and he had a plan. Once he enlisted in the Army National Guard, he was eligible to get reimbursement for his credit costs. Most of the classes were held in our town, so he could work and go to school. He registered for the law enforcement program.

Kevin was diagnosed with a "learning disability" when he was in first grade, and school was always a challenge for him. He and I worked every night during the school year. He could listen and learn but reading and writing were a mystery to him. When he was in first grade, I met with his teacher and the principal of the school. The teacher asked in a very patronizing voice, "Do you read to him? Do you have books in your house?"

They didn't know us at all. "Yes, he loves his library in his bedroom. He asks me to read to him every night. We have newspapers in our house. We go to the library often," I responded. I was an administrator in Kevin's school, and I decided then and there that I would never talk to parents like these people talked to me.

Kevin never wanted people to consider him disabled. In middle school, his classmates told him they thought he was faking that he couldn't read just to get out of doing the work. He was mortified and that made him work even harder.

"How come everyone, my sister, my friends can complete their homework in a few minutes and get an 'A'? I have to work and study, and it takes me hours to complete the assignment and I'm lucky if I get a 'C'?" he asked after one particularly long night working on his assignment.

He would never take the alternative assignment because that would make him look different. When he got to the end of the first semester in his freshman year, he wasn't passing his classes. He knew that I was furious. After I read his report, we sat down.

"What is going on, Kevin?" I asked. He could hear the frustration in my voice. "You are missing half of your assignments. I know you did them."

"I don't care, Mom," he responded. "What good does school do for me?"

"Don't give up, Kevin," I responded. "You are smart and strong. You are brave. High school is just a step along the journey. Some people will tell you that high school is the best time of your life. I can assure you that is not true."

"Why would you say that Mom? What do you know anyway?' he responded as he stood up, ready to walk away.

"I have worked with kids with disabilities almost all of my career," I responded. "I have seen kids achieve things that others thought were impossible. Kevin, you can do this." He looked at me like he thought I was crazy. "Kevin, I can help you, if you want me to. But this is up to you. Do the work and turn it in. All I expect is for you to do your best. Do all the work and do your best."

Kevin accepted the challenge. From that point on, he turned in all his assignments. Most of the time he maintained a "C" average and the rest of the time he made the "B" honor roll. I saw him develop into a young man with an unbelievable ability to persist through challenges. He loved history, economics, and political science.

After high school, my son enlisted and was compelled to serve. He found his calling as a soldier. The traits that make a good person, and the traits that make a good soldier were already a part of him. He embodied the Army core values: Loyalty, Duty, Respect, Selfless Service, Honor, Integrity and Personal Courage.

LDRSHIP is an acronym for the seven basic values of the United States Army:

1. **L**oyalty - Bear true faith and allegiance to the U.S. Constitution, the Army, your unit, and other soldiers.
2. **D**uty - Fulfill your obligations.
3. **R**espect - Treat people as they should be treated.

4. **S**elfless Service - Put the welfare of the nation, the Army, and your subordinates before your own.

5. **H**onor - Live up to all the Army values.

6. **I**ntegrity - Do what's right, legally, and morally.

7. **P**ersonal Courage - Face fear, danger, or adversity [physical or moral].

Army Creed:

I serve the people of the United States and live the Army Values. I am disciplined, physically and mentally tough, trained, and proficient in my warrior tasks and drills. I stand ready to deploy, engage, and destroy the enemies of the United States of America in close combat.

Kevin wrote these in a notebook, and I later found them in his handwriting beside his bed.

Kevin couldn't believe that other people could be soldiers and not entirely support their core values. He told me about one day when he was in his Advanced Individual Training at Fort Benning.

"Hey, mom," Kevin started one night when we were sitting outside by a bonfire. "I can't believe that people can be in the Army and not support what is right." I looked at him as I took a sip of my beer. Sometimes he just wanted to know someone was listening.

"When I was at boot camp," he reminisced, "Some of the guys were talking about their college experiences. They were joking about how boot camp would never help them when they got their real jobs as teachers."

Somehow, the conversation shifted to education for

people with disabilities and one of the guys expressed his opinion, "People with disabilities have no place in schools. They are just a drain on resources."

Kevin put his head into his hands as he waited for me to say something. Of course, Kevin knew he had a learning disability, so I asked him, "What did you do?"

He said, "I thought about it and listened. Finally, I knew I had to say something." I said, "Hey dudes, my mom has worked with people who have disabilities for most of her career. You would be amazed at what people can do given the chance."

It was a great answer. I asked him, "Did you tell them you had a learning disability?" He chuckled and smiled his smile then said, "Are you crazy?"

Kevin wanted his chance to serve his county and he was thrilled when he was first deployed. He went to boot camp in the middle of the summer at Fort Benning, GA. How a guy from Minnesota could move from the relative coolness of Minnesota summers to the sweltering heat of Georgia, I could never understand. Of course, the military didn't give him the choice. He was one of the few northern guys at boot camp during those months, he told me.

When he left for boot camp, Kevin told me not to write him until he contacted me. He was very independent, and he didn't want to be different. I was so excited the day that I went to the mailbox and found a letter addressed to me in his blocky printing. It was a surprise, I must admit. He wasn't great at writing when he was in school, and I knew the effort that it took to send a letter to me. I asked him about that later and he told me that he and the other guys were told to "write home." He did what he was told to do.

He told me about the day that his group was sent on a run. It was hot and humid and several of the guys dropped out due to heat exhaustion. Finally, at the halfway point, 2.5 miles into the run, the rest of the guys were told to turn around. The leader ended the run for the day. They would have to run it the next day. Kevin was so mad, "I wanted to finish it," he said in the letter. "We were already halfway through it, and I was fine. We were just going to have to do it again. What a waste."

I asked him how the training was going. He said, "If you can make it through two- and three-a-day football practices, you can make it through boot camp." Giving up was not in his nature.

His nickname in boot camp was "Doughboy." I look at the picture that was taken at the beginning of boot camp, and he was a young man with the face of a boy. He holds an expressionless pose in the picture. I knew that he was where he wanted to be, and he was thrilled to be a soldier. I asked him why he wasn't smiling in the picture. "I'm fine, mom," he said. "You're not supposed to be smiling when you are in boot camp." I knew he was happy then.

Posted for family and friends: Week 4–Surgical Intensive Care Unit

October 16, 2013

Hurry up and wait–Kevin said that is the military way. We are waiting

for transport to his new hospital. Once he gets settled, he will be on a coma stimulation program. Friends are encouraged to visit but advised to call ahead so that you don't arrive during a scheduled "rest" break! I am hopeful that once therapy starts Kevin will again begin to show responsiveness. He has never liked to just lie around in bed. Thank you for your prayers and continuing love and support.

October 18, 2013

Kevin continues to wean off the vent–the good news is that he was able to breathe spontaneously for over 8 hours before he tired out. Some family members spent the day with him and reported that opened his eyes and reacted to stimulus. Slow and steady is good. We continue to pray that Kevin knows how much everyone wants him to laugh and smile again. May God bless all of you.

October 19, 2013

No one would have guessed one month ago the events that would follow. Kevin is lifted each day by so many people. His brother and I are sitting with him this afternoon as he rests. He had a two-hour session sitting in a chair–we can't even imagine the strength and energy that takes for him. When we walked in, I gave him his baby blanket that he has carried with him through all his deployments. I found it in his bed at his apartment yesterday. I gave it to him telling him that I found it and he clearly gave Connor and me a "thumbs up" with his right hand. It wasn't just a little movement. It was clear and definite. I pray each moment of every day that Kevin knows that we want him back.

October 22, 2013

Continue praying for Kevin's recovery. Kevin's grandparents were at the hospital again today. It was another good day and Kevin lifted his head off the headrest (3rd day in a row) and he opened his eyes and seemed to respond to names and voices. He likes to have stories read to him! He also lifted his left arm up and clearly pointed his finger as his grandfather read a chapter from the book, "Visiting Tom." Every day is filled with small blessings. Thank you for being a part of Kevin's team. God does perform miracles.

When Kevin was in kindergarten, I suspected that he was struggling with written language. How did I know? Things like picking out letters on signs came easily for his sister. This wasn't easy for him. He tried so hard, but it just didn't seem to make sense to him those squiggles made up letters. He loved to listen to stories, though. Every night I read to him. He loved the stories with heroes. He saw himself as a hero. He would act out the stories with the other children when they were playing. He had the whole collection of "He-Man" figures. He played with these for hours as he told the stories to no one, only to himself.

When I asked his teachers about the possibility that he might have a learning disability, they told me he was okay. "Boys mature slower than girls," they said. "Don't worry. He just needs some time to mature." He wasn't fine, though. He struggled with reading and writing all his life. Nevertheless, he never gave up. If given the choice, he would always choose to be like everyone else. He would choose to write the story, rather than draw a picture. He did most of his work on a computer, and he survived with spell check.

Kevin told me that once he was called out by his

commander after an IED incident. The soldiers were told to write their recollection of that specific incident. They were given a piece of paper and a pencil and told to talk to no one– just write what happened. I knew this would have been a challenge for him. I asked if he could have used his computer. He told me that wasn't an option. The next day, the officer called him out in front of his squad. "I can't believe you have a college education. You write like %^&*$."

"What did you say?" I asked. "Did you tell him you would have been able to write better if you could have used your computer?"

"Are you crazy," he responded. "I just stood at attention and said, "Yes, sir."

Later, he told me that he was riding with that officer on a mission. As they were talking on those long hours patrolling the roads outside Al Assad base in Iraq, the officer brought up that incident. His comment was that he couldn't believe that someone so smart and competent in the field wrote so poorly. Kevin told me that he admitted to his learning disability to the officer. "Why didn't you tell me?" the officer asked him.

Kevin's response was, "It is fine, sir."

My son was like that. He worked harder than most people, and he rarely let on that those tasks were difficult. He just pushed through the struggles. Until now, that worked very well for him.

Posted for family and friends: Week 5–Long Term Care Hospital

October 24, 2013

Kevin's dad spent the morning with him. He was pleased to see Kevin move his arms and open his eyes. Kevin also spent the day breathing off the vent. Progress is evident, small though it may seem. The Care Team meeting was productive. His whole family was present, even though some attended by phone. We felt like the team was encouraging. The doctor said each step no matter how small is important. So tonight, we say a prayer that God continues to provide Kevin with these opportunities to make the many small steps that make up his journey. May God bless you as you keep him in your prayers.

October 24, 2013

I read this prayer tonight–please share it tonight and the hundreds of prayers that are said will surely shine God's light on Kevin:

Lord Jesus, since you love Kevin, now spread your wings above him and shield him from harm. Let angel guards sing over him: this child of God shall meet no harm. Amen

October 26, 2013

Several people from Kevin's father's side of the family spent the morning with Kevin. They left a wonderful description of their visit in the journal I have in the room. They are absolutely amazed by Kevin. They had not seen him since he left the first hospital. We are seeing more and more consistent movements and responses. Kevin is truly beginning to wake up. This afternoon a friend and I visited Kevin. He gave me a "fist bump" and then he patted MY hand. Kevin has a heart of gold–he seemed like he was reassuring me.

October 27, 2013

Praise to God and thank you for your continuing prayers. We know that with God all things are possible. Visitors left a note today. They saw lots of movement and responses and the nurse reported Kevin was trying to say something. They thought it was something like "Get me out of this place." Each small step is one closer to achieving that and everyone who has stopped this weekend is amazed at Kevin's progress. This afternoon my parents and Kevin's brother and I visited. Kevin really seemed to be putting the pieces together. He reached for my face, and he also checked out his own face. We all told him we love him, and he clearly mouthed the words "love you." How sweet it is to see him mouth those words. His uncle and aunt made a brief stop on their way to the Vikings/Packers game, and we're absolutely thrilled to see Kevin's progress. They told him they would wave to him with each Packer touchdown.

October 29, 2013

Kevin is off the ventilator support and breathing on his own through the trach! His sister called and the nurse reported he is consistently squeezing hands to communicate. He has had a new trach with a speaking valve put in. He is continuing to wake up and show us that he is coming back. Praise be to our Father, Son, and Holy Ghost.

October 29, 2013

Kevin was sleeping when I arrived this afternoon. He works third shift, so a nap at 4:30 p.m. is perfectly understandable. Once he discovered the book I was reading aloud to him, he began to feel the pages. He lifted it up and studied the cover. He is trying to talk but hasn't figured out how to use his speaking valve. He is swallowing well and that is a good step. I told him he was in an accident, and he is in the hospital. I told him he has many, many people who care for him and are praying for his recovery. He needs our prayers more than ever as he starts this next very hard phase–relearning just about everything after over four weeks in a coma. With God all things are possible. Thank you for your prayers.

October 29, 2013 (added)
"For I know the plans I have for you," declares the Lord, "plans for welfare and not evil, to give you a future and a hope." Bless Kevin and all of God's children. –Jeremiah 29:11

I learned that boot camp involves constant tests of courage and strength. Besides the physical fitness courses, the men often had hand-to-hand combat. Kevin excelled at that, but he had to fight his way up from the bottom. He wasn't an imposing looking young man in the beginning. He stood just over 6 feet tall and was about 210 pounds when he arrived at Fort Benning. By the end of his AIT, he was a lean 175 pounds, and he had lost his boyish face.

As a boy, besides football, Kevin dabbled in wrestling. When he was in elementary school, he was in the youth wrestling program for a year. He learned quickly, but decided he'd try gymnastics, hockey, and basketball in the following years. He never wrestled again until he was a senior in high school. He decided he wanted to enter the local Christmas vacation "Open Wrestling Tournament." In his usual manner, he threw that idea out at the dinner table a few days before the tournament started. It wasn't a big deal to him. No one was more surprised than the high school wrestling coach when Kevin ended the tournament in 2nd place in his weight class. "Where was this guy all through high school?" he asked me. That was Kevin. He wasn't one for attention and the limelight. He did his best, always. He was fine with being in the background. He was the kind of young man who pulled the heavy load without complaint.

In boot camp, as the hand-to-hand combat rounds continued, Kevin fought his way to the top. He battled everyone with the same intensity. In one of his infrequent letters, he told me officers and enlisted men all fought. He wrote about one specifically tough round. He fought and the first guy tapped out. Another one jumped into the ring and Kevin fought him until that guy tapped out, too. The third guy jumped in, and Kevin was beginning to tire out, so he wanted to end that fight as quickly as possible. He put the guy into a Full Nelson. The guy tapped out and said to him, "Hey–that move is illegal." Kevin's response was, "I didn't think anything is illegal when you are fighting for your life and the lives of your soldiers." He was like that. He let me know that his stock went up that day with the officers.

Posted for family and friends: Week 6–Long Term Care Hospital

November 1, 2013

Kevin had some awesome events this afternoon. He was really trying to communicate. I finally recognized that he was signing some letters. I went out into the nurses' area and asked if anyone could use sign language.

Yes! He was signing letters–x, s, t, a–not words but clearly signs. I shared some apps on my iPad, and he was alert to them. Erica called and he listened to her. I played back a voice message from him, and he listened intently. He used his voice to make some sounds. The nurse heard him. We couldn't make out what he was saying but perhaps it was "What happened?"

November 3, 2013

Another good day–Kevin seems to be a bit more awake each day. His personality is shining through as well. Kevin has a good work ethic, and he was really working on his muscles today, especially his right arm. I could tell that he was frustrated that it isn't as strong as his left arm. He keeps doing arm curls and I keep counting the reps. I told him he would get it and he gave a "thumbs up." He also shook his head "no" when I asked him to give me the mouth swab back. I laughed. He is working so hard, and he does get tired. I was told that many people are following his progress and that he is loved. He closed his eyes at that and promptly fell asleep. May God's love shelter him throughout the night and your prayers lift him up.

November 5, 2013

One of my friends drove us to the hospital tonight. Kevin was sleepy when we arrived, but we got him motivated with a good leg massage. And neck rub. He really enjoyed that, and it woke him up. He is mouthing and whispering words. He asked about his job. He wants the dog I promised him. He is looking forward to visitors because he really tried to talk when we mentioned that. The nurse commented on how much more he is doing in the past few days. He is still waiting for his move to the rehab floor. Maybe tomorrow!

November 6, 2013

Kevin moved to his new room on the hospital rehab floor this afternoon. When I arrived, he immediately said, "Take me home." He wanted his cap on his head and he was ready! He started to do his exercises and he even moved both legs several times. I haven't seen that before. He successfully rolled to his side and counted "1-2-3" and tried to pull himself up. It is really hard work. I take rolling over for granted like so many things. Keep those prayers coming–with God anything is possible.

As the weeks continue to pass, I am struggling more and more with the layers of things that I must address. People who work with me think that things should be going back to the way they were. They think that my job should be the most important thing in my life. Truly, work is important, but it is not the most important thing. I know that. I try hard to balance my job responsibilities with the care for my son. I go to work early and use FMLA leave for the appointments with the doctors and other professionals who are making major decisions for Kevin. I am responsible for him.

When he didn't awake from the concussion within 24 hours, and things started looking grim, I called a friend of mine who is a lawyer. She helped file a petition with the courts for temporary guardianship/conservatorship. As a young single person, Kevin was responsible for himself. When he was incapacitated, he was not able to make his own decisions. He is my baby–of course I would be his guardian and his conservator. I fully believed that this was temporary. I wanted to be able to tell him when he awoke that his apartment, his car, his bank account, and his job were waiting for him. I wanted him to be able to return to the life that he had suddenly left. I had no idea what that would look like. When I walked into his apartment for the first time after the accident, I could tell that he expected to return. It was surreal to be walking into someone's home to look for accounts, passwords, and all the trappings of the business side of living. Armed with the court paperwork, I tracked down everything that I could think of. Of course, there are always things that a person doesn't even know that they don't know. Those were the mysteries that would jump up and catch me off guard. Those were the things I wish I could have asked him about. Those were the things that brought tears to my eyes at unexpected moments.

It is incredible the amount of time and work involved in making all the decisions for an adult. The people at my job couldn't really comprehend this. I went to work for the day, and then jumped into my car to make the nearly 90-minute drive to the city and the hospital. I would stay there with him if I could. If not, I would drive back home where I would check the mail and sort out the tasks involved with the business side of his life and mine. I'd head to bed at midnight and wake-up at 5 a.m. to start the whole process over again. Someone once told me that a person can do anything for a time. It is when there is no light at the end of the tunnel that things become unbearable. There is always light at the end of the tunnel.

Posted for family and friends: Week 7–Long Term Care Hospital

November 8, 2013
Happy Friday! Kevin continues to make incremental improvements. He is waking up more and more and that brings new challenges. He is frustrated that his muscles don't respond as they did before the accident. He works hard to communicate, and we often don't understand him. Today, he really started to communicate with the staff. He told one of his nurses to "shut up." She said that's okay–"We'll take it!" A few of the Mason brothers visited him and I could tell he really appreciated that. It is hard to see him when he must work so hard to communicate. He gets frustrated and he isn't cognizant 100% of the time. People ask me if he is still in a coma–I respond that he is waking up. When he is "on" he is doing great. It isn't like he is there all the time. I take these moments when he is lucid, and I thank God for that gift. Today, he took my hand and lifted it to his mouth and kissed it. He did it twice. He asked me to tell him it will be okay. Of course, I told him it will. Yes, I trust God and I believe he will be okay. May God's love hold Kevin up through these days. May the prayers of God's family hold Kevin up.

November 9, 2013
Kevin participated in the Tough Madder event in 2012 when he returned from his last deployment. It was a nasty cold rainy day and Kevin, and his teammates were ready to go. I was an observer, and it was an event to see. Before a team could even get to the staging area and starting line, they had to scale a wall that was at least 8-feet tall. This event is a great metaphor for Kevin. Three Saturdays ago, we didn't even know if Kevin was going to be able to get to the starting line of the race. In the past two

weeks he has scaled that wall and is now at the starting line. Each day has shown us that Kevin is still the fighter he has always been. He is working hard to start the race. The other thing about the Tough Mudder is that no one can finish by himself. It is only through teamwork. Each of you is part of Kevin's team and your prayers push and pull him each step of the way. And through the grace of God, Kevin continues. I know he will get to the finish line, and I know that will be accomplished with your prayers and with God's will. If you visit Kevin, please remember how hard it has been to accomplish even the smallest step. Thank you for your continuing prayers.

November 10, 2013

This morning, I read this verse after a friend sent it to me in an email. I talked to some of you who visited Kevin for the first time this week. Then, I went to the hospital to visit Kevin. Three of Kevin's rugby teammates were also there along with their families. Kevin was really motivated by the stories that his mates shared. At one point, one of the guys said he could probably beat Kevin in a fitness test now. Wow! Kevin responded with a word I can't repeat, and he told us he wanted to sit up. So, with the help of his teammates, he did, several times. It was amazing to see pure determination on his face. He will overcome with the help of all of you and with God's grace.

James 1:2-4 reads: Count it all joy, my brothers, when you meet trials of various kinds, for you know that the testing of your faith brings steadfastness. And let steadfastness have its full effect, that you may be perfect and complete, lacking in nothing. *Kevin truly has an army of prayer warriors at his side.*

November 12, 2013

Amazing afternoon. Kevin is working on standing up with the help of the physical therapist. That is a chore after being flat on his back for so long. Once he can stand up, he can do a pivot transfer and he won't have to use the lift. Yeah! The sweetest thing I heard today was Kevin's voice. It started as a whisper then he said a little louder and finally with determination and clarity, "My name is Kevin Ash!" Sing praises!

November 13, 2013

The trach is out! Yes! Kevin pulled it out, but the doctors said they would not be putting it back in. The next hurdle is to pass the swallow test. Then it will be time for real food and a cool drink of water. Kevin doesn't talk a lot yet, but when he does, he uses complete sentences. His medical team commented about that. Kevin is also moving a lot. The team commented that he is getting stronger very quickly. He is determined. His memory is beginning to trigger. He is very afraid at times as he is remembering his tours of duty. I tell him he is in Minnesota, and he is loved, and so many people are holding him in prayer. Please share this verse in your prayers tonight:

> So do not fear, for I am with you; do not be dismayed, for I am your God. I will strengthen you and help you; I will uphold you with my righteous right hand.

I am wearing out. The temporary guardianship/ conservatorship time is coming to an end. I want to extend it for another temporary timeframe. I can't, though. The options are Kevin can manage his own financial affairs (he can't at this time), or Kevin needs a permanent guardian/conservator. I would need to go to court again, to appear before the judge when my lawyer friend presents the petition. It is not what a parent ever wants to do. I have had to do so many things during these two months that I never wanted to do. Kevin is having to do so many things that he never thought he would have to do. He has a much bigger mountain to climb than I do. These are the least of the things I can do for the baby I brought into this world. I will never give up on him. Never.

Appearing before the judge and testifying to all the things that Kevin can't do breaks my heart. To have to say that he doesn't know the day of the week, the month of the year, or how old he is, breaks my heart. To say that he can't walk on his own, eat on his own, hold a job or manage his finances breaks my heart. To agree that he needs a permanent guardian/conservator is not something I want to admit. I ask if this can ever be revoked because I hope that one day, he will be able to live his life. I find out that we would need to return to the court and prove that he can manage his own affairs. I wonder why I can't just take my baby home and be his mother. I need to have a financial bond in place because I am managing his accounts. I tell the bondsman that I would never steal from my own son. He worked so hard and did everything he was supposed to do. He saved his money from the time he held his first job. He bought what he needed with cash. He lived sparsely. He served his country and his company. I would never hurt him. I am told that doesn't matter. There are bad people out there, so I write a $500 check to cover the bond and I go home.

I will eventually find out that every cent, every decision

that I make on his behalf must be documented for the courts. It seems like his life is no longer his own.

Posted for family and friends: Week 8

November 16, 2013

It is truly amazing what Kevin has accomplished in one week. While he is still not alert and responsive some of the time, I see the cumulative effect of each tiny step. One of his regular visitors told me, "I now see only each progressive accomplishment when I visit." Kevin asked his nurse (with a voice–not a whisper) "I need you to help me find a knife." When she asked him what he wanted it for, he pointed to the seatbelt on the wheelchair. He is thinking all the time and he is frustrated that it is slow progress. So, every night when I leave, I tell him how amazing he is and how he has hundreds of people who hold him in their prayers.

November 17, 2013

As Kevin continues to awaken, it is both a challenge and a blessing. Tonight, his awareness was so painful for him. He has lost so much of his time and his memories are deep and sometimes painful. His vision is very poor, and his muscles are weak. He works very hard to use his voice. He was frustrated and angry. I stayed with him longer than I intended and before I left, I said what I always say. "You are amazing, you are smart, you are strong, you are a warrior, you are brave, you are loved by so many who pray for you every day, you are not alone." He took my hand and brought it to his lips, and he kissed it. Habakkuk 2:3 reminds us not to despair; slowly, steadily, surely, the time approaches when the vision will be fulfilled. Just be patient and have faith.

November 19, 2013

I arrived at the hospital this evening with a resolve to keep encouraging Kevin to move forward. I started with the affirmations that I usually end with when I visit. "You are strong, you are brave, you are good, you have so many people praying for you, you are not alone." I shared the posts with Kevin, and I told him I write a post every night. I asked him what his day was like so I could post that tonight. I was secretly hoping for a long description of the day's events. (I know that even before the accident Kevin wasn't that chatty!) Kevin surprised me by whispering "It was a good day." He also signed "good" with his hand. So, pushing forward I asked him to give me one word to share with his Caring Bridge readers. He whispered, "Thank you." So, even though that is two words, I pass Kevin's words to you. Thank you for believing and for your trust in God. Thank you from Kevin. Someday he will share his story with all of us. He has an amazing story to tell. I look forward to hearing it.

November 22, 2013

"Underneath are the everlasting arms…" Kevin had a full day of therapies today and the therapists were pleased. His vision is still very poor and that makes it hard on him and the team. He did ask what happened, where he was, and what year it was. He also spent a full ten minutes on the exercise bike. He asked the therapist, "Can I be done now?" So, by the reports it was another good day. I know that your prayers and God's everlasting arms hold up Kevin and our family as well. We cannot do this alone.

November 23, 2013

Each day God's light shines through Kevin. Today I had a conversation with Kevin's doctor. He told me that the past five days have each shown Kevin improving and he has come so far since the accident. It is a long journey, and it will take time and patience. I spent the afternoon with Kevin, and he is so worried that he can't see. I told him he can hear, and the world is still beautiful. If I had to condense those hours that we spent together into a few sentences I would share this. Kevin touched my face and told me that he loves me. He told me I am beautiful. He told me he loves his dad, and his dad is a good man. Then he asked me to call him tomorrow and he said his phone number (and got it right) and he told me he'd see me tomorrow. He suggested we meet at his apartment in Owatonna. I told him "Not yet." I know that day will come. Tonight, I leave with 1 John 4:7

Beloved, let us love one another: for love is of God; and everyone that loves is born of God, and knoweth God... for God is love.

Kevin was on life support and his brain was swelling. He was in an unresponsive state. I try to stay in the moment. I try not to think too far ahead. The movie that I make in my head continues to spin. What will happen to us? What will happen to Kevin? I know he can't see. I can tell by how he acts with me. He panics and I know he is no longer here with me. He is somewhere else, in his mind.

"Where are my boots?" he says. "Who is that guy in the corner? Shush! Don't talk. He might hear us. He might come over here. I am Sgt Kevin Ash, United States Army," (and he gives his social security number.) Then he is quiet. His face is impassive. He thinks he has been captured.

"Incoming!!!" he screams out in the room. "Ready!" He lifts his weapon that is nothing. He looks around the room. He is not here. He hears blasts. He hears gunfire. He is in a fight for his life.

"You are not my mother," he says with a tone I have never heard before. My soul sinks. "You are not my mother. Where is she?" I know that he isn't even with me when that happens. Yet, I cry. I am silent and I walk out of the room, very quietly.

"I am your mother," I want to say. "I was with you before you were born, and I will be with you until I die. Even then, I will be with you in eternity. You are supposed to have a long and happy life. You are supposed to have a family and I am supposed to hold your children and watch them grow up. We are supposed to be together until I die, and then I will meet you in heaven." This is not the way this story is supposed to go. This is a nightmare.

Shortly after Kevin's accident (time is now defined as "before his accident" and "after his accident"). As I drove home I was crying. I asked God, "How could you let this happen to my son? He is in a coma." Each day we prayed the Lord's Prayer over him before we left the hospital. Every day we prayed many prayers. Along Interstate 94, in the pouring rain and through my tears, I heard God and felt His Words which gave me peace in my heart–How could I let this happen to your son? He was my son first. Remember what happened to Jesus. You cannot understand.

A few days later, we had a decision to make. Continue with life saving measures or take him off life support. My parents, my two other children, my brothers and sisters-in-law met, and we prayed that I would be able to do the right thing. As we were praying, Kevin whispered the words, "Don't. Give. Up."

We heard God's message. My son lived.

The doctors told me to bring the things that were important to him as he gradually became more awake–pictures, objects, books, movies. He would grasp onto these things as he awakes. I went to his apartment and looked at the things that were there. He had models that he had built of tanks and airplanes–memories of his military life, perhaps? I brought those to the hospital. He had figures that he had painted, goblins and monsters and heroes. I brought those. He had pictures of his dad, his grandparents, his sister, his nephew/Godson, and me. I brought those. He had a Bible, and he had Game of Thrones–the whole set of books. I brought those. He had a few medals from his deployments. His camera was there, and I brought that. I packed the bag and took these trappings of his life back to the hospital room. He was alive and yet he couldn't see them. He was blind.

He began to crawl out of the coma. He listened and he couldn't remember the events that brought him to this place. His memories consisted of battles and things I couldn't know. He remembered his name, address, rank, and numbers. He was afraid. He feared everyone. He saw only what was in his mind. The things that I brought him didn't help; he couldn't see them. I prayed for him. I told him he was a child of God and that had redeemed him. He cried out, "Jesus use me."

Posted for family and friends: Week 8–Long Term Care Hospital

November 24, 2013

Rejoice and be glad in it. Thank you to the visitors who have been stopping in to see Kevin. Yes, despite all the trials in our journeys, it is still a beautiful world. Kevin continues to waken, and each day brings me some smiles and some tears. He is realizing the things he can't do and since he can't see his mind imagines that this must be from the war. He needs assurances that he is here in Minnesota, that he is safe and that he will make it through this journey, too. He is a child of God and God has him in His hands. When I tell him this, he nods "yes." How hard it must be to sort out his surroundings when he suddenly can't see them. How often I have seen the staff come in and begin their duties without telling him what is going on. I can see the panic in his face when that happens. I wish I could take this from him and yet I know and trust in God's plan. Please visit if you can and keep your prayers strong. God bless you.

November 25, 2013

When it seems darkest, God shines a light. It is hard to see Kevin struggle to make sense out of this senselessness. He is working so hard and truly there are times when he wants to give up. I saw the hand of God today at this kind of moment. It came through the nurse aide who talked to Kevin and told him how much he has still to give, and how brave and strong he is. She told him she knew he has this–he can do it. He nodded yes and kissed her hand. Thank God for the small things as many small things become huge.

November 26, 2013

I want to give thanks for each step in Kevin's journey and today Kevin took 10 steps! Yes, he had a person on each side and his arms were on their shoulders. He took those steps and that is what counts. I can feel the collective praise swelling across this nation for those steps. Give thanks and sing praises to God. May Kevin continue his progress. This is truly a Thanksgiving to remember.

November 27, 2013

Do not be anxious... Kevin had a wonderful visit with my friend last evening. He is starting to converse, and I am starting to see his personality shine through. He likes to sing–that's a little-known fact about him. He had solos when he was in choir in junior and senior high school. When things start to overwhelm him, he likes to hear a simple lullaby or cheerful song. Overwhelming it can be–his vision is poor, and he has hearing issues because of his IED exposures in Iraq. Despite the challenges, Kevin continues to display the determination that has served him so well. When his situation begins to wear on him, I remind him that he is loved, and he has many people praying for him. He is God's child, and he will never be alone. He asked me to hold onto him and to never let go. He told me that he is fragile, and he doesn't want to break. I told him we will never let go–he said, "Thank you." Amen to that.

November 29, 2013

Kevin continues to become more alert. This comes with challenges in orienting to today. While it is hard to see the struggles that Kevin has as he works so hard to pull up memories. He continues to fight through. Today, he asked for a shave, haircut, and a shower because he was rating himself a "2" right now on his appearance. Once he finished, he felt a lot better. I would rate him a "10" for determination, perseverance, and looks!

"We can't keep him here forever," the doctors tell me. "He needs to go somewhere else." I suppose that I knew this, but in the movie in my mind, he will awake from this nightmare and have his bags packed. We will walk out of the hospital together. He will pull his baseball cap on his head and jump into his car, open the window, lean out and say, "Hey, Mom. I'll talk to you later." With a jaunty wave he will pull out and drive back out into the world. He will pick up his life where it so abruptly stopped two months ago. He will call me and say, "Hey, Mom. I got your message. I'm calling you back."

That was the last message he left me on Saturday morning, September 21, 2013. I have his cell phone, and finally figured out his password. I checked his messages. I was desperate to understand what happened during the months before the accident. How could this have happened? It made no sense. It still doesn't.

Nothing has been easy for Kevin. As I learned of the events that led up to the accident, I got more information about the end of his military career. I called one of his fellow soldiers. I learned he could potentially be eligible for service at the VA hospital. "Do you have his DD214?" he asked. I don't even really know what that is, and I presume he has it–

somewhere. The Federal government has been shut down. I can't get any records from them currently. I travel many places looking for the next stop on this continuing journey in Kevin's life. The doctors tell me that he needs a skilled nursing facility. He has a PEG tube for feeding. He still can't eat on his own. They list all the things he can't do.

I want to scream at them, "He can talk. He can sing the songs from his childhood. He took 10 steps. He has emotions. He has joys and fears. He responds to us. He has come so far from that first day of the accident. He is only 31 years old. Nursing facilities are for old people. He is a young man."

But I can't scream these things anywhere, except in my head. I need to work with these people. Kevin needs me to speak for him. He deserves nothing less. He is my beautiful baby. He is a combat seasoned veteran. He has value. He cannot live in a warehouse just waiting for death. He has lived through many things already. These things are a part of him, even if he can't talk about them–even if he doesn't remember them. The people who work with him see the endless days and nights that will turn into years for him. The people who are in these homes are there until they die. My son is not dead.

I am packing up my son's belongings yet again. Each time this has happened, he has not died. Still, he can't do this job himself. The first time I did this, he was still unconscious. I felt so out of place as I went into his apartment. I felt like I was trespassing. I washed his dishes and his clothes that he had left out before he went to play rugby that fateful day. I cleaned out his refrigerator. I emptied his trash.

The second time wasn't any easier. People kept telling me to stop paying his rent–let his apartment go. I couldn't do that. In the movie in my mind, he would go back to his apartment. I wanted it to be clean and ready for him with his clothes washed and hung in his closet and his dishes neatly put into their place in the cupboard. I wanted him to know that I kept everything in place for him–that he had a place to go back to.

The third time, I go into his apartment and begin to box and bag up his possessions. So many of the day-to-day items were things I had given him for his apartment. Things like the microwave, the toaster, pots, and pans can be replaced. I send those to the secondhand store. Other things are harder to pack. Things like his notebooks and games, medals, and pictures are reminders of things he can't use right now. I don't have the energy to sort through them. I carefully box and bag them. I label the boxes and bags with the room location just in case he asks for something. In the movie in my head, he will ask for the picture that was in his living room. I will know right where to find it.

What do these things mean to him? They are waiting for me to figure out their riddle. Today, these items are in the storage locker that I rented. Why did he keep these things? What did they mean to him? Or were they simply the trappings of his life? These things do not define his life that was or what it will be. As I pack each thing, I touch the pieces of his life–memories and questions fill the space. Cleaning out a person's space when they die is hard enough. When a person dies, he has moved beyond this place. These objects will mean nothing to him. The hardest thing is packing up a person's life when he is still alive, and doing that over, and over again.

Posted for family and friends: VA Hospital—Week 9

December 1, 2013

Kevin had visitors today–his dad's side of the family met him in the hospital lounge. Kevin was alert and amazed that people were there to see him. We constantly reminded Kevin of our love and where he is. We need to stay grounded in our faith, our love, our hope, and our presence. Tomorrow will be a busy day–Kevin will be moving to the VA hospital, a Level 1 Trauma hospital. This move will bring a new team and intense care for Kevin. We all know that Kevin needs that.

December 2, 2013

Kevin arrived at the VA Hospital today at 10:45 a.m. His team members began arriving immediately and introduced themselves to Kevin. He is in very good hands. The VA is committed to providing Kevin with all the treatments and therapies he needs. It was a busy day and Kevin was engaged and connected throughout, although he was emotional when he thought about all that has happened over these past few months. At one point he asked how all the bills are going to get paid. I assured him that he has many, many people who care about him and who pray for him daily. We leave this challenge of paying the bills in God's hands as well.

December 4, 2013

Kevin continues to adjust to his new routine at the VA hospital. His team is working hard to gain his trust and to let him know they are working in his best interests. Today was the first day Kevin has not had one of his visitors. The winter weather is going to be a challenge and I couldn't get to the hospital to see him. When I talked with his nurse tonight, she told me that they want to see improvements every day. So, when it is a status quo kind of day everyone is a little bit sad. Kevin is working hard, and he is in God's hands. God holds him, and all of us, in His hands. If we cannot be there in person, please let Kevin know that we are with him in spirit. He is a strong person, and he can make it through these challenges.

December 5, 2013

One of the guys from the rugby team visited tonight and he sent me a message about how good Kevin was doing–he conversed, answered questions, and even asked his own questions! Nate has been in this journey since the beginning. He told me that Kevin's progress in the two weeks since he last visited is remarkable.

I called Kevin earlier today at the nurse's suggestion. I really expected to just have a chance to tell Kevin I am thinking about him and to tell him he is not alone. Imagine my surprise when he talked to me on the phone. He said, "Mom?" I asked him if he had a good day. He said, "No." His tone was the one people use when they mean "duhhhh." So, I said, "Do you want to tell me about it?" He responded, "No, I don't want to talk right now." And then he threw the phone! The nurse picked up the phone and told me, "Let's try it again." I laughed and said I didn't think that would be a good idea because he didn't want to talk right now. He is communicating how he feels–amazing. I see God at work every day. Thank you for your prayers.

Psalm 145:5–I will meditate on your wonderful works.

December 6, 2013

He is talking more and more and asking questions. He answers questions appropriately but not always accurately. He continues to amaze me. Today, he wanted to talk to his sister on the phone. He wasn't very loud, so I was trying to be helpful by repeating what he was saying so Erica could hear him. At one point he asked Erica a question. I repeated the question and Kevin turned toward me and said, "Mom, I just asked her that!" I left the room so they could talk!

Kevin finds pleasure in singing old familiar songs. He was smiling and I was laughing tonight when we sang "Old McDonald Had A Farm" and he suggested that he had a pigeon (what does a pigeon say anyway?) and a snake! I say a "thank you" to God every night. Yes, Kevin has a long way to go and he has come so very far already. Praise God!

December 8, 2013

Each day I am more amazed–even on days when Kevin experiences a world of confusion and seemingly huge contradictions. His team is present and patient and understanding. Today, I was talking with Kevin about his past and the present. He is struggling to make sense out of the fragmented memories. I told him that there are people all over the world–people he doesn't even know who read his posts and that he has hundreds of entries in his guest book. He wanted me to read the entries to him. It brought him to tears as he listened and then he said, "I didn't even know that so many people care about me or even know I'm here." Each day is another day to look for God's hand and each day is another chance to pray. Kevin is not alone. He has all of us sharing this journey. And we are never alone (Hebrews 13:5)

My son has dreams of the past, and he has dreams of the future. His life has changed so much since the accident that took his memories, his physical ability, and his sight. Yet, he is still alive, and God has a purpose for his life. I know that. He thinks that he is in a dream. He asks me to wake him up. He is living in a nightmare that has become his reality. When doctors ask him questions, he tries to answer. He has always wanted to be able to give the correct answer. They say he is confabulating. What does that word mean, anyway? I looked it up: In psychiatry, **confabulation** (verb: **confabulate**) is a disturbance of memory, **defined** as the production of fabricated, distorted, or misinterpreted memories about oneself or the world, without the conscious intention to deceive.

I suppose that is what he is doing. He has no intention to deceive. His memories are distorted or misinterpreted. It is another thing that he has lost. I wish he could see the pictures that I brought him. I have a picture of when he caught his fish. He was so proud of the little fish as he held it up for me to see. I have a picture of his race car set that he got for Christmas one year. He was ecstatic about that present and his smile was so bright and wide. I have a picture of him with his sister and brother outside of our camper. They all wear bandanas around their heads. It was hot that day.

I wish he could look out the window and see the weather. It has been a snowy winter and the drifts are up to the windows. We can hear the wind blowing, but he doesn't know if it is winter or summer unless I tell him the month. The doctors aren't convinced that he can't see, but I am. I know my son. They say, "He answers questions correctly some of the time, therefore he can see." I tell them that he was always good at figuring things out. It narrows down the possible answers and the laws of probability say he will get the answers correct some of the time.

He defies the "usual." Of course, all people are different. Of course, no brain is the same as other brains. I ask, "What are the best practices for people who have brain injuries and who are vision and hearing impaired?" If this is what Kevin has left, how do I maximize it? I am a teacher. I know that we underestimate people all the time. I have seen children who literally lost half of their brain learn to read, write, and function. I know that my son responds well to challenges and goals. If we want him to have the best results, what should be we doing to help him achieve those results?

The answers the therapists and doctors give me aren't very satisfying. They said, "For memory issues, rely on lists and pictures." But he can't see those. What can we do? "For blind people, use verbal lists," they tell me. But his memory impairment doesn't allow him to use auditory lists without help. What do we do? "That is a big challenge," the therapists say. "Surely, my son isn't the only one with these challenges," I declare. They look at me with sadness in their eyes and walk away.

They don't realize yet that I will never give up on my son. I will be there for him, and I will do everything in my power to help him come back to life–to have hope. I know that his brain is powerful. While he isn't responding consistently yet, he says the most profound things at times. Yesterday he told me, "I don't understand what happened. Half my brain does and half of it doesn't." The nurses tell me his descriptions and the details that he provides are astonishing. One day I was reading a book to him. It was about a Ronin. My son has always been fascinated by samurai. "I don't even really know what a Ronin is," I say. "Do you?"

The aide was cleaning his room as we talked. Kevin thought for a moment and said, "A Ronin is a samurai without a master–a samurai whose master died." I didn't tell him that I had looked it up before I asked him the question. You know what? He was exactly right. I congratulated him. The aide looked at me with a shocked and perplexed expression. My son is amazing. How can I help him through this nightmare? I agree with him–we are in a terrible dream. It doesn't end. I work hard to stay in the moment. When I try to imagine what his life will be like, the thoughts shake me to my soul. I can't think about that. I choose to focus on what I can do at this moment to make his life better.

I remember hearing that the average person only uses a portion of the brain power that is available. I hold onto the stories of the people who have literally lost half of their brain. With perseverance and a lot of hard work, people can continue their lives. Some stories tell of people who have learned to talk, to read, to function in life again, despite loss of their brain. As a teacher, I know people can rewire their brains. It takes hard work. My son is not afraid of hard work. I'm not afraid of it either.

Posted for family and friends: VA hospital–Week 10

December 10, 2013

Never doubt that your prayers are felt, and your messages are needed. Tonight, was rough and Kevin had a setback. I was so afraid that he was going back to a coma. While his nursing assistant and I tried hard to get him to respond it looked like nothing would work. He appeared to have had a seizure and he was not responding to anything. The doctors were consulted, and we waited. Finally, I told Kevin that he is strong and smart and brave and loved by so many. I told him his posts have had thousands of visits, and people have left hundreds of messages and countless prayers. I asked him if he wanted me to read the messages to him. He gave us an almost imperceptible nod–yes. I read to him, and a big tear slid down his cheek. The aide on one side and I on the other cried with him as we told him that he is loved. He began to sob and then he began to talk again. We cried together and promised him that he is not alone. As it turned out he had two more visitors tonight. His brother arrived and one of the guys from the rugby team arrived shortly after that. When I left the guys were talking and all was better. Just know that when you read these posts and if you send a message and say a prayer you are truly saving Kevin's life. Thank you and God bless you.

December 11, 2013

I went to see Kevin with some trepidation. When I arrived, the nurse caught me to tell me it had been a tough night and the day had been tough too. Kevin was silent and distant when I got to his room. My sister sent a present which he did open–it is a drum and the perfect size for him to hold. As it happened, the rec therapist was scheduled for the early evening. At first it looked like Kevin was not going to interact. However, after she gave him a tender shoulder, arm, and neck massage, he started to relax. By the end of her visit, he was talking about the bands he likes, his pets, and his family and friends. He even laughed a few times. He repeated patterns on his new drum, and all was well. He told me he was tired, and I said, "When you head to bed, I have to go home." He said, "Okay, I'll see you later." What a bright way and normal way to conclude a rough 24 hours. I said, "Sleep well my son."

December 12, 2013

"Touch it at any point and the whole web quivers." (Stanley Kunitz) On September 21 our universe was shaken. Since that day, Kevin has shown all of us what it means to suffer incredible adversity and still move forward every day. Today the nurses reported that he attended the Christmas party, and he enjoyed the festivities. It was hard for him to head back to the unit, though. He wants to go home. He told me, "I want my life back." Kevin will have his life back–he already has begun to reclaim it. We are blessed to share his life. I read the guest book messages and I have no doubt. I feel the prayers and I know that this is true. Rock on, Kevin. You are a son of God and your story continues to amaze us all.

December 13, 2013

As I left Kevin tonight, he was amid a flashback. I felt so helpless as I tried everything, I knew to bring him back to this moment. He would touch it and suddenly be back in that war zone. So, I assured him again that he is held up in prayers and that he is cherished, that I love him. I left feeling despair. As I drove home in the dark, I began to reflect on all the progress Kevin has made this week. He is eating pudding and soft food; he is sitting unassisted for 5 minutes. He is standing for several minutes. He is talking out loud and he is singing, and even laughing at times. He is compassionate, polite, and gracious. Yes, his situation can seem dark and yet we still have many blessings. Kevin will get through the darkness and in each day, we must keep our eyes on the light. I pray that Kevin has peace and sleeps well tonight.

December 14, 2013

Kevin finally slept last night and when I called this morning his team was letting him sleep in. On the rehab floor, therapies continue, even on Saturday. His dad visited him today. I read an article about Maria Shriver today. The final quote of that article resonated with me–"You have to be willing to let go of the life you planned in order to make the life you're meant to live." I pray that Kevin and all of us will achieve this. Truly, God is in control.

December 15, 2013

Sunday at the VA hospital is a little more relaxed with only a few therapies. Kevin had OT and Rec therapy today. He continues to ask very good questions about what happened. He was very engaged today. He asked his rec therapist to help him continue to wake up. He is working so hard, and he amazes everyone. We watched the first 45 minutes of "White Christmas" and we decorated the Christmas tree that Grannie and Grandad sent. It has been a wonderful afternoon.

December 16, 2013

At this time of the year, it is so easy to get caught up in the commercial side of the holidays. For generations, our service members have been across the world during the holidays. Kevin had three Christmas holidays while on active duty. He asked me what happened while was on his tours. I couldn't give him any answers. I know that what he experienced forever impacted him. Kevin served to make the world a better place. The VA staff understand that. They tell him now, in his hour of need, they are here to serve him and help him recover.

Matthew 5:9–Blessed are the peacemakers for they shall be called the children of God.

I would never have predicted that I would be spending Christmas like this. I think back to the Christmas times that Kevin spent with the family. As a January baby he was nearly one year old at his first Christmas. He was a chubby little guy with blue eyes and blond hair. He was the second grandchild on both sides of two large families. He was lucky to have three great grandmothers, and both sets of grandparents, a total of nine uncles and three aunts. He was cherished by a large extended family. There is a picture of him with his sister and his extended family at Christmas. He was happy and the world was a wonderful place.

We moved away from our family two years later. Times were tough and jobs were hard to find. Still, I knew that Kevin was fascinated by the military. I joked with his dad that Kevin would play with sticks for a sword or a gun, and a garbage can lid for a shield. Where these ideas came from, we don't know. Even though his father had served in the Navy, we weren't what one would consider an active military family.

It was a snowy, dark November day. In our little town, many people were hunters, so this weekend was the fabled "Hunters' Widows Bazaar." Churches, organizations, and community members brought their wares to the high school where they set up tables and sold what they had made. Leave it to Kevin to find a camo outfit that was just his size. "Mommy buy that for me," he begged. While I'm pretty sure it was hunting camo, he saw it as his very own military uniform.

I told him, "No. I don't have any money." I tried to convince him.

"Just use a check," he said. Clearly, he didn't yet understand that if you don't have money, you can't use a check. He was relentless.

He wanted that outfit so he could be a soldier. Needless to say, I ended up getting it for him for Christmas that year. Then, he begged me to sew a matching camo outfit for his favorite stuffed animal–a lion. From that point on, he and Lion were together. He packed up that stuffed animal, still wearing camo and carried him through all three deployments. When he began to awaken, he asked for Lion. I found Lion and brought him to Kevin. When Kevin felt him, I asked, "Do you know what this is?"

In a voice that expressed such amazed happiness, he said, "It's Lion?" He hugged that now ragged stuffed animal with the paint of its eyes rubbed off to his chest. He hugged Lion as he slept.

Kevin didn't fight battles for the sake of having a war. He fought to defend others. He wanted to be a protector of the weak. I don't know how he developed that concept, but it was present from the time he could express himself. He had a kind and loving soul. He began to see the world as a place where things weren't always fair or just. He was troubled by that, and that knowledge drove him further towards the idea of service to others. Joining the military was a calling for him, not to wage war, but to be a peacemaker.

Posted for family and friends: VA Hospital—Week 11

December 19, 2013

Kevin is trying to make sense of his current condition. Today, he struggled and escaped into fantasy. It seemed like a reasonable path when you think about it. What he is dealing with is huge. He was able to let go of the escape strategy through songs and shared memories. I can only imagine how hard it is to see how much progress is being made when all you feel is the mountain left to climb. So, with his amazing ability to ask profound questions, Kevin asked me, "I don't understand what the lesson is that I am supposed to learn." With tears in my eyes, I had to choke them back to tell him. Sometimes we don't know the answers. God has a plan. Trust God and trust others and know that you are loved by so many people. That is the lesson. I asked him if he wanted to hear from all the children who are sending him Christmas cards, and from the people who have sent cards. He said, "Yes." I read many cards and he shed a few tears. He held a handful of cards and closed his eyes. I said my goodbyes and told him that he is very loved. He said, "I know." Yes, perhaps the most important lesson for all of us is "trust God and know that you are loved."

December 21, 2013

One of Kevin's aunts and uncles and Kevin's brother joined me today at the VA Hospital. Kevin genuinely enjoyed the large group. We were in the family lounge and that was a nice change. Kevin responded to questions and even had a few of his own. He told us he wants a red Mustang, and money for Christmas and he smiled. Connor had a chance to spend some 1:1 brother time with Kevin. Kevin said something funny, and Connor told me that when he laughed Kevin had a big old belly laugh too. Inch by inch and step by step Kevin makes progress–a smile and a belly laugh–what a great way to end our visit. I hope you all realize how much your prayers support Kevin. I know that he has a powerful shield of prayer around him.

December 22, 2013

We are truly amazing creations–when I think about all the complexities that make up each one of us, my head spins. Kevin struggled through the late night and early morning hours last night. He had very lucid conversations with the staff followed by periods of agitation. At these times I pray that he is surrounded by light and love and that prayers hold the demons at bay. Truly, he is a child of God. Kevin has always told me he wants his life to make a difference for others. At times like this I envision the light shining through his darkness. I pray that tonight he knows the comfort and peace that we all shower on him.

God of our life, there are days when the burdens we carry

chafe our shoulders and weigh us down; when the road seems dreary and endless, the skies grey and threatening; when our lives have no music in them and our hearts are lonely, and our souls have lost their courage. Flood the path with light, run our eyes to where the skies are full of promise; tune our hearts to brave music; give us the sense of comradeship with heroes and saints of every age; and quicken our spirits that we may be able to encourage the souls of all who journey with us on the road of life, to your honor and glory. –Prayer of St. Augustine

(May Kevin hear this prayer in his heart and soul as it is spoken from hundreds of voices tonight.)

December 23, 2013

"Trust the Lord with all your heart and lean not on your own understanding." *Kevin has had a couple of agitated days and he is tired, and I haven't seen him awake since our awesome visit on Saturday. It is so hard to see him so quiet and sleeping during the day. I know in my heart that he is healing, and God is holding him. Yet my brain sees him so silent, and I think of those terrible weeks when he was in a coma. I think about all he has accomplished now compared to just three weeks ago and I know that prayers continue as we trust the Lord and His plan. Tomorrow is a new day. May Kevin's sleep be filled with rest and peace tonight.*

December 25, 2013

Kevin and I spent the afternoon together. I read him the Christmas story and we sang some Christmas songs. He told me he was annoyed when I arrived. He didn't want to be at the hospital on a holiday. So, we made

the best of it by taking several laps around the unit as I pushed him in his wheelchair. He enjoyed that and didn't want to stop. He is still in the wheelchair, and he can't see, so I spent a lot of time describing the route. We stopped in the rec room and played catch. I told him to throw the ball at me. He told me he couldn't see me. I said, "Throw it at my voice." He did and it hit me right in the mouth! Good thing it was a soft ball. The staff got a chuckle out of that! When staff walked by, I asked him to introduce himself and ask their names. They got a chuckle when he asked Mohamed if he was "the" Mohamed. After that all the staff wanted to have "the" in front of their names. He does have a good (and dry) sense of humor. Kevin continues to ask questions as he tries to make sense of his situation. He asks the timeless question of "why." We don't know the answer to that question and so we put our trust in God's plan. When I left, I assured Kevin that his team and all of you are working hard to help him recover and fulfill his plan, whatever that will be.

Chapter 2

Posted for family and friends: Month 4

December 26, 2013

Kevin had a full day of rehab therapies today after the Christmas break. I was back at work, too. I called and Kevin and I talked with him on the phone. He sounded just like himself. It was nice to hear him talk. The nurse reported that it was a productive day and Kevin is making improvements as he is doing more of the physical part of moving from the bed to the chair on his own. He still needs assistance, but he is successful. That is important. I came across this quote from an American author, Laurence Shames, and I thought that it sums things up very nicely: "Success and failure–we think of them as opposites, but they're really companions–the hero and the sidekick." *It is a good thing to keep in mind. It takes many, many times of trying before success. Then, when success happens, it is so sweet. Keep trying, Kevin. We won't give up and neither do you.*

December 27, 2013

There are so many verses in this Psalm that help us through these days. 118:5 "out of my distress I called on the Lord; the Lord answered me and set me free." 118: 7 "With the Lord at my side, I do not fear. What can man do to me?" *And all the other verses... Today, my friend and I visited Kevin after his care team meeting. The team is reporting positive steps. Even the times of agitation are steps in the right direction. We know we need to pass through the storm to get to the light. Kevin is in a storm at times, and he is angry, and he knows the reasons for his anger. As the doctor said, he has very little that he can control right now, and he can be angry. The VA Hospital is the best place for him right now. They understand his anger and his fears. My friend and I tried all our strategies, and nothing worked until we asked him if he could open his heart to the love that surrounds him. He said he could do that. My friend asked him how we could show him our love. He said, "Blow me a kiss." From that moment on he began to calm. We told him that he is loved and that he is God's child. When anger tries to consume him, he can take the love that is in him and around him and move onward and forward. He was exhausted (and so were we) and he asked to rest. So, the staff tucked him into bed, and we pulled up his Freedom Quilt and bathed him in love and said, "Rest well knowing that you are loved." Your prayers are so important to Kevin and to all.*

December 28, 2013

My good friend reminded me that progress can often dip and spin and that it has. I visited Kevin today and he was tired and just getting ready for a nap. He was calm and clear and asked about his sister and his brother. I told him that Connor is on a vacation with his dad and then we talked about planning a vacation in the future. Kevin suggested

Florida–he was there once a long time ago. Then we called Erica and they chatted for several minutes. Kevin told me sleep was calling him, so I said my goodbyes. A tiny tear collected in his eye. I asked him if he was sad and he said, "No, I'm happy to be back." I am happy, too, that he has once again made it back from that dark place that he has been in for these past few days. So, keep sending out your light and he will continue to find his way.

December 29, 2013

Kevin has had a quiet weekend. His dad and stepmom visited yesterday, and his aunt visited today. I was so happy to hear from his nurses that all was well. Kevin is struggling to make sense of this–it continues to baffle him. Certainly, it is impossible to understand. Kevin says it just seems like a bad dream. However, his spirit is strong, and he has a sense of determination that is second to none. He tried his hand with drawing yesterday and he even signed his name. The staff were amazed. He and I played cards and he did a great job counting points in the cribbage game. Today he started a craft project by sanding the wood for a model airplane. While these things seem small, each one is a testimony to Kevin's ability to adapt and succeed. He asked me today, "What will people think about me being in the hospital so long?" I told him that people admire him and care for him. People rejoice in each step of this journey.

May the God of hope fill you with all joy and peace as you trust in Him. –Romans 15:13

December 31, 2013

A year ago, I would never have guessed what would happen. As this year ends and I think back, I am filled with hope for the future–not just for

Kevin, but for all of us. As I think about Kevin's question, "What is the lesson I am supposed to learn from this?" I realize more and more that it is to trust. Whether the day that has passed has had moments of sadness and pain, or happiness and peace, we must trust God. As Kevin and I spent time together today, I had the pleasure of watching him do the work with his therapists. He is working and progressing more and more each day.

First, he whispered, "My name is Kevin Ash," then he spoke out loud, "My name is Kevin Ash," and now he is writing his name–Kevin Ash. Yes, there will be good days and days where things aren't so good. However, the trust we have means none of us is alone.

Psalm 90: 12–Teach us to number our days that we may get a heart of wisdom.

I sometimes feel like I have lost my child completely. It is my greatest fear–to lose a child. I think most parents would agree with that. We bring our children into the world with hopefulness. We are filled with happiness that comes from pain. We bring our children into the world with the belief that we will protect them and create for them a successful, happy life. We are lulled into a false sense of security and power. We can't always protect our children from the adversity and accidents of the world.

When I was a young child, my parents would pack all six of us–my brothers and my sister and me–in our big station wagon. We would get up early in the morning, and my mom and I would pack a bag of sandwiches. Sometimes these would be peanut butter and jelly, sometimes ground bologna and sometimes ground ham. I remember getting out the meat grinder and making the sandwich meat, mixing it with Miracle Whip and ground pickles in the big metal bowl. I'd slather the concoction on the fresh, homemade bread. Sometimes, we'd have cookies to add to the bag. Then, we'd all pack up into the station wagon and drive a few hours to wherever we were headed. Six young children and two parents contained in a vehicle on the highway could have been a dangerous place. I never once thought about the dangers that we might face.

Our car was "air conditioned" when the windows were open. The noise of the wind through the windows of cars still bothers me today. I generally sat in the "way back" of the station wagon. My seat faced where we had been, not where we were going. I generally couldn't hear any conversations with the wind coming through the open windows that was our air conditioning. I passed the time reading or looking out the window. I never worried, though. I always knew where we had been, even though I couldn't see where we were going.

On one of these trips, we traveled to the city to visit a couple who were friends from my parents' college days. We were rural children who played outside every day. We seldom thought about the traffic because we didn't ever see a lot of cars. On this sunny Saturday, we were playing in the house. I was playing "house" with my sister and the other girls. The boys were playing Mr. Potato Head and Battleship. We heard the doorbell ring. Doorbells didn't usually ring in our lives. I remember stopping and listening to that unusual sound.

First, I heard my mom and her friend moaning, a sound I don't recall ever hearing before. I was so surprised that this sound was coming out of my mother's mouth.

I found out that a young neighborhood girl had been hit by a car down the street. She had died. I had no concept of how that could have happened. Watching my parents' and their friends' faces reflect the fear and tragedy that was encompassed in that message will always stay with me. My mother said, "Instead of planning this young girl's next birthday party, they are planning her funeral."

I overheard the child's mother talking to my parents' friends. I will forever remember what she said. She was talking about what clothes her beloved daughter would wear for the burial. "I want her to have the anklet socks with the lace around the cuffs," she said through her tears. "She always wanted those socks. I always told her that they weren't necessary, and she didn't need them. Now, she will have them. I wish I had her with me now. I would buy her those socks, even if she didn't need them." I saw my mother, her friend and this child's mother encompassed in grief. My mom and her friend were grieving for this child's mother. I felt their pain and loss in my very soul. I had never thought that a child, like me, might die. My mother and her friend were surely fearful thinking that this could have been so easily one of their children. Later, I heard my parents often say, "There, but for the grace of God, go I." I carry this memory forever.

When I became a mother, I remember thinking of this

tragedy that happened so many years ago. I remember thinking that I would always cherish each day that I had with my children. Nothing is guaranteed.

Now I'm sitting in hospital rooms every day. I go to work and head out to see Kevin every evening. As I drive I-94 to 494 to 35E, I keep thinking of Kevin, my practical child. He was the second of three children, and he exemplified the middle child. Kevin was a team player. He never saw himself as the "superstar" and he was uncomfortable being the center of attention.

Middle school is a tough time for many young people. They are half children and half teenagers. When he was in middle school, his music teacher discovered that Kevin had a wonderful voice. The teacher was so excited to have Kevin sing, and put him in a solo position singing, "Lean on Me." Kevin performed the song in the spring concert so well that he received a scholarship to attend a summer music camp that year.

I loved to hear Kevin sing. As he got older, he began to step back from the "solo" roles. He preferred to be in the chorus, not in the limelight. "Kevin, please try out for the Carolers group this year," I remember begging him. I wanted him to try out for the elite singing group in high school.

"No, Mom," he was adamant. "I am not going to try out. I don't want to do that." Despite my pleading, he was insistent. He felt his contribution to the choir was enough.

When Kevin went to boot camp after high school, he was marked to be a squad leader. He exemplified the Army Core values then, and throughout his military career. We went to

Fort Benning, GA to watch the graduation ceremony where he "Turned Blue." I can see the squads and companies march onto the parade field on that hot late summer day. We sat with families who all had someone out on that field. We all were looking to see our person who was one of many. I scanned the groups and I remember smiling when I saw Kevin marching. After the ceremonies, families were invited out to meet up with their soldiers. Kevin hugged me and introduced me to the officers and a few of his fellow soldiers. All graduates of boot camp have a picture taken. When I compare the picture from the start of boot camp to the picture at graduation, I see the boy who has truly become a man. "Why didn't you smile?" I asked him. He just looked at me with a little smirk. "Really, Mom," he said. "Soldiers don't smile."

We helped him walk from his boot camp barracks to his Advanced Individual Training (AIT) barracks after the graduation ceremony as he stayed to combine both training into one. All the soldiers who were staying for AIT had a little bit of time before they had to report, but he wanted to be ready.

Kevin moved through the ranks steadily and was a sergeant by his final deployment. As a middle child, he demonstrated the ability to be more independent. He didn't let what others thought about him define him. He wanted to fit in and fulfill his role. He wanted to play his part.

Once he committed to something, Kevin was deeply committed, but he always looked for different ways to get to the final goal. He wasn't interested in finding the easy way out. Rather, he wanted to find the best way to reach the goal, even if it was the most difficult way. As a student who struggled with reading and writing, he often suffered from harassment by his peers. They didn't understand that his challenges in reading and writing didn't determine his ability to understand complex issues. He thrived in classes where discussion was valued. He observed, and formulated theories and was able to clearly articulate well defined hypotheses and analyses. Parent/Teacher conferences were not pleasant most of the time, however. His peers and his teachers formed their judgment on his abilities from his reading and writing skills.

When he was in high school, his favorite classes were of the social studies, history, and geography subjects. He often shared his thoughts about these topics at the dinner table. I remember reporting to conferences early in his high school career. Kevin and I assessed the situation in the gymnasium. "Which teacher should we see first," I asked him. Ever the practical one, he scanned the lines of parents and students, and selected the shortest line to go to first. It happened to be the social studies teacher. I expected that this teacher would be more positive than the English teacher, so I was happy to walk over to that line. When we sat down with the teacher, I was surprised to hear that despite above average test and quiz scores, Kevin's projected grade was slightly below average. "Kevin doesn't take notes in class," the teacher pointed out. "I require students to turn in their notes each week, and this is a large percentage of their grade. He hasn't turned in any notes, so that really pulls down his grade."

As we left that conference, I was frustrated. He passed his tests and quizzes; he loved the discussions. He can talk about all the concepts with us at the dinner table. "Why don't you just take notes and turn them in?" I asked. "You are capable of getting a really good grade in this class. Why don't you just do this? It is an easy thing."

"Mom," he replied, "I want to learn. If I must, I'll listen and take notes at the same time, I fall so far behind, I can't learn anything. What would you rather have me do–take the notes and not learn, or learn and not take the notes?" That was a great point. My son taught me so much about looking at the world through a different lens. Later, I went back to that teacher and explained that Kevin would not be turning in his notes each week. I explained the reasons and that I was okay with learning and passing the tests and not turning in the notes. "That's fine," said the teacher. "But he will get a zero for that anyway. I won't give him special treatment." It was the way it worked. He never expected special treatment, and he worked incredibly hard to compensate for his challenges. I was so proud of each passing grade he received, even though it was often just an "average" grade because I knew the cost of every point that he earned. High school was not the best part of his life as it is for many people. It was the time that he learned how to persist with grit and determination. He learned how to make things work and how to succeed. He built the foundation that he would bring with him into the future. He showed me that he would be able to survive through challenges, misunderstandings, and hardship.

As a child, I had a strong Christian faith. I was brought up in the church, and some of my earliest memories revolve around that. My grandmother had a strong faith, and I spent a lot of time with her. I didn't know it at the time, but many of the words of wisdom she gave me were verses straight out of the Bible. In my childhood, my life was my family, my school, and church. Belief in God and Jesus was a part of me, and I never questioned that. Kevin and his siblings were brought up with that faith as well. The church community was a big part of their lives, too.

When Kevin was in confirmation classes, he struggled with reading and writing as well. It was a huge challenge for him. He worked so hard to complete all the requirements, which included taking and submitting notes from the sermons. He struggled with this requirement, but never asked for any exceptions. Sermons were different from class discussions, so I think perhaps he thought that he could listen and prepare his summary. He wasn't quizzed or tested on sermons either, so it was a little different from school. He wasn't fond of standing up in front of an audience, though. When the group had to select, memorize, and present their personal verse. He selected John 11:35–"Jesus wept." I asked him why he selected this verse. Kevin smiled his famous half-smile, almost a smirk, and responded, "It is the shortest verse I could find." What he said was true. If I knew how Kevin's life would unfold, I would say his choice was prophetic.

John 11 is the story of Lazarus, brother of Martha and Mary. Lazarus dies, and Jesus raises him from the dead, but that is only part of the story. The power of Jesus made the blind man see, and the lame walk before he raised Lazarus from the dead. Lazarus had been dead for four days before Jesus could get to him. Martha met Jesus along the route. She was angry that Jesus had not been with her brother so that he could have lived. Jesus assured her that her brother would live. Both Mary and Martha knew that their brother would be resurrected on that last day. Jesus' spirit was troubled. Mary and Martha wanted their brother to live. The people who watched this unfold thought that if Jesus could make the blind see and the lame walk, he could have made Lazarus live. Jesus wept. He chose to bring Lazarus back to life, even though he had died many days ago. Did he cry because he loved Lazarus, Mary, and Martha like his family, and they had lost their brother? Did he cry because he had to make a choice? Did he cry because he knew what was about to happen? Jesus wept. Jesus sacrificed himself for others. When Kevin selected this verse, God knew the path of his life, even though we did not. It is only after Kevin left that I could see the importance of Kevin's choice of this verse.

January 15, 2014

I met with Kevin's doctors today. They are so pleased with Kevin's continuing progress. Some days are better than others (and isn't that true for all of us!) Kevin still has many obstacles ahead, and his determination, persistence, and grit keep shining through. His sense of humor is noted by all who work with him. He is still in a very confused state, and that is part of the recovery. Forward movement is the goal. Each first down is worthy of celebration. I have no doubt he will get to the goal line. Kevin and I talked about what he might say if he were to tell his story. At first, he couldn't imagine he had a story to tell. We talked about the first sentence. "My name is Kevin Ash. I was born on January 25, and I have a story to tell." Yes, first a whisper, then out loud, and finally a roar! I can't wait to hear his story. Roar, Kevin, roar!

Psalm 146–Praise the Lord oh my soul.

January 16, 2014

Tonight, I was so pleased to hear about Kevin's day–his nurse reported that Kevin had very appropriate conversations. He worked hard and accomplished the goals for the day. He was resting quietly when I called tonight. My heart felt peace when I heard the report. A friend of mine told me tonight, "sit down, and I will give you peace." *That advice reminded me of a spiritual that I remember singing with my grandmother.* "Sit, down, servant, sit down and rest while. You have come over a mountain, sit down, servant and rest awhile." *So, tonight Kevin is resting after a long climb and so am I. Tomorrow, we begin again.*

January 26, 2014

I have already learned so much in this journey with Kevin and he keeps teaching me. Waking from a coma is very gradual, sometimes painful, and always an amazing process. This weekend, Kevin made a leap forward in his recovery. He started recalling the night before the accident. He also started realizing that he slept through much of the last four months. He describes it as sleeping and waking moments with times of nightmares. He is so articulate, and he amazes us all. He describes it as time travel. Tonight, before I left, he asked me to pray with him. We asked for the love of Jesus to keep the nightmares at bay. We finished with the Lord's Prayer and 1 John 4:16–God is love.

One can find statistics that indicate that middle children are more likely to be trailblazers and risk-takers. They are more likely to affect change than any other birth order. They have an openness to experience that leads to a willingness to try new things. Middle children are more likely to be focused on fairness. They perceive injustices in their family, and they are attuned to the needs of others. Middle children align with the underdog. They practice what they preach.

Now, so many months after the September 21 accident, Kevin began gaining more awareness that his life had changed so very dramatically, and he begged to understand why this had happened. I sat holding back my tears for so many days. I tried to answer him, but I couldn't find a reason that made sense. I searched for a reasonable response. I didn't feel very satisfied with my answer, but I had a response for him. "I don't know why this has happened to you, Kevin," I would start. "It doesn't make sense. It is senseless. You had an accident, it is unusual that what you are experiencing came from that accident. Yet here we are. All I know for sure is that you are a child of God. God loves you and He will be with you always. He knew you before you were born, and he has plans for your good. Always know that. You are a child of God."

One snowy night, Kevin asked yet again, "Why did this happen to me?" Kevin's memory was very short, almost nonexistent, and he often asked the same question dozens of times. Each time, for him, was the first time he had asked it. I could see the aide in the room listening. I gave him the answer that I always gave him. "I don't know. What I do know is that you are a child of God. He knew you before you were born. He has plans for you."

Kevin closed his eyes for a moment. I sat holding his hand and I closed my eyes, too. I prayed that we would have God's grace and mercy. I prayed that Jesus would shine his light through Kevin.

Kevin squeezed my hand, and I opened my tear-filled eyes. His eyes were open, too. He spoke, "Jesus use me. Jesus, use me. Jesus, use me. Jesus, use me. Jesus, use me." Tears flowed from both of our eyes.

Jesus wept.

Posted for family and friends: Month 5

January 27, 2014

As Kevin and I talk, I know he wants to make sense out of this crazy world. He is working so hard. He is making gains every day. Still, he tells me he is scared. He wants to get home. I can only try to imagine how the demons and dragons try to overcome him in his waking dreams. He hears the affirmations that I speak to him, and people pray for him. I read this today and it is so true: " 'I need to know,' we tell ourselves.

'No,' God answers in that still soft voice, 'you need to trust.' "

I know we can never go where God is not.

Matthew 28:20–I am with you always even to the end of the age.

January 31, 2014

After a long, rough night, Kevin finally fell asleep at 3:30 a.m. He was very tired today. He needed to sleep, but not too much. He was tired but calm and very present when I saw him tonight. We talked a lot about trust and faith and how much he has accomplished since the accident that put him into the hospital. We talked about the pleasures of eating food.

As a dutiful son he told me he misses my cooking. We both smiled. Then we talked about our favorite foods. We talked about goals and then we prayed The Lord's Prayer together. Galatians 2:16 reminds me that faith is wholehearted trust in God. Whatever it is, I trust God's plan. It is not for me to understand. I am grateful that Kevin is here. He has lots to share with us.

February 3, 2014

I got the report from the day staff that all was going well. Kevin had a full day of therapies, and he was tired when I called at 3:00 p.m. I felt relieved as I had to work late tonight. When I checked my phone on the way out of the office at 6:00 p.m. I had a voice message from Kevin. He was agitated and wanted me to help him. Nothing can tear at my heart more than my child's cry, "Help me, mom. Help me!" I took a deep breath and closed my eyes. I regretted that I had not gone to the hospital. Then I sat still and said a prayer. I thought of all the people who hold Kevin in prayer and all the team at the VA who truly care for Kevin. I thought of God's hands around Kevin and Jesus' light enfolding him. I called when I got home and talked to Kevin. He was still agitated, but not as much. He asked me why I was calling him. I told him I just wanted to tell him that I love him always and I told him to be at peace. He is in good hands. He asked me if, I was sure. "Yes," I said. Kevin is in God's hand, and he is in our prayers. He is safe.

February 5, 2014

He will sustain you–Psalm 55:22 *Another late night at work. It was so nice to pick up my phone after work and see Kevin's name. He left a voice message telling me he had a good day and that he will see me soon. I know that this journey is one that has ups and downs. The good days happen, and I cheer. The bad days happen, and I shed tears. Through each day, the one constant is God's love. It is such a relief to cast these burdens to God. I know that He will be with us each step of the way. When Kevin cannot walk, God holds him up. When I feel the sorrow of a bad day, God carries me through. God's love surrounds us no matter the circumstances and that is the true blessing. Through Him anything is possible.*

February 7, 2014

Tonight, my friend and I brought a lovely takeout meal and joined Kevin when he had his dinner. We told him he was our date. He smiled. We had a good dinner conversation. It was a short visit, and it was good. In this Friday night I pray this for all of us:

May you be content with yourself just the way you are. Let the knowledge settle into your bones, and allow your soul the freedom to sing, dance, praise, and love. It is there for each one of us.

February 11, 2014

"I love you, Mom," these are the words Kevin used to greet me tonight. He took my hand and kissed it. What a gentleman. I told him last night when I called that I would visit on Tuesday. It feels like perhaps he is beginning to retain his thoughts from day to day. I hope that he is. We talked tonight about how some days are rough and hard, and how the next day can be better. Kevin was wearing his rugby jersey that his Bokspring rugby team buddy sent him. He talked about how tough rugby players are. He said, "People were talking about being strong and tough so I picked this shirt to wear today to show them how tough I am."

He also said, "Six months is a long time." When I asked him if he knew what happened six months ago, he said, "Something bad." Then we talked about how good he is doing. He said, "Thanks for telling me that." As humans we tend to focus on the things that went wrong or the bad things. Instead, we need to celebrate the good things. Kevin was able to see that today. He was so grateful to know that his story inspires others. He told me to tell all of you, "Thank you for your prayers." Yes–after a rough day yesterday, tonight was a better night. Thank you, God, for shining your light in this dark world.

February 14, 2014

I called Kevin tonight. He had a good day but woke from a nap and has been disoriented for most of the evening. He has been frustrated and, in his time, traveling place. I told him he is my Valentine and I love him. I was reading tonight, sitting with my parents by their fireplace. We are drinking tea and talking about memories and good books. Tonight, I read this Swedish proverb: "Shared joy is double joy; Shared sorrow is half a sorrow."

I pray that this love surrounds all of us tonight. Have a blessed evening. Tomorrow is another day.

February 15, 2014

Emily Dickinson wrote: "Hope is the thing with feathers / That perches in the soul, / And sings the tune without the words, / And never stops at all," *Kevin woke from a nap yesterday and he was disoriented for the whole night and most of the morning. He finally fell asleep around noon and slept until supper. When he woke this time, his nurses said he was oriented and now he is quiet and calm. He told me a few weeks ago that he is so afraid of falling asleep because he never knows where he will wake up–what year it will be. Tonight, he ate his meal, and he is relaxing in his room. He tells me he feels such relief when he is "back." It is so important to let Kevin know he is surrounded by people who care. Even if he is sleeping, his soul is aware of us. I'm confident that is true. My promise to him is that all of us who care about Kevin send him hope and a smile even when we can't be at his side. We whisper to his soul–have hope, faith, and trust. We can tell him, "God's grace and love will carry you though." Tomorrow is a new day.*

February 20, 2014

What describes a traumatic brain injury? Kevin describes it as time travel and a big jigsaw puzzle dumped on a table. A friend's brother describes it as a library where someone has pulled and dumped all the books onto the floor. A neuropsychologist describes it as a tornado through the mind. In all these descriptions, the theme is the same–chaos and pieces that are mixed up and present but in unusual places. Kevin tells me he knows the pieces are there, but he can't find them. Sometimes he puts a few together but they don't connect with anything else yet. I can only imagine how disorienting this would be. I am so amazed that Kevin keeps moving forward. With God all things are possible. Tonight, I think of Theodore Roethke's poem, "The Waking":

I wake to sleep and take my waking slow. / I feel my fate is what I cannot fear. / I learn by going where I have to go.

God is good. He can move mountains. Have faith and trust in God who is the true light that guides us.

February 23, 2014

Kevin and I have been talking about his thoughts. Perhaps this seems odd, but we have always had conversations about how we think of things.

Kevin thinks metaphorically. (Is that a right brain thing perhaps? He is left-handed!) He is so disoriented without his sight and the brain injury itself has tossed his mind into a chaotic land. When he loses his way to the time traveling place, as he calls it, he is experiencing old memories or pieces of memories. We all want our worlds to make sense and he is grasping to make sense of this crazy accident. We talked about the chapters and books of his life. These pieces are real to him, and they are sentences and words, and pages of his past life. We are working on putting those memories in order and at the same time creating completely new experiences in this new reality that is his life now. It is hard, hard work. Trust, Faith, Love, and many prayers are the only path. I see the miracles and I continue to pray for God's will to be done. My new nightly prayer is Psalm 23. The Lord is my shepherd.... and I trust in him.

February 24, 2014

Late night work and so I got an update on Kevin from his nurse. I am so thankful for his nurses and the rest of the staff at the VA. They really do care about Kevin and that makes it a little easier on the days that he doesn't have visitors. As I was coming home tonight, I thought of the musical Godspell that was popular a long time ago. I had the sheet music, and I played those songs on the piano many nights–even into the years after my children were born; I put Kevin and his sister to bed, and later their brother. They always seemed to enjoy going to sleep with that music. Tonight, the song, "Day by Day" kept running through my mind. "Three things I pray...." *Tonight, I pray that Kevin continues to make progress toward recovery. I rejoice that he has so many people praying for him. I pray that each of us can see the miracles that surround us. No problem is bigger than our God.*

February 25, 2014

Today, both of my boys sang "Happy Birthday" to me. It was beautiful and brought tears to my eyes. Five months ago, I could only pray that this would happen. Today it happened. We spent some time playing cards. Connor won, but Kevin smiled the whole game. Kevin's team reported that he had a very good week, and it was the best so far. I get caught up in the bad days, and this was just the reminder I needed. It is all about the small steps that keep adding up to progress.

In October 2002, I wrote this poem. It seems like it is the message for today:

All have gifts and challenges. Experiences lace our lives.

Past, present, and future lie in the white spaces between the words. Possibilities are yet to be defined.

Events occur. Stories unfold with abundant truths. Opportunities continue so that the lesson is learned.

Even before Kevin signed his enlistment paperwork, he was beginning to plan for his military future. He researched all the branches of the military. I thought he might enlist in the Navy because his dad was in the Navy. I asked him why he didn't pick that. With the honesty that is Kevin, he said, "I thought about it, but I really don't like to swim." We laughed. All of Kevin's grandfathers, including his step-grandfather had served in the Air Force, so I thought he might pick that one. But he was more interested in the Army. He wanted to be in the infantry. He loved to play chess and other games of strategy. He thought the infantry was the foundation of a successful career. He decided on the Army National Guard mostly so that he could work on his law enforcement degree while in the Army.

Even though reading and writing were a struggle for him, he worked hard at the community college he attended, and he was on the Dean's List almost every term. He laughed when he finally earned his Associate Degree. "I think I am the only person who took over six years to earn a two-year degree." That may have been true, but he also served two tours of combat duty during that same time.

Kevin was filled with anticipation when he received his deployment papers for Kosovo after boot camp and his advanced training. This was what he was training to do. He returned to Minnesota for a few months, and continued training so that he would be ready when the day came for activation and deployment a few months later.

Kevin approached the upcoming deployment like he approached everything. He looked at what he needed to do, and he did it. He would often get up early in the morning and go for a run through the community.

His little brother Connor adored Kevin and wanted to be just like him. I think his brother became such a good student and athlete partially because of the role model that Kevin was to him. They were 13 years apart in age. Kevin loved having a little brother to take to the middle school events. He called his brother a girl magnet. "What middle school girl doesn't love a cute little toddler?" Kevin volunteered to watch Connor a lot in those years, and they went to many concerts, sporting events and even after school dances together. Connor grew up watching Kevin studying for classes and working out.

One Saturday morning when Kevin was in the first of the three deployments, Connor woke up early. I could hear a pounding through the house. I got up to find my youngest son doing jumping jacks in the TV room. When I asked him what he was doing, he responded, "Getting ready for fitness testing." He was only about 7 years old at the time. Another time, Connor woke up early on a Saturday morning and woke me up, too. "Mom," he said, "Let's go for a run." I wasn't thrilled about that idea. I finally relented and agreed to go with him. "I'm not running, though," I said. "I will bike, and you can run." The route he picked was about a five-mile trek down a hill to the river, and then back up the hill to home. Off we went and his brother set a quick pace. As we were heading back home, up the hill, a guy in a pickup truck came up behind me. He opened his window and called out to me, "Wow! That kid must have done something really bad." I laughed all the way home.

The first deployment ceremony was difficult for our family. We didn't really have any idea what to expect. Connor was excused from school for the day, and he sat close to his brother whenever he could. The soldiers were filled with more excitement than trepidation. The families had several sessions where the commanding office and chaplain met with us. We got a lot of paperwork, and some reassurance. This mission was a United Nations peacekeeping force. The governor and several other dignitaries from the military and government spoke. I can still see the freshly shaved heads of the soldiers as they sat through the speeches. When I saw their faces, I could see how hard they were trying to look solemn, but the excitement in their eyes wasn't as easily hidden. For Kevin, especially, this was what he had trained and prepared to do. Just before he boarded the bus the next morning at 4:30 a.m., he hugged me and told me he would be okay. He would see me again. Someone snapped a picture that I still have today. I had a sad smile, red eyes, and messy hair. He had a brilliant smile and bright eyes. He was ready to go, and no one was going to take this moment of happiness from him.

He and the other soldiers gathered on a base in Germany and spent some time there. He told me that they all were permitted a few leave days to take a tour in Germany. He was a young guy from Minnesota who had never been out of the United States. He was on an adventure doing exactly what he had planned and prepared to do. When he called me to tell me about his leave, I asked him what he saw. The guys had been given the choice of touring some castles or touring Auschwitz. It didn't surprise me at all that he picked Auschwitz. Kevin described how that tour impacted him. The reality of Nazi Germany and the gas chambers where over 1.1 million Jews died or were killed sobered him. Of course, he knew the history, but he said that walking through the camp and seeing it was truly life changing. That made the history a reality. It made the mission to Kosovo even more important to him.

Chapter 3

I drive to the VA Hospital almost every day. I pull out of the parking lot at work, turn right, and head to I-94. From there, I can turn on any number of state highways. It depends on the traffic, the weather, and sometimes simply how I feel. I think I know every possible route now.

Each day is a routine. I get up, go to work, leave work and drive. I have my favorite parking place in the vast parking lot outside of the VA Hospital. Then I get out and walk to the main entrance. I give a slow little wave to the security guard. He doesn't ask where I'm going. He knows the answer by now.

I carry my bag of work, a book to read to Kevin, and my computer. Some days I just sit in his room and look at him. Some days we talk. Some days we walk and walk around the floor. As I push his wheelchair, I describe the pictures on the walls, call out the room numbers, say hello to the various people working on the unit. I must be prepared for anything. I want to be there when Kevin awakes from this nightmare.

I want to give him a proper accounting of what has transpired during these many months. I want him to know I love him, and I will always be here for him.

While I drive, I search my mind for memories of Kevin. I don't ever want to forget anything. Sometimes I feel like a nature explorer. I search for each memory like it is an elusive butterfly in a vast wooded land. There are so many other memories in my mind, but I want to find the memories of Kevin.

We lived together for the first 19 years of his life. That is 6940 days in which I could have memories–I should have memories. I search and search for the snippets and flashes of moments with Kevin. When I capture a moment in my mind, I catalogue it and vow that I will never forget this moment of Kevin's life before the accident when this nightmare began. I want to be able to share these with him. The doctors tell me that sharing memories helps people with brain injuries put the pieces together. I would share pictures, but Kevin can't see them. I share music and sing the songs from his childhood through his life. I create a playlist for him so that he has his music. All he has to do is ask, but he doesn't. He can't remember to do that.

Kevin left when he was 19 so during the next 12 years, I have far fewer memories except of the times he chose to share something with me. Even though I haven't been with him, I cherish these memories of what he told me, what we talked about just as much as the memories that we experienced together. When I search my mind, I feel sad that I only have a fraction of the memories of those 6,940 days in those first

19 years. I want to remember everything. I want to remember everything he told me, or we talked about for the next 4,383 days of memories. I want to be able to help him pull his memories out of his ravaged brain. I pray that he will remember. So, I drive, and I search for the memories of Kevin so that I can share these with him–so that I can help him regain his life.

Posted for family and friends: Month 6

February 26, 2014

*It is hard to watch from a distance as Kevin works on recovery each day. His life has changed. He has so many people praying for him. So many people would like to be physically in his room with him each step of the way. Yet, this is not possible for any of us. Tonight, Kevin found himself back in 2001. That was a big year: he graduated from high school; 9/11 happened; he decided to enlist in the Army National Guard; he enrolled in the criminal justice program. Yes, it was a big year, and the memories are flooding over him. With that, Kevin knows something isn't right. It is 2014. He worries that he will not be able to make sense out of this chaos. He asks for help, and we do our best to reassure him. Paul said it best in Philippians 4:6-7–*Be anxious about nothing. Be prayerful about everything. Be thankful for all things. The peace of God passes all understanding.

I pray that Kevin sleeps well tonight with the assurance that he is truly loved.

February 28, 2014

A few days ago, I spotted an eagle while I was en route to see Kevin. Eagles are such regal birds. Native Americans cherished them. Eagles seem to appear for me when I need encouragement. Each month that passes brings new challenges. Kevin is more aware of his confusion, it seems. He is more aware of things in general and that also means he is more aware that something terrible happened. His life changed in an instant. He tries to connect the dots and sometimes he makes up stories of things that could have happened. He isn't sure if things are real or imaginary. Sometimes at night he just lies in bed, not sleeping, not talking, just trying to think. It breaks my heart–it is so painful to see. So, I go back to the eagle that I saw a few days ago. Isaiah 40:29-31– "He gives power to the faint, and to him who has no might he increases strength. Even youths shall faint and be weary, and young men shall fall exhausted; but they who wait for the Lord shall renew their strength, they shall mount up with wings like eagles."

I pray that Kevin will soar with wings like eagles. That prayer fills my heart.

March 2, 2014

Trust is such a powerful word–trust God as He knows what He is doing. Kevin had such a good night on Friday. He was happy and then his reality hit again. He isn't getting as agitated now. Rather, he is very quiet and appears to be contemplating his situation. Today, his brother and I visited him. The first thing he said was, "I want to go home." He looked perplexed. We talked about the accident. He talked about what was on his mind: where he will live, what he will do. He talked about the things he still needs to do for the Masons. He wanted to be sure I knew that he has Veterans' benefits. I told him we are working on getting all his things in place. Kevin and his brother talked about hockey and baseball. Kevin assured him that he would be at some games this spring (if spring arrives!) Then his brother asked him if he wanted to have a thumb war. They proceeded to have a great time and the visit ended with smiles and hugs all around.

We all need to trust in God. Kevin is here through the grace of God who holds him in His hands. God has a plan, and He knows what He is doing. Praise God.

March 3, 2014

Sometimes the little gifts mean the most. Today is my mother's birthday. I left a message last night on Kevin's phone suggesting he call his Grannie and sing "Happy Birthday" to her. He left a message for me today telling me he had called her and sung "Happy Birthday." He told me he had a great day, and he completed all the things on his list. I talked to my mom, and she was so touched by Kevin's strong voice singing her that song. When we consider how many steps he has made to get to this point, we know that God is with us. What a great present. Little things sometimes mean the most.

March 6, 2014

Henry David Thoreau wrote: "I went to the woods because I wished to live deliberately, to front only the essential facts of life, and see if I could not learn what it had to teach... I did not wish to live what was not life, living is so dear."

Kevin suffered a traumatic brain injury. That has changed his life and it has changed him forever. It has taken our family down a path we never wanted to be on and didn't plan to be on. At times I see the pain of the knowledge of his new reality in Kevin's face and I feel my heart tear apart. Progress is slow and sometimes it seems like I am one of the few who sees it. I hold on to faith and I know that the secret to life is choosing to live the life that is in front of us. I give Kevin affirmations and I remind him that he is not alone. He will live the plan that has been set before him. As Thoreau said, "living is so dear." I kiss him good night and pray that he feels surrounded by love.

Kevin wanted to be a police officer. He saw that as a way that he could help others and be true to himself. He enrolled in the local community college and declared Law Enforcement/Criminal Justice as his program. He embraced the discussions, and his professors recognized his discussion and leadership abilities. He quickly became the student that the professors identified as the group leader. Kevin liked the psychology classes. He wanted to learn why people choose their actions. He was very much a rule follower, but he questioned the rules that he didn't think made sense. He wasn't afraid to ask the important question, "Why is this what people believe?"

Kevin was hired as a security officer at a local business. While that job can seem boring to some people, Kevin enjoyed greeting each person who entered the building. He asked about their days. He welcomed each person. He built on his communication skills, and he liked his job. The people at the company liked him as well.

Kevin thought the police should support all people equally. One day he told me that he had been out jogging, and he observed a minor accident at one of the street corners.

He stopped and stayed with the two drivers until the police officer arrived. Both young drivers were distressed and anxious. He tried to keep them calm, and he encouraged them to remain patient. When the officer arrived, Kevin described how that person interacted with the two drivers. The officer was short tempered and was quick to cast blame. Kevin was disappointed in the officer's reactions. "A person can get answers with kindness," Kevin told me. He commented that he always wanted to be that kind of officer if he was ever in a similar situation.

When Kevin was in high school, he stood up for what he thought was right. His school had an alternative lunchroom area for students who were trying to get their lives back in order. Some of these students were trying to quit smoking, others had been in a treatment program, and others just felt like they didn't belong anywhere. Some of the adults in the community volunteered to be in the room as mentors for these students. They would play cards and sometimes just talk. Kevin went to that room often to talk with kids who felt like outcasts. He believed he could make a difference for others. I saw that repeated throughout his life.

March 8, 2014

I spent most of the day with Kevin. Kevin sent me a message this morning asking me what time I would arrive. I hope he remembered that I told him yesterday that I would see him on Saturday! Kevin spent some time with Scooter, a therapy dog. It was fun to watch them get acquainted. Kevin misses his dog. We talked about pets and Kevin and Scooter played "fetch." After that, we tried a walk to the gift store. Sadly, that was a rough experience. Kevin closed his eyes and started saying, "I'm going to wake up from this dream now." He started getting very upset and he was very distressed. I'm sure it feels like a nightmare. We hustled back to the floor and his nurse coached him through his deep breathing exercises. I talked through the past five plus months, and he calmed down. I know he understands some of what happened. It doesn't make sense, but Kevin is smart, and he knows something about brain science. I told him the old memories are all there and we just need to put them in order. He needs to reconnect the neurons to his muscles and relearn things he used to do. It is sort of like being reborn. So, we started doing math and spelling and other exercises and I think Kevin appreciated doing these tasks. It was reassuring to him that he can think through problems and make his brain work for him. The rest of the day was productive. Kevin went to PT and completed 15 minutes on the recumbent bike. He pushed it and the therapist was pleased. He had a good lunch and was very successful eating with just some guidance from me. By the time I left, he was tired and was ready for a rest. I drove home with tears in my eyes and prayers in my heart. Tomorrow is a new day. Each little step forward leads to progress.

March 9, 2014

We have surrounded Kevin with prayers that he would awake from the coma state after his accident. Each day I see him awakening more and more. Now, I ask for prayers that he can come to grips with his new reality. Today, he asked, "What job will I be able to do?" He said, "I want to make a difference and help people. How can I do that?" Then he told me he was slipping into a hole and was going under the water. He begged me to stay with him. I held him and rocked him and told him he is not alone. Please pray that he feels our love. God holds him and

God has plans for him.

Philippians 4:6–Do not be anxious about anything but in every situation, by prayer and petition, with thanksgiving present your requests to God.

Kevin came home from his first deployment and attempted to reconnect with his high school friends. It was much more difficult than he expected. Some of his friends seemed so immature to him. He had seen combat and he had seen cities torn apart by war. He walked through Auschwitz and felt the silence of a million souls. Other friends had moved on to careers and families. Kevin told me he felt that he just didn't really belong. Still, he continued to participate in the community. He connected with an acquaintance whose father had the local Taekwondo company. He attacked Taekwondo with intensity and rapidly passed through the belts. The concepts and principles fit for him:

- COURTESY (Ye Ui)
- INTEGRITY (Yom Chi)
- PERSEVERANCE (In Nae)
- SELF-CONTROL (Ye Ui)
- INDOMITABLE SPIRIT (Baekjul Boolgool)

The philosophy, based on ethical, moral, and spiritual principles, fit for Kevin. He truly wanted people to live harmoniously in the world. He was committed to stopping oppression of the weak and poor. He believed that to be strong, one would show humanity, fairness, wisdom, spirituality, and trust. He wanted to be part of creating a better society. He worked hard and was very successful.

Kevin also continued to watch anime and he was fascinated by Samurai. He read *The Art of War,* a Chinese treatise dating from the 5th century BC. He taught himself about military strategy.

"There is nothing outside of yourself that can ever enable you to get better, stronger, richer, quicker, or smarter. Everything is within. Everything exists. Seek nothing outside of yourself." –*Miyamoto Musashi, The Book of Five Rings*

"All men are the same except for their belief in their own selves, regardless of what others may think of them."

"The ultimate aim of martial arts is not having to use them." – *Miyamoto Musashi, A Book of Five Rings: The Classic Guide to Strategy*

He began studying *The Book of Five Rings,* a Japanese swordsman's study on the arts of confrontation and victory written in the 17th century. He incorporated what he read into his beliefs.

"Timing is important in dancing and pipe or string music, for they are in rhythm only if timing is good. Timing and rhythm are also involved in the military arts, shooting bows and guns, and riding horses. In all skills and abilities there is timing... There is timing in the whole life of the warrior, in his thriving and declining, in his harmony and discord. Similarly, there is timing in the Way of the merchant, in the rise and fall of capital. All things entail rising and falling timing. You must be able to discern this. In strategy there are various timing considerations. From the outset you must know the applicable timing and the inapplicable timing, and from among the large and small things and the fast and slow

timings find the relevant timing, first seeing the distance timing and the background timing. This is the main thing in strategy. It is especially important to know the background timing, otherwise your strategy will become uncertain."

He studied the Samurai, who were the important Japanese military class warriors. The word Samurai comes from the Japanese verb *Samurai*, which means to serve (someone). Kevin was happy to sign another contract with the Army National Guard, and he was happy to volunteer with most of his squad when the call came for deployment to Iraq. He told me he volunteered because he felt it was the "right" thing to do.

Along with anime movies, Kevin liked playing games of strategy like War Hammer. He studied the strategy books and created his deck of cards using what he had learned about strategy. He cultivated a group of friends who played the same games.

Kevin joined approximately 3,700 National Guard soldiers in this deployment as part of the 1/34 Infantry Division. The remaining 1,300 soldiers in the group came from various states across the country, including Iowa, Nebraska, Kansas, Wisconsin, New Jersey, Kentucky, Idaho, and Washington.

The National Guard website reported that this deployment was the longest continuous deployment in Iraq.

Guard unit recognized for record deployment

By Sgt. Mary Flynn | National Guard Bureau | October 05, 2007

ARLINGTON, VA – A recently returned Minnesota National Guard unit is getting the kudos it deserves this week. The House of Representatives passed a Concurrent Resolution October 1st that commended Soldiers from the 1st Brigade Combat Team, 34th Infantry Division on completion of their record deployment to Iraq. The unit's 22-month deployment is the longest continuous deployment of any military unit during Operation Iraqi Freedom.

The 1/34th Brigade Combat Team received alert orders in July, 2005. They mobilized in September and trained throughout the fall before finally deploying in March, 2006. Originally set to return in February, 2007, the unit was extended four months as part of the President's "surge" strategy.

During its deployment, the 1st Brigade Combat Team completed 5,200 combat logistics patrols and secured 2.4 million convoy miles. They discovered 462 improvised explosive devices prior to detonation and captured over 400 suspected insurgents. They completed 137 reconstruction projects and helped start two Iraqi newspapers.

Over 1,400 members of the 1st Brigade Combat Team reenlisted during their deployment, and 21 members became United States citizens.

The 1/34th BCT is part of the famed Red Bull division, which has a long history of service. The division was sent to France during World War I but did not see combat until World War II when they were the first division deployed to Europe. Coincidentally, the division has the distinction of having spent more days in combat than any other U.S. Army Division during World War II. The U.S. Rangers can also trace their roots to the 34th Infantry Division: 80 percent of the 1st Ranger Battalion consisted of volunteers from the 34th. (www.nationalguard.mil)

When the team was deployed out of Minnesota, we gathered at the National Guard Armory again. The mood was somber. This was the second deployment for Kevin and many of the other soldiers and their families. It was different from the peacekeeping mission to Kosovo.

We had a "family event" at the National Guard Armory before Kevin headed to Mississippi for training prior to his deployment to Iraq, Anbar Province. Kevin's brother was excused from school for the day, and we gathered with the other families of the men in Kevin's company. We heard the governor speak, as well as other dignitaries. They talked about the honor to serve. I watched Kevin and his fellow soldiers sitting at attention, eyes forward, expressionless, except for their eyes. In their eyes I could see the excitement.

The CO met with the families and told us his goal was that all of those under his command would return alive. "Hold it," I thought to myself. "What are you saying? Your goal is that they will all return alive? They may die?" This was a National Guard. I think people thought that the National Guard help when there is a tornado or some such natural disaster. Those people who enlist do their drill sessions and their two-week camp once a year. They play army, but they are the combat types. Kevin's experience was different. He received his deployment papers before he left Fort Benning. He had returned only to deploy again less than two years later.

The CO told us, "We will be the best trained force in Iraq. We will have night vision goggles. Do you know why?" he asked. "We will have night vision goggles so that we can run their missions at night. It is harder to see us at night."

I remember the feeling of trepidation when I left those sessions. I wanted to hug Kevin, and tell him I loved him, but he just brushed me aside. As I looked into his eyes, I could see that he was proud to serve. He was ready and would be a good soldier.

Kevin was happy to be leaving. He boarded the bus with the same smile that he had when he left for Kosovo. The Company headed to Camp Shelby near Harrisburg, Mississippi. He spent about 5 months in training before heading to Iraq.

Kevin continued to call me when he could. He liked to tell stories about his time at the camp. One of the training requirements involved learning to recognize and create Improvised Explosive Devices. He would tell me about the IEDs he built. "What are you doing that for?" I asked him. He responded by telling me that if he could build an IED he would likely be better equipped to recognize one.

During that time, Kevin attacked his training like he his life depended on it. He worked on his marksmanship and on firing large weapons and grenades. He studied for his classes, and he read books on warfare. He requested that I send him audio tapes so that he could start learning the Arabic language. "You don't even like English," I said with laughter in my voice. Kevin said, "Arabic is the language I am going to be hearing. I want to have some understanding of what the locals are saying." He was committed to being the best soldier possible. He was filled with anticipation about the upcoming tour of duty and the chance to implement what he had been learning.

Posted for friends and family

March 12, 2014

Kevin is working toward the next phase and that will mean a move from the hospital to a new place. While we don't know where this will be located or exactly when it will happen, we do know that Kevin is getting ready. He is no longer in need of acute medical care. He is more and more awake and aware of his new reality. As he moves toward this next step (and as we move with him) I realize that I need to let go of the past to open the door to the future. What happened on September 21, 2013, changed reality for all of us. I trust God and I pray each day for Kevin and that he will continue to be surrounded by caring and loving people as he moves forward on this journey. Your continuing prayers mean so much.

March 18, 2014

What is God's plan for Kevin? God knows and we must take comfort in that. Kevin asked me what purpose he can fulfill. I said that perhaps it is to share his story in a book or a screenplay. (He thought a screenplay would be better than a book!) I asked him if he could tell me what he would say. His response was, "This is the story of great leaders in unexpected places and people who were never expected to be great leaders."

What a thought that is. Kevin inspires me every day. He continues no matter how hard it is. He finds the inner strength to keep going. What a title–Unexpected Leaders.

Keep praying. Keep leading. Keep moving forward one step at a time.

March 19, 2014

Kevin keeps working–every day. He never gives up. With that being said, it is so hard to come to grips with this new reality. Tonight, Kevin could not accept that this is reality. He yelled, "Wake up, wake up, wake up..." He asked me, "Why can't I see you?"

It was heart wrenching. I explained the accident and I assured him that he is loved. I wanted to say, "It will be okay." Of course, things will not be the same. It will not be "okay" in that sense. What is important is to hold on to faith and knowledge. That God is in control. God has known us before we were born. He holds our lives.

Alfred, Lord Tennyson wrote, "More things are wrought by prayer than this world dreams of." Pray on...

Searching for Kevin's next location is difficult. I want to bring him home with me. He wants to go home, and he tells me often. Yet, the VA staff tell me that isn't an option. I live by myself, and I have to work. My house is not wheelchair accessible. I don't have the resources to ensure that he has the care he needs.

When he was at the long-term care hospital, the staff told me he would need to likely go into a nursing home where he would have skilled nursing services. Instead, we were able to have him go to the VA hospital. Now, even though he no longer needs that high level of care, he still can't go home. I ask, "What are his options?" The only answer is that he will need to be in a group home environment.

I know that isn't what he wants. I know that isn't what he needs, but I am told that is the only option available to him. Because the rugby accident happened after he was discharged, he doesn't have a high enough service connection to get assistance from the VA to help with his day-to-day care. I complete the paperwork for disability assistance and medical assistance to cover the cost. Because he can't see and he is also hearing impaired, and he can't walk on his own, and he can't remember things, he is certified to have a 1:1 personal care attendant with him for 13 hours per day and awake staff at night. The only place available will be a group home shared with three other individuals with disabilities.

I want recommendations from the staff and am surprised to learn that no one has been to any of the places that they recommend. They hand me a list of places that someone found on the computer. I started the vetting process.

The first group home that I look at is near the VA hospital. The location is good, and the staff tell me that it has good reviews. I called and made an appointment to visit the house. The house looked like a typical rambler, and it was located on a block where I learned that the company had many group homes. When I walked into the house, the first thing I noticed was that there weren't any chairs to sit in. I asked about it, and I was told that all the residents are in wheelchairs, so they don't need any other chairs. Other chairs would make it more difficult to wheel the residents in the space. "Where do guests like me sit when we visit," I ask. The person who gave me the tour looked at me like she had never heard that question before. I was not impressed. There was a TV in the living room, but it didn't appear that there was much of anything else. It was the first of many visits across the state where I saw the same conditions repeated over and over. I looked at private and corporate homes. The houses were only part of the issue. Not one of the people who worked in these homes understood the complex nature of my son's situation, and none of them seemed even interested in partnering with me to find a path that would help Kevin lead a rewarding life considering his current condition. Yes, the facilities could provide food, shelter, and basic care, but they didn't know how to help him through the maze that was this new life. They saw him as a person who was not able to contribute or do anything. They saw him now and could not even imagine that he had a life before this life.

During the past months, I researched everything I could find about working with blind individuals who also have brain injury and PTSD. I was horrified to find that very little exists to help people like my son. The strategies that work best with individuals with brain injury require them to use their sense of sight and hearing. The strategies that work best with individuals who are blind require them to depend on their memory. I went to conferences and talked with companies that say they have the best materials to help people with disabilities. I ask them, "What types of materials do you have to work with people who are blind, hearing impaired, and have brain injury?" I am horrified to learn that they have nothing. "Surely, there are other people who have similar challenges as my son has," I say. All I get in response to my questions is a sad expression. I start building my toolbox of teaching tools that I modify as I go along. I use music and rhythmic drumming, modeling clay, Velcro, and anything else I can find. Kevin still has the sense of touch.

Kevin loved going to movies. Before the accident, he would sometimes go to the theater for an entire day and watch 2 or 3 different movies in a row. I thought he might like watching movies again. If the movie is something he has watched many times before, like Star Wars, for example, he seems to enjoy it. He knows the story by heart already. If it is a new movie, it is much harder. The theaters have subtitles for the hearing impaired, but I can't find anything for people who are blind. One day I was at a store looking for movies that Kevin might like, and a salesperson asked me if I knew about Secondary Descriptive Audio movies. I went home and I started my research.

The 21st Century Communications and Video Accessibility Act of 2010 identified the FCC's involvement in providing rules for video description. The rules took effect on July 1, 2012. In less than two months Kevin became so disabled that he needed descriptive audio.

I had to laugh because I just don't need to cry any more tears. Tears don't make it better.

Movies in theaters need to have special equipment and tracks to do this, but some DVDs have this available. If the movie has this available, one must be able to read the fine print on the back of the movie under "languages." I learned to look for this feature and started buying movies with SAP or English Secondary Descriptive Audio. I educated a lot of salespeople about this feature in the process.

Kevin lost so much in the rugby accident. Besides the obvious things, he also lost access to everything he did for fun. He had a high-quality camera that he took with him on his runs, and he liked taking pictures of nature and sporting events. Not only could he no longer run, but he also couldn't see to take pictures. He liked building and painting models, and he no longer could see to do that, nor did he have the fine motor skills necessary. He liked to play his card games, and computer games, and he couldn't do that either. He liked Tae Kwon Do, and he no longer had that physical capacity to do that. He couldn't swim or even take a bath because of the PEG tube. He couldn't go on a bike ride. He lost a significant amount of hearing, and his memory was significantly impaired. He could listen to books but listening without discussion was also difficult.

I struggled to see how any of the group homes would be able to meet his needs. The staff were bewildered by the type of accommodations he needed. They didn't know how to adapt for his needs, or they thought he needed them to do too much. After visiting groups from northern to southern Minnesota and from the metro to the rural communities to the west, I asked the staff at VA, "What happens if I can't find any group homes that could meet his needs?" The unsatisfactory answer was that he couldn't stay there much longer. And they would not release him into my care.

March 20, 2014

What a great day. It has been so many months since the accident. Kevin, his Recreational Therapist, and his OT took a drive and stopped to get lunch: hamburgers and French fries. They sent me some videos of their outing. Kevin looked giddy with pleasure as he narrated the ride. He belted out, "Take Me Out to the Ball Game." He ate his meal without any assistance (and he was proud to say that.) It was heartwarming, especially after the pain of yesterday. I am reminded every day that our lives are precious and fragile. Truly, God is good. As Paul says in 1 Corinthians 13:4-5, "Love is patient; love is kind..." Love matters most of all.

March 21, 2014

It seems like a lifetime ago that we were in such a terrible place not knowing if Kevin would even survive. Tonight, I was blessed to spend the evening with Kevin. He talked about his hopes for the future. He wants to get on with his life. He is determined.

I know God has a plan. I know that Kevin continues to be surrounded in prayer. Kevin needs us now as much as he did six months ago. The next six months will bring marvelous things. I know there will also be heart wrenching hard times. I do trust in God and the power of prayer is indisputable.

Tonight, I share these lines penned by D.H. Lawrence as a prayer for us all:

"And if tonight my soul may find her peace in sleep, and sink in good oblivion, and in the morning wake like a new-opened flower then I have been dipped again in God, and new-created."

Chapter 4

A lot has been happening. I feel the pressure of finding Kevin's next location. I feel like the staff are frustrated with me, and the county case manager assigned to Kevin is frustrated with me. They don't seem to understand that I will not accept a house that is not good for him. This is his life–I am his guardian and his advocate. I won't let him go to a place that won't be able to help him continue to move forward.

I know that the deadline is fast approaching. He will be discharged by the end of April. I am frequently told that they have kept him longer than they wanted to while I try to find a home for him. I pray that I will find a place.

I stopped at the grocery store on the way home and ran into some people in our community. During our conversation, they told me that they have a group home that they built in the memory of a son who had died. They have an opening. The home is in my town. I am going to see it.

I was more impressed than with some homes, but this is the first home that is within minutes of where I live. I think,

"If it can't be perfect, at least it will be close enough for me to visit frequently. I can even stop during my lunch."

The next thing is to get my selection approved by the powers that be. Everyone has an opinion. Kevin hadn't lived with me for many years before the accident. His county of residence was different from mine. His county case manager was identified by the county in which he lived. That person had to agree to a placement outside of her county, even though that county had no residences available. The VA staff had to agree. Because this home located near my house was newer, it didn't have much more than a name on the licensing site. No one was very encouraging to me about my selection. In fact, they were not happy about it at all. While Kevin would be much closer to me, they would all be required to drive much farther to do their required checks. However, I finally got Kevin's move to this residence approved and plans continued to move forward for Kevin's discharge pending completion of all the required paperwork.

Wherever Kevin was going, I needed to know that Kevin would continue to work on building the neuro pathways to regain as much brain function as possible. I learned about the Rancho Los Amigos scale.

The Rancho Los Amigos National Rehabilitation Center has been in operation for over 125 years. Their mission is to revitalize hope for people with life changing illness. The cognitive scale that they developed helps rehabilitation teams and families build treatment plans for people like my son. I learned that the scale has 8 levels, with the 8th level being the closest to "normal." A person must demonstrate 100% of the criteria to move up a level. Many people demonstrate the elements of several levels at the same time, but the classification stays at the level where all the elements are met. Kevin was identified as a Level IV with elements of Level V when he was proposed for discharge. The cognitive Level IV that is subtitled: Confused and Agitated, or even Level V that is subtitled: Confused and Inappropriate, make my mind quiver. It sounds so dismal. While my logical and rational brain understands that was where Kevin was, my emotional brain doesn't want to accept it. I keep looking for the signs that he had "graduated" to Cognitive Level VI, subtitled: Confused and Appropriate.

Kevin was confused and frightened. He didn't understand what was happening about him. He did scream and use abusive language. One day I walked into his room and there were three staff around him. Kevin was in his wheelchair, and he was using his arms to point like he had a rifle. He was making shooting sounds and pointing his "pretend" rifle around the room shooting. The staff were afraid; I could see it in their eyes. Each time someone would try to talk with him, he would scream, "SHUT UP!" and then return to firing his pretend weapon. I asked if I could talk to him, and eventually, the staff let me do that.

"Kevin, it's Mom," I said. "I'm here with you. You are here with me. Put the gun down."

"Get away from me, Mom," he responded. "Leave me alone." It was heartbreaking. "I want to die. I want out of here. Just shoot me."

Sadly, I knew where he was coming from. His life was a nightmare, and neither he nor I had any idea what was going to happen next. "Kevin, I love you," I assured him. It took some time and a lot of assurances, "You are a good person. You are kind. You are brave. You are strong. You are a child of God. God has plans for good for your life." He eventually put down his arms and let me come by him. I hugged him and he hugged me. That was all I could do. I wanted the nightmare to end, too.

As a teacher, I looked at each of the Rancho Los Amigos elements and observed to validate where Kevin was. I felt myself shift into a different way of thinking at these times. I needed to be objective and logical, and I also wanted to be his mother. The hospital staff and my other two children struggled with seeing me flip back and forth between mother and educator. My youngest son told me once, "I hate being with 'hospital mom'."

I knew that my son was an enigma. While every brain is different, and every brain injury is different, Kevin seemed to always be even more outside the "average" in his responses and challenges. The usual medications didn't work for him. The levels with his blood tests were generally at the very high or very low acceptable thresholds. He would have sudden spikes or drops in certain levels. He challenged our thinking. On top of that, he was blind. He could not use the visual cues that all of us depend on to trigger our memory.

Posted for friends and family: Month 7

March 22, 2014

Kevin wrote a story today. I asked him if he could draw a dog. He worked on it, and then told me the story as he attempted to write the words:

Frankie, the Dog

Frankie the Dog grew up in a small town. He liked to do tricks like rolling over and playing fetch. Everyone loved him. The end.

Maybe he will become a writer of children's books? I asked what he thought about that. He laughed. Then he started to write some more. I asked him what he was writing. He told me, "A letter." I asked if he wanted to say it out loud and I would write it. "No," he said, "It's personal." I say hurray to that. Keep moving forward, Kevin. You will achieve wonderful things.

March 23, 2014

Kevin drew a picture. He wanted to get some flowers, but the gift shop doesn't have any. He drew fireworks instead.

March 24, 2014

Kevin went on a ride again today! He is approaching the end of his stay in a hospital setting and that is exciting and scary at the same time. Six months is a long time. I am so grateful that Kevin has been surrounded by prayers this whole time. The fact that he continues his recovery is a miracle. Now, he is getting ready for that next step. It is another world of unknowns. Please pray for wisdom as we must select the place that Kevin will continue his journey. I asked him tonight if he wanted to tell me a story. He said, "Would anyone want to listen?" I told him that many, many people are listening already.

This is the story he told:

Once there were three brothers. They were globetrotters who were born in a small town. They came back to that small town, and they saw a lot of people. One day they went for a walk down the road. A wizard appeared and said he would grant them one wish. They argued about what they should wish for. Finally, the oldest one said, "I'm the oldest, so I will make the wish." And he did and they were happy.

I asked Kevin, "What did he wish for?" Kevin said, "He wished for happiness."

March 27, 2014

Kevin was tired today. Despite that, he kept pushing forward. He seems less likely to be really agitated these days. I pray that he may be moved up a level in the Rancho scale soon. He was joking with the staff, and they really enjoy seeing that side of him. The speech therapist asked him a question and he said, "No hables ingles." That story made many people laugh. Sleep well, Kevin. You are loved.

Ezekiel 36:26-27–I will give you a new heart and put a new spirit in you.

March 28, 2014

In 2006, Kevin deployed to Iraq from Mississippi. We took a trip to visit him in Mississippi before he left and spent some time at the art museum in Jackson. Georgia O'Keefe's work was on exhibit. I remember one of her quotes, "To create one's own world in any of the arts takes courage." Today, Kevin and I listened to his high school senior concert

CD. He sang along to the recording, and he impressed the staff. I reminded him that he can sing no matter what. He gave me a little smile.

Helen Keller said it so well, "Life is a succession of lessons which must be lived to be understood." Kevin showed me some things today–love and the power of forgiveness are a window into our soul. What new things will he show us as he gets ready for his next stop on this journey? He told me he is going to miss the people at the VA when he leaves because they have helped him a lot. God bless them all.

March 29

Kevin is working hard to get stronger. The thing about a brain injury is that it is like rebuilding the circuits for potentially every part of the body. We take this process for granted. I see Kevin trying to use his brain to tell his body what to do. It takes phenomenal concentration. I am amazed. Today, Kevin was able to tell me that images of missions in Iraq were in his mind. I was so proud of him. He was able to recognize that these were memories, not reality. That's a huge step. Even the process to discern memories from reality takes effort. Kevin is a soldier.

Ephesians 6:10-13–be strong in the Lord and in the strength of His might.

March 30, 2014

Sometimes I try to imagine this new reality that Kevin faces. I close my eyes and hold my body still. I tell my brain to make my legs move and my fingers close. I tell myself to roll on my side. And then I think of how each movement must be planned and thought about. I think about trying to reorganize the fragments of memories without the accompanying sight. I feel the anxiety build under my skin. I can't really begin to imagine what it is like. Then Kevin tells me he wants out of this dream, and I hold him and tell him we will get through it with God's help. I tell him I love him: he is loved. And tomorrow we begin again.

April 2, 2014

There is an Ojibwa story about how a caterpillar spins a web that holds the world together and then one day becomes a butterfly. Kevin's journey is showing me how pain, frustration, confusion, joy, and wonder are all elements that pull our humanity together. His story continues and each day the caterpillar spins another length of the thread that connects us. I watch in awesome wonder to see each step that reflects God's miracles. His story is an amazing connection for so many people. I cherish every prayer.

April 5, 2014

Kevin knows that his time at the VA hospital is nearing an end. After over six months in a hospital, it is a miracle that Kevin is healthy enough to take this next step. The hardest thing is that the specific location and discharge date are not finalized. So, truly, the waiting is the hardest part. Kevin and I chatted with another young man and his mother today. Kevin gave that young man some words of encouragement. He told him he can overcome this. As a sergeant, Kevin is a higher rank, and he used a little military lingo. Both mothers and sons smiled at this. Kevin showed compassion and kindness. Despite Kevin's own challenges, he thinks of others first. I pray for Kevin and all of those who have served our country and now need our love and prayers.

1 Corinthians 13:13–"And now faith, hope, and love abide, these three; and the greatest of these is love."

April 7, 2014

It has been seven months since Kevin, and I have been out to dinner together. Tonight, we enjoyed a dinner of ribs, baked beans, French fries, and coleslaw at that famous BBQ restaurant that had its start near Hayward, WI. "It was delicious," to quote Kevin. Before we went on our outing, we had a good conversation. Kevin does think about his future. He wants to continue his education. He wants a job. He has a lot of ground to cover before that will happen. Yet, without hopes and dreams, we would not accomplish anything. Kevin made a few phone calls tonight–he thinks about all of his family and friends who love him. He is blessed to have all your prayers holding him up. Love is the greatest gift of all.

April 10, 2014

Kevin and I talked about life today. We chatted about his cousin's new baby, his great-uncle's surgery, and his hopes and dreams. At one point I said, "A penny for your thoughts."

He said, "Life is rough and hard, but life is good." One of the staff walked in and joined the conversation. She asked what hopes and dreams I have for Kevin. I told her I want Kevin to live as independently as possible, to continue to learn new things, to have a job, to travel to visit family across this nation. Kevin piped in, "To live a life like normal people."

I praise God and give to Him my worries and concerns. His will be done. Blessed be God, because he has not rejected my prayer or removed his steadfast love from me!

April 11, 2014

It was a busy day; we had a full team meeting with all the therapists, specialists, doctors, and lead nurses. The team is planning for Kevin's discharge sometime in the next few weeks. Then, Kevin and I went to the U of MN hospital for testing of his vision. The testing took over two hours and Kevin did a great job handling the whole process. I was so proud of his composure. Thankfully my good friend was able to meet us there as it was a challenge to navigate the building and give Kevin the quiet support he needed. We will get the analysis from that doctor in a week or so. It is in God's hands. As I travel this journey with Kevin, I am reminded that we are transformed through the challenges that we face. When we put these challenges in God's hands and when we rely on Him, we will get through the darkness. We trust in God's plan and time, and we know we are not alone. Thank you for your prayers that surround us every day.

April 13, 2014

We stopped at the chapel this afternoon. I asked Kevin if he wanted to stay for a while in the quiet. He sat and then said this prayer: "Lord, please take care of the young people. Keep them safe even when they don't think they need to be safe. Help them respect their parents. Help us be at peace."

Well said, my son.

Mark 6:31–Come with Me by yourselves to a quiet place and get some rest.

April 14, 2014

I spent the better part of the day with Kevin, and I was able to observe most of his therapy sessions. He is getting stronger physically. He can follow multiple step directions. He can feed himself. He can identify objects and describe their function. He is becoming more aware of time and place. Kevin continues to have many great insights. After the final therapy of the day, Kevin and I went back to his room. He became very sad. When I asked him what he was thinking, he asked me, "Why is life so hard for us?"

I don't have an answer for him. I just know that faith and trust in God's plan is the only thing that makes sense. The Easter story tells it all. We will face trials and trouble. We can proceed without fear. We have God's promise through his son that we will overcome this world. Kevin's story is full of miracles. His story continues. His recovery continues to show us these miracles.

Psalm 91:11–For he will give his angels charge of you to guard you in all your ways.

April 16, 2014

I got a phone call late this afternoon from the neuro ophthalmologist at the VA. She told me that we got the results from the visual evoked potential test that Kevin had last Friday. The results validated that Kevin is totally blind in his right eye. He has some response in his left eye, and I pray that he will be able to continue to recover enough vision to see movement, light and dark, and objects. The doctor reinforced the importance of repetition in rebuilding all the various pathways in his brain including the pathways in the occipital lobe. His brain is slowly recovering, and I pray that he continues to get stronger in every way in every day. The doctor will be having another specialist from the U of M hospital consult with her on Monday. Kevin and I will meet with her on Monday afternoon to discuss the next steps including strategies to help Kevin build upon what he still has. While this was not totally unexpected news, the fact that recovery for his right eye is not possible is hard to take. I am grateful that there is still a possibility for some recovery in his left eye. So, tonight I say a prayer of gratitude for that.

April 18, 2014

It has been a busy week, and we are still waiting for the approval for Kevin's discharge date. We are waiting on the county approval for the financial assistance. Kevin wants to leave, and it is so hard to tell him each night that he must stay yet another night at the hospital. I try to give him something to think about as we wait. Tonight, he told me, "This part of my story is done."

Maybe there are a few more pages, I told him. We must trust that all will be according to the plan. This story is just beginning. –Ephesians 2:1

April 21, 2014

Today is the 21st day of the month. Since September 21, 2013, I find myself pausing each time it is the 21st day of the month. This is the eighth time now. Kevin's progress continues and I say many prayers of thanksgiving. Today, he worked on biking in PT. He went for 30 minutes and traveled over 8 miles. As he pedaled, I talked with him about what he would see if he were riding on the back roads in Buffalo. He was amazing. When he had to bike uphill in this story, we increased the resistance and he kept pushing. When he had to sprint to the end, he did that, too. He had a smile on his face and the workout felt good. I look forward to the day we get his tandem bike so that he can ride despite his blindness. So, tonight I share these lyrics from the song "Broken Hallelujah:"

This is my broken song.

April 27, 2014

Tonight, is Kevin's last night at the VA hospital. It has been seven months and one week: 219 days. Today, Kevin, Connor and I stopped at the chapel as we took one last walk through the VA facility. I asked Kevin if he wanted to say a prayer. This is what he said: "Thank you, God, for all of the people I have met and who have helped me through this adventure. Thank you for those I have not yet met who will help me through the next one." We ended with our Lord's Prayer. Tomorrow begins the next book. Life is not perfect and with each other and our prayers and with God all things are possible.

Chapter 5

Kevin believed that hard work would result in success. He believed it because it worked for him. Meritocracy is one of the founding principles of our country. He didn't expect life to be easy for him and he certainly had experiences that supported that belief. When things got hard, he continued to push through the challenges. When he was a senior in high school, he had to pass a written language test. It was so difficult for him, and he worked so hard to pass it. He couldn't use any of the accommodations that had worked for him in the past. He had to hand write the essay and he couldn't use a dictionary, computer, or spell check. He struggled. It took so much more time than the typical high school senior required. Still, he persisted for hours to complete the essay. A lot of people would have given up, but Kevin didn't. One of the teachers wanted him to take the easy road and request that the requirement be waived for him. Kevin wouldn't allow that. He insisted that he would complete the essay, and he did. I'm sure his peers and most of the teachers had no idea about that particular event. It showed me how strong Kevin's resolve could be.

I look back at the training he received in Boot Camp. I bought him a copy of the camp yearbook. At the time, he thought I was being just plain silly. He didn't think anyone would ever look at it again. I look at it often. Along with the pictures of all the guys who were at Boot Camp with him, there are pictures of each of the steps through training starting with the Medical Processing, Record Processing, and Orientation. Once that was completed, the new soldiers were sent to their units and introduced to their drill sergeant. Following that, PT (physical training), Drill and classes consumed the days.

Kevin enjoyed all the classes from First Aid, Tactical Communications and Biological Warfare to Rifle Marksmanship, Landmine Warfare, Hand Grenades, Reinforcement, and AT-4 (used to disable tanks.) He was good at all these events, and he worked hard whenever he had to. He told me that he didn't understand how anyone would "fail" at any of these sessions. Still, he told me about soldiers who were unable to complete Boot Camp, and who left unsuccessfully.

Kevin liked the big weapons and was excellent with the M-203 Grenade Launcher. He learned Rifle Bayonet fighting techniques. He loved hand to hand combat. The pictures in the yearbook show soldiers smiling throughout the training. He learned urban warfare techniques. Kevin was in his element. Kevin could repeat The Infantryman's Creed in both the Minnesota and Southern accents. He not only knew it by heart, but he also absorbed it and made it his own.

Faith Alone

I am the Infantry.
I am my country's strength in war,
her deterrent in peace.
I am the heart of the fight—
Wherever, whenever.
I carry America's faith and honor
Against her enemies.
I am the Queen of Battle.
I am what my country expects me to be–
The best trained soldier in the world.
In the race for victory,
I am swift, determined, and courageous,
Armed with a fierce will to win.
Never will I fail my country's trust.
Always I fight on–
Through foe,
To the objective,
To triumph over all.
If necessary, I fight to my death.
By my steadfast courage,
I have won 200 years of freedom. I yield not–
To weakness,
To hunger,
To cowardice,
To fatigue,
To superior odds,
For I am mentally tough, physically strong,

And morally straight.
I forsake not–
My country,
My mission,
My comrades,
My sacred duty.
I am relentless.
I am always there,
Now and forever.
I am the Infantry!
Follow Me!

Adversity was something that Kevin knew and expected. He was not willing to submit to the challenges that face him.

Posted for friends and family: Month 8

April 29, 2014
It was so nice to stop by this morning to say hello to Kevin on my way to work. I enjoyed a few minutes of conversation while I drank my coffee. How nice it was! The staff reported that it was a good day. Kevin was sad at times as he is trying to make sense of his new house. He knows he isn't at his apartment. He is still adjusting very well. After work, I stopped by on my way home. We had a nice conversation in the living room and enjoyed freshly baked chocolate chip cookies from a neighbor who sent them as a welcome to the neighborhood. We sang a few songs

together, talked about books and talked about movies. Then it was time to say goodnight.

Thanks to God for the opportunity for Kevin to be so close with a great, caring group of people. I pray for his continuing recovery.

April 30, 2014

Kevin had another good day. The guys have him using a pillow as a punching bag. He also is doing kicks. He did over 400 reps and was sweating and smiling all the way. He told me that he isn't scared anymore. He said, "I'm so glad I'm home." Then he told us he wanted to go to his room. It is a nice family-type home. Life is good.

May 1, 2014

Kevin is gaining strength every day. I saw him standing straight and tall tonight and he had very little support. He is working so hard. He is also collecting his thoughts, and his memory is gaining strength as well. It is hard when he wants to go home. He knows he isn't at his house, and he isn't at my house or his dad's house either. He knows that something has changed. He is sad and even angry about what happened. I tell him I love him and that the people he is with care about him deeply. Still, I know that we need to hold him up in prayer as he is held by God. There are good things ahead for him. God has a plan for all of us. We trust and wait as it unfolds.

May 4, 2014

What a beautiful Sunday. Kevin and I went to church, and it warmed my heart to hear him recite the Doxology and pray with the church. He listened intently to the message, and he enjoyed singing the songs. Later this afternoon I brought my little dog Daisy to visit. She is wearing the

Army bandana that Kevin bought for her before he left the VA. The group home staff enjoyed seeing Daisy and the wonderful look of pure enjoyment on his face. Kevin petted Daisy and rubbed her belly with a smile on his face. I think therapy dogs would be a great addition to Kevin's Sunday routine. Praise God from whom all blessings flow.

May 6, 2014

It was good to hear Kevin call this house his "home." I know it is tough for him; he is beginning to connect the dots. He is beginning to realize how much his life has changed. Still, he works and works. He smiles as he does the physical activities. We watched him take 8 steps tonight. It may not seem like a lot yet compared to where he was just a few weeks ago, this is like finishing a marathon. Each night I give Kevin affirmations. Tonight, I realize that Galatians 5:22-23 is true, and I praise God.

"The fruit of the Spirit is love, joy, peace, patience, kindness, gentleness and self-control."

Kevin is blessed with the Holy Spirit.

May 8, 2014

Kevin is doing so well. I am so proud of him–tonight we had a great conversation about the weather. We've had storms all day. Last night we had an awesome lightning show. I so enjoyed it when Kevin added comments and shared his thoughts. (He likes sky-to-ground lightning best.) He told me about his boxing. He really enjoys doing that. The aide told me Kevin makes him work hard to keep up. He told me he asked Kevin if he wanted to stop. Kevin paused for a few seconds, smiled, and said "no" as he began punching with a smile on his face. It was a very good day.

May 12, 2014

Kevin has had two good weeks without agitation. When I saw him tonight and asked about his day, he told me it was rough. He said, "I've been time traveling." My heart dropped because that means he had hallucinated and was not oriented. I was glad to hear him recognize it and he was so happy to see me. He sang a little bit and I read him some jokes to make him smile. I reminded him that he is loved. His prayer warriors surround him. When I left, he was snuggled into bed. I pray he has a restful night.

May 16, 2014

May 16, and it has been almost 8 months since the accident. In the grand scheme of things, it has been just a blink of an eye. Kevin keeps working and he wants to continue his life. We talked about that tonight. He would like to be home–and that means living on his own. It is hard for him as he knows he needs help, but he wants to be able to be on his own. However, humans need friendship. There is nothing more powerful than knowing that God holds us for eternity and our friends care for us on Earth. Tonight, Kevin had two friends visit. It was a beautiful thing. I pray that he will continue to move toward that time. Even when that comes, I pray his friends surround him and keep him safe.

May 28, 2014

Kevin came over to my house today. He sat in the shade and played bocce ball. He really had fun playing with his nephew. We also tried croquet and badminton. Bocce ball was the best, though. His nephew did a nice job using his voice to help Kevin locate the target ball. Kevin smiled during the whole visit. He was tired when it was done. I am so proud of him. He is working hard to remember things. Each day he shows us more and more. It is still a very long road ahead of us and we ask God for His help each step of the way.

May 30, 2014

Kevin was at Connor's high school graduation ceremony today. Since January Kevin has said he would be at Connor's graduation, and he did it. He listened to the speakers and when his brother's name was announced, Kevin raised his arm and said, "Way to go Connor." He stood and saluted the graduates–a fitting response for a school with deep military foundations. What a beautiful day.

Graduation is a rite of passage. It marks both an end and a new beginning. Graduation is the closing of one chapter of life and the beginning of a new chapter. My youngest son graduates from high school this year. He is 13 years younger than Kevin and 16 years younger than his sister. He has lived most of his life with the knowledge that his brother was serving in combat zones. My youngest son entered kindergarten in 2001. His world was defined by events such as 9/11, Columbine, and the disappearance of Jacob Wetterling. My youngest son has almost always lived in a world filled with impending disaster. He knew that his brother was one of the brave souls who willingly stepped forward to defend his country. His brother was his hero.

My daughter was the oldest child, and her graduation party was supposed to be perfect. We planned it for weeks. She wanted a backyard party, complete with lawn furniture, lawn games, and a buffet table with a watermelon bowl filled with fresh fruit. We invited both sides of the family. She was the oldest grandchild on both sides and her dad, and I were both from large families. We expected a lot of people.

On the day of the party, we were happy to see that it was a lovely sunny day. We began setting up the areas as we had planned. We set up the food tables last and put them in the shade on the deck next to the kitchen door. As we were working on the set up, we noticed that it was beginning to cloud over. I thought that it was so nice that we would have a bit of cloud cover so our guests wouldn't be too hot in the sun. About 20 minutes before the start of the party, it started sprinkling even though the weather forecast had not called for rain. We all grabbed golf umbrellas to keep the rain off the food. Suddenly the sky opened, and it poured. Everyone was looking at me, so I ordered everyone to take the food into the kitchen and out of the rain. The downpour lasted about 10 minutes. It stopped just before the party was scheduled to start, but all our beautiful food arrangements were in disarray. I took a deep sigh and said, "I guess this is a good reminder from God that life isn't perfect." It was a great party, even though it wasn't perfect.

Kevin's graduation party, four years later, was a much more relaxed affair. He wanted his party in the morning. I think he wanted to go to other parties rather than stay at home on his own. He picked the food: cinnamon rolls, fresh fruit, and an egg bake hot dish. He loved the cinnamon rolls that his grandmother baked. Since she was coming from out of state and couldn't bring her cinnamon rolls, we ordered the cinnamon rolls from the local bakery. He liked those, too. The party went off without a hitch. Kevin was so happy to be done with high school. He was ready to get on with his life. It would be 13 more years before my youngest child would graduate. I had no idea how our lives would change in those years.

When Kevin graduated from Boot Camp, his little brother watched the ceremony with pride. He was fascinated by all the equipment and the weapons that were on display, and by the demonstrations of combat that were a part of the ceremony. I look at the pictures of my two boys and see the pride in their eyes–Kevin's pride at being a soldier and his little brother's pride in Kevin. Kevin's sister watched her brothers as only a big sister can. She was so proud of them. Kevin called her his "favorite sister." She laughed, saying, "I'm your only sister!"

His younger brother watched the deployment ceremonies as his brother left for Kosovo and Iraq. Each time Kevin deployed, I could see his little brother hold back his tears and his fears. We prayed every night The Lord's Prayer instead of that old childhood prayer:

"Now I lay me down to sleep.

I pray the Lord my soul to keep.

If I should die before I wake, I pray the Lord my soul to take."

"Why don't you want to say, "Now I lay me down to sleep?" I asked my youngest son one dark night.

"I don't want to think of Kevin dying before he wakes," he said in a solemn voice that only the young can use. He had already lost his innocence that the world was always safe.

When Kevin returned from his first deployment safe and sound, I could see the relief in his little brother's eyes. This was to repeat two more times before his little brother would graduate from high school. With each deployment, Kevin's little brother would hold his breath, pray, and wait until his brother was back at home.

During Kevin's second deployment, his little brother had to write a paper for his fourth grade Language Arts class. The assignment was "Who is your Hero?" He wrote about his big brother. He described Kevin as kind and helpful to others. He described how his brother would take him places with him and play games with him. He talked about his brother being a soldier. At the end of the essay, this little boy wrote, "I wish I could change places with my brother. Then he would be here instead of in Iraq. I don't want him to die."

By the time Kevin was deployed for the third time, his little brother was no longer so little. He had just finished his junior year in high school. He and his brother Kevin were both a full six feet tall and rugged. They had both lived through a lot. As Kevin prepared for his deployment, our family gathered together. Kevin, his brother, his sister, and her partner and their son spent a wonderful day at the Mall of America. They played together at LEGOLAND, went to the Amusement Park, and enjoyed each other's company. I had to work, and so it was a true sibling day. It was a day that they each talked about separately many times after that. It was a day that memories were made and a day that we all hold close to our hearts.

Now, as Kevin prepared to graduate from the VA

Polytrauma unit, his brother was preparing to graduate from high school. My daughter and her family and Kevin and I were all together once again. The high school graduation was held on the lawn of the school. It was a beautiful, sunny spring day in Minnesota. Kevin could feel the sun, and hear the birds, the music, the hum of the quiet conversations of the families of the graduates. He couldn't see his brother, so I whispered into his ear as he walked past us. As the ceremony ended and the graduates passed us during the recessional, we were all standing. As his brother passed by, and I whispered into Kevin's ear, he raised his hand to his head and saluted his little brother. That is a picture I will hold in my heart forever.

The Lord's Prayer

Our Father, which art in heaven,
Hallowed be thy Name.
Thy Kingdom come.
Thy will be done on earth,
As it is in heaven.
Give us this day our daily bread.
And forgive us our trespasses,
As we forgive them that trespass against us.
And lead us not into temptation,
But deliver us from evil.
For thine is the kingdom,
The power, and the glory,
For ever and ever.
Amen.

Posted for friends and family: Month 9

June 2, 2014

With God's help we all have an opportunity each day to make a difference in someone's life each day. Kevin shows me each day his strength and his ability to keep pushing forward. He inspires me. He makes a difference in how I see the world. He had a tough day, but he was still able to do a full PT and speech therapy session and an outing to the park for a birthday party for one of his housemates. He has been officially moved to a level five on the Rancho scale. That is a huge, huge step. Tonight, I shared with Kevin again that he has many people praying for him. No matter how tough it is, he is not alone. He is held in God's hand and as we watch him, we have the chance to witness miracles daily.

June 3, 2014

Good news–Kevin is scheduled to have the PEG tube removed next week! This is from the days that he had tube feedings and medications sent directly into his stomach. It will be a few weeks before the site heals and then Kevin will be able to have a bath and go into a swimming pool. I think it would be good for him to go swimming again. He had a good occupational therapy session today. He was tired at the end of the day, but we had a good visit. He continues to amaze me. Kevin is one of the strongest people I know.

Psalm 27:14–Be strong and take heart; wait for the Lord.

June 5, 2014

"For we are his workmanship..." When I talked with Kevin this morning, I suggested that he have a goal of walking 20 steps by June 25th: in twenty days. His aide told him, "You can do that. One step today and two steps tomorrow and so on." Tonight, when I saw Kevin, the staff reported he had walked 26 steps today with moderate assistance! What a celebration we had. So now his goal is 50 steps by the 25th. Truly, God plans our steps, and we walk with his grace. I look forward to watching His plan for Kevin unfold. Kevin walks with God's hand upon him.

June 14, 2014

Kevin enjoyed a nice visit with his dad this afternoon. Kevin told me he was happy to see his dad. Later, I asked Kevin to share some words of wisdom with me. He thought for a moment, and told me, "Drive safely." That is a good reminder for all of us! Kevin has been working on getting in and out of a vehicle. He did an amazing job of that tonight. We asked him to show us what he could do. Not only did he remember all the steps in the process, but he also did the whole thing by himself. We were just next to him to prevent any unsteadiness. I am so amazed at how determined Kevin is. He continues to show all of us that he will continue to make progress. Each day someone reminds me that Kevin has a team of prayer warriors surrounding him. I know he is not alone.

Deuteronomy 31:6–God goes with you; He will never leave you.

June 15, 2014

The old Irish blessing says it best:

"May the wind be always at your back. May the sunshine warm upon

your face, the rains fall soft upon your fields, and until we meet again may God hold you in the palm of His hand."

Kevin enjoyed church this morning. It is busy and the music fills the sanctuary. He does not get distressed. He sings along and he listens. He had a great day and when I stopped in this afternoon he was smiling, and he looked the best I have yet seen him. We took Daisy Dog for a walk and Kevin held the leash the whole way, while I pushed him in his wheelchair. It was so good for all of us. While none of us know what the future holds, we continue to follow the road and God holds us in His hand.

June 16, 2014

Kevin looked great again today. He seems stronger and a little more in tune to where he is. He really wants to continue towards being more independent. The flip side of this is Kevin is asking what happened to him. I went through the events that started on September 21, 2013. He listened and asked a few questions. Then he hit his default switch and said he wanted to go to bed. We talked a little more about how important it is to get his mind and body connected again, and how painful it is to have to start at the beginning. He pushed through the desire to check out through sleep. He is a determined warrior. He will make it through this, with God's help and your prayers. Thank you for surrounding him with prayers.

June 17, 2014

Kevin is gaining more and more awareness and that is both good news and heartbreaking. Tonight, he was very conscious that he couldn't see me. He kept saying he wanted to see me. I explained that the injury caused cortical blindness and that he can see some shapes with his peripheral vision. He got very quiet. I asked him what he was thinking. He said, "I'm feeling sad because I'm afraid I will never see you again." I had to catch my breath before I answered him. We don't know the future. We have faith and hope, and God has a plan.

Please pray for Kevin tonight.

June 19, 2014

Remember how an old-fashioned roller coaster worked? It creaked and climbed up to the top of the ride and then exploded down to rise again. The riders would smile and laugh, scream, and cry. Each day for Kevin can be a roller coaster ride. He made it through the rough day, and he managed to ride it through a good night. He had a really good therapy session today. His right arm is responding. However, he did ask if it was "dead." No. His right arm is slowly responding. He is slowly regaining his strength. He is able to laugh and smile. He knows how he feels. He will continue to gain, and this momentum will continue. Prayers mean so much. Thank you.

June 20, 2014

Kevin passed the swallow test! Yippee! He has just removed one more medical need. Everyone at the group home cheered. Tonight, we went to a movie–Dragon 2. He made it through the whole movie. He even laughed a few times. It was hard because he couldn't see the screen. He did seem to see some movements out of his peripheral vision. I am so proud that each day is a new day for Kevin. He does get discouraged and depressed at times. Yet, throughout this journey he shows us and starts again every day. He says a prayer for others, and he keeps moving forward.

June 23, 2014
Moving day is right around the corner! Thursday is the big day. The group home is moving, and Kevin and his housemates will be in their new custom-built house on Thursday evening. It is exciting and yet Kevin still wants to be home. He received a letter from his Mason brothers. They hold him in their prayers. Tonight, Kevin asked if he must be able to see before he can come home. "No," I said. "You don't need to see. You are working so hard. You are home. You are where you need to be for now." Truly, Kevin is in our hearts and prayers. He is God's child. He shows us how strong he is, and he will be home one day. He called his Grandad tonight and sang "Happy Birthday." His Grandad told him that was the best present ever. Kevin shines his light every day.

Colossians 4:6–Let your speech always be with grace.

Pack up and move–again. Kevin has moved a lot in his life. We have learned to travel with few material possessions. Possessions weigh a person down. Possessions mean it is more difficult to move quickly. Military life is rather transient. There is something that is different about home, though. We have places where we sleep, and places where we live, but these places aren't always what we would call our home. Home is where we are loved and where we belong. Home is the place where we are safe and where we can sleep in peace, trusting that all will be well when we awake. Home is not a place where everyone is a stranger.

Kevin wants to go home. He is living in a place that he doesn't see as his home. He can't go to his home because he can't care for himself. He can't stand on his own or prepare his own food. He needs someone to assist him with almost everything he does. I try to be with him as much as I can, but my work requires me to be there, too. I feel my heart break when Kevin asks me when he can go home. I don't know. I pray to God that Kevin will have a miracle.

This whole story doesn't make any sense. I don't understand how an unremarkable tackle could cause this much damage. The doctors don't have any answers. They say, "These things happen sometimes. We don't know why. Every brain is different."

I spend time searching the Internet for anything I can find on traumatic brain injury, traumatic brain injury and blindness, brain injury and veterans–anything that might help me understand. I search the professional medical journals for studies that might apply to what I see with Kevin. When I find something that seems to apply, I share it with Kevin's doctors. One day I discovered some research on the cumulative effect of repetition of blows to a person's head. The research suggested that this repetitive blows to the head is cumulative and will reach a point where that person's brain becomes very damaged.

When I asked Kevin's doctors if this could possibly be the reason he has such severe symptoms, they don't want to talk about it. They tell me, "He had a concussion. He has brain damage. This happened when he was playing rugby."

I tell them, he played football. He was a good player. He took a lot of hits, but he never lost consciousness. He was in the infantry. He was exposed to a lot of IED blasts. He was different when he came back from his deployments. Could this have started before the rugby accident? Could this be an explanation for his extreme difficulty metabolizing medications and the other symptoms that generally happen with a much more significant accident?" People who see Kevin as he is always assume that he was in a terrible car accident. If they know he is a military veteran, they always assume he had been blown up.

The doctors told me, "It is too hard to prove. Yes, he had symptoms of anxiety, depression, nightmares, and reported blackouts after deployment, but they are related to his symptoms now."

In his third and final deployment, Kevin began to deteriorate quickly. Despite being given a medical clearance to be redeployed a third time, he was still having night terrors. He was angry and he wanted to be alone. He would get into fights with the guys in his quarters. Each time that happened, he would be reassigned to new quarters. He moved a lot during those 7 months before he was evacuated out. He didn't want to be with anyone, and no one wanted to be with him. I wish I had known what was going on in his head.

"If he had some of the symptoms before the rugby injury, and now he has those symptoms and more, couldn't they be related?" I ask over, and over again. "It's not like the rugby accident caused the first symptoms to disappear." It felt like Kevin's condition was at least partially related to his time in the service and the blasts he was exposed too.

My questions were met with little or no response other than, "Don't put your energy into this. It would be too hard to prove anything before the rugby accident. Anything before that accident is too hard to prove."

Kevin's medical care was provided by the VA. His rugby accident happened within the required timeframe after his final deployment. He had a 10% service connection for tinnitus from his deployments. But his day-to-day care was not covered. As his guardian, I had to apply for public assistance to get help with that. I wanted to be his caregiver and have him live with me. Neither social services nor the VA supported that idea. As I lived alone, they said I would not be able to provide for his care without other people. The only place that could happen was through the group home model.

When he was discharged from the VA hospital to the group home near me, I thought that if I could see him frequently every day, I could help him adjust to that housing. He would get angry with the staff when they would tell him that the group home was his home. This was not his home. I would tell him that this was the place that he lived in. That was much more acceptable to him. After all, he had handled moving from place to place for a long time.

Kevin depends on me to speak for him. For so many people, he is only a list of symptoms. People do not know him like I know him. They see him as a very damaged person. They don't even see him as a person. They describe him in terms of his challenges.

Now that he doesn't have the PEG tube, he no longer needs skilled nursing care. That changes the requirements. He has been raised to the Rancho Los Amigos Level V. When I read the characteristics, it makes me feel sick. I often pray every day that God will be gracious and merciful, and that Kevin will be able to come home.

COGNITIVE LEVEL V

CONFUSED AND INAPPROPRIATE

A person at this level may:

• be able to pay attention for only a few minutes;

• be confused and have difficulty making sense of things outside himself;

• not know the date, where he is or why he is in the hospital;

• not be able to start or complete everyday activities, such as brushing his teeth, even when physically able. He may need step-by-step instructions;

• become overloaded and restless when tired or when there are too many people around;

• have a very poor memory. He will remember past events from before the accident better than his daily routine or information he has been told since the injury;

• try to fill in gaps in memory by making things up (confabulation)

June 25, 2014

Kevin looked happy today. He is at his best when he is active. We met with his vision case manager from the VA. She will advocate for him and help us get the resources he needs as he adjusts to life where seeing is done without eyes. He demonstrated his punching skills, and he smiled all the way. She asked him what he likes to do now. He said, "stand." How amazing it is to see the joy in a skill we take for granted. About a week ago, one of the care staff told me that he asked Kevin if he wanted to punch him. Kevin said, "Why would I want to knock down the guy who gives me a hand up?" Today, his care staff told me that Kevin added a new goal to his list for the day–to do something nice for someone. Kevin is truly one amazing guy. In God's hands this terrible accident will lead to eventual good. I trust in God's plan.

Ephesians 3:20-21

Now to Him who is able to do immeasurably more than all we ask or imagine, according to His power that is at work within us, to Him be glory in the church and in Christ Jesus throughout all generations, for ever and ever!

Amen.

June 26, 2014

Kevin didn't sleep well last night. He had some bad dreams. It is all part of making sense out of his life. Despite that, he had a great physical therapy session. He walked 100 steps by June 26–that was his goal. He accomplished that and more. What will he achieve in the next month? All is possible with God. Kevin and his housemates moved into a new custom-built house today. The house is fully accessible, and it is beautiful. All the rooms are spacious, and each room has a bathroom. Nice! The team was busy unpacking and setting up the house. It was a busy night. I am so thankful for the family that built this home and their mission to serve Kevin and others who need care.

June 30, 2014

Kevin continues to impress the therapists at the VA. Today, they let him try a bicycle. The report was very good–Kevin needed some supports to keep his feet on the pedals, and once they figured that out, he did great. He smiled all the way. They also talked about getting him into a pool next. He will enjoy that as well. When I saw him, he was relaxing in a recliner in his living room with his housemates. He was tired yet he still got up and walked across the living room. While he still needs assistance he continues to strive for that next step.

As Alfred, Lord Tennyson wrote, "More things are wrought by prayer than this world dreams of."

July 1, 2014

Kevin continues to try to make sense out of these past nine months. When I arrived this afternoon, he was sitting at his desk drawing pictures. It was so nice to see that. I brought him a movie, "Wolverine." I asked him if he knew anything about that. He told me that Wolverine was a Marvel character. He told me that his main characteristic is his hands. Then he drew a perfect picture of the hand with the sharp claws. After that, he had a nice dinner. Kevin is doing a good job managing his own meal. After dinner, it was time to work on standing and walking. Again, nicely done. He was sweating at the end, so he sat in the recliner for a while. We talked about the X-Men characters and the plot of that movie. I asked him if he had a favorite character. He thinks Wolverine is amazing. He fights for good. We talked about society's tendency to ostracize those who are different. I asked him what Wolverine looks like, he said, "Elvis." The whole group laughed. We all like to hear him laugh. Joy is in the little things.

July 2, 2014

It is another holiday approaching and I am reminded of how grateful I am for living in the United States of America. I am grateful for Kevin's service to this country and the many others who served with him and before him. I am grateful for those who care for him both physically and spiritually. He continues to show that indomitable spirit that made this country great. He never gives up. He keeps working toward his goal and he pushes himself and all of us. Today he walked 200 feet with minimal assistance. He surprised all of us as he took off his shirt. He continues to reach for those next steps towards independence. He is building new pathways each day in his brain. What he does each day despite the huge challenges makes me proud of him, those who have challenges, and all of those who stand with Kevin. God blesses us and I am grateful.

July 6, 2014

After a great day, Kevin had a rough night. He had bad dreams. He was able to tell me that when I saw him this morning. It tears at my heart to see his pain. As he realizes his new reality, he struggles with adjusting to this world. He is aware and he can articulate his depression, frustration, and confusion. I continue to assure him that he is loved, and he is not alone. He has an army of prayer warriors surrounding him. Tonight, Kevin gave this prayer: "God bless this day and the people who are here. Thank you, God, for this day."

I trust God's plan and I know that we are in His hands. Even when the road seems like it goes on forever, Kevin continues moving forward. He is an inspiration. Please continue your prayers and messages. Please visit if you can. Your thoughts and prayers mean so much to Kevin and our family.

July 7, 2014

Monday brings continued awareness and confusion for Kevin. He worked through several tough patches. He wants to be able to be independent. He asked several times what he needs to do to move to the next step. He describes it as a tunnel that he must crawl through. I'm sure it feels like that: dark, endless, and fraught with all sorts of unexpected twists and turns. He likes to complete his list each day. Even though he has trouble remembering what he has done, he checks to be sure he has completed his list. His care team works as hard as Kevin does. I was so happy to see him walk across the living room. He smiled as he relaxed in the recliner. He was feeling good about that. Each step is slow, and it takes so much thought and effort. I know Kevin will keep pushing through the tunnel.

July 8, 2014

Hard day. Kevin ran a fever all night. It broke this morning, but he slept all day. He was awake at dinner time, and he was eating well and taking plenty of fluids. I asked him what I could do to help him feel better. He said, "I want to go home." He and the staff are all working hard to achieve that goal. I wish I could make it easier. It is not easy. We need to pray and trust in God.

"Precious Lord, take my hand. / Lead me on; let me stand. / I am tired; I am weak; I am worn. / Through the storm—through the night— / lead me on to the light."

–African-American Spiritual

July 12, 2014

Kevin had a long trip to the VA on Friday for therapies. Transportation back to Buffalo was delayed so I couldn't see him in person before I headed out of town overnight. He called a couple of times and told me he was back and ready to be picked up to go home. It was a hard night for Kevin. He didn't sleep much, and he was tired when I stopped in as I got back in town. He needs us now as much as ever. Please surround him in prayers.

July 12, 2014

Kevin slept most of the day after a rough night. However, he did get up for me. He seems to still have a summer cold. He also told me he is doing "poorly." He said he was having a lot of dreams and they were bad ones. I asked, "How can I help you?" He said, "You can't; no one can change the past." That is true but we can create the future. I started singing some old familiar songs and soon Kevin was joining in. Then we played a game where I tapped some rhythm on his legs. He copied me perfectly. Then we did some mental math. He did all the math perfectly. Finally, we played "The Last Word." I gave him about 30 topics, and he was able to provide words for each category. I asked him, "How do you feel now?"

He said, "Better, I know a lot of things." Yes, he does. He is creating his future. He was tired after dinner, so he headed in for his evening routine. I pray he sleeps well tonight.

July 13, 2014

It was a lovely day today. The humidity dropped about 30% from yesterday and the sun has been shining. We went to church this morning and Kevin sang along. He stood up for the final song and it brought tears to my eyes. God helps us see even when we are blind. This afternoon, Kevin and his assistant and I went to show him the fitness center. He toured the facility and even did a few exercises. He had the best smile on his face when we finished. Of course, he was tired mentally and physically, but he still worked hard to get out of my Jeep with very little assistance. I pray that he sleeps well tonight and that he knows that he is recovering. Through God all things are possible.

July 14, 2014

Despite a night of "time travels" Kevin had a good day of therapies. His OT and PT at the VA hospital are a great team. Kevin went for a walk today and his assistant reported that Kevin walked two full blocks! That was great news. He was tired after a difficult night and a hard workout, and I worked late tonight so I didn't get to talk to him tonight. His team continues to work diligently for Kevin's successes. I am so grateful that he has a team of prayer warriors and a compassionate team of caregivers. It reminds me of something Woodrow Wilson once said. "The difference between a strong man and a weak one is that the former does not give up after a defeat." Yes–that is Kevin's story.

July 16, 2014

Kevin was up most of the night again. He was talkative more than agitated. He is making good conversation these days. We went to a potluck picnic and prayer meeting tonight. We had hotdogs cooked over a fire and all the usual picnic food. We sang accompanied by a guitar and people offered their prayers. Kevin quietly said his prayer. I don't think anyone heard it except his caregiver and me. He asked God to bless those who try. He asked God to show the people of the world the way to try and to have peace. It was a beautiful prayer.

Psalm 23–The Lord is my shepherd; I shall not want. He makes me lie down in green pastures. He leads me beside still waters; he restores my soul.

July 18, 2014

Kevin slept well last night. I know he was happy to have a visit from his dad, Dan, this morning. I understand they visited for a few hours. The staff reported that Kevin wanted to go to bed after his dad left and that he didn't want to get up. It is hard for him to keep putting the pieces together. It is emotionally draining, and it takes a lot of mental effort. I talked to him and encouraged him to take a walk or do some exercises. It is hard to watch from afar. He is in good hands and God holds him close. So, tonight I am confident that Kevin is in God's hands.

July 19, 2014

Kevin slept well last night. He had a hard time getting motivated to get up this morning, though. Fortunately, we have cell phones, and his care givers are willing to work through the rough spots with him. I talked with him several times today. He knows I am not in Buffalo, and he wanted to be sure that I will be coming back. Kevin is determined and he is always willing to keep working hard. He is such an inspiration. When it feels like we are holding on by a thread, we know that God is shining the light of love around us. There are angels everywhere. They share the hope and love that helps us hold on to that thread.

Isaiah 30:21–"This is the way; walk in it."

July 23, 2014

It was good to see Kevin today after returning from my trip. While it was hard for him, it was good to get the reports from the staff. One evening, the staff told me that they heard a click. He had unbuttoned his seat belt and when they turned, he was standing up! On one hand that was great, but on the other hand it was a bit of a surprise. When asked what he was doing, Kevin said, "I'm going to bed."

We went to the fitness center tonight. Kevin met with a trainer. It was amazing to hear their conversation. Kevin was very engaged and answered questions with complete accuracy. I am excited for Kevin as he will begin working out with the trainer next week. Kevin was even smiling. He tires quickly though, so after we returned to the house, he was ready to relax. Prayer's work! Thank you

What are the things that make us who we are? This is something that I have thought about a lot as I drive to and from Kevin's appointments and as I sit in hard vinyl chairs and wait with him to see one of his doctors or therapists. I think about that question a lot.

Some people judge our physical appearance. Kevin had acne when he was in middle school. He was tormented by a few kids for that. He hated it. Even though he worked hard at everything, some of the other boys called him terrible names, like Pizza Face and a faker.

One day, it got too much for him. In the locker room, after football practice, the name-calling started. He finished gathering up his clothes and headed out. He was walking home when one of the boys caught up with him and started badgering him. Kevin turned and punched the boy. It didn't turn out well for Kevin. He got called into the office the next day and was suspended for hitting another student. He knew he was wrong. We talked about it, and I made him clean the house and deliver a package to a friend (riding his bike in the pouring rain.) I told him that would never, ever happen again. The other boy should not have tormented him, and Kevin should not have let his anger rule his behavior. Kevin never had another incident, but he did stand up for others by doing the right thing.

One year, one of the other football players quit the team

mid-season. The coaches were furious with the player and told the rest of the team that the player who quit had abandoned them. They told the team that this boy did not deserve anyone even talking to him. Kevin told me, "Everyone deserves to have someone say hello, and treat them with kindness." Kevin said hello to this other student every time their paths crossed. One of the coaches called Kevin in before practice one day and asked why he was defying the order. Kevin said, "Do unto others as you would have them do unto you." The coach stopped the meeting and sent Kevin out to practice. Kevin would do the right thing. Does doing the right thing define us as a person?

When Kevin was in high school, he went to the Junior Prom one year. I was so surprised when he told me he was going to go. He didn't have a girlfriend, and proms cost quite a bit of money. I asked him, "Why are you going? I didn't think you liked that kind of thing."

Kevin told me the story. The girl had planned on going to prom with her boyfriend. She was excited and had bought her dress and made all the plans to have her hair and nails done. She was ready. A week before the big day, her boyfriend broke up with her. She was heartbroken. Kevin asked her if he could be her date instead. She agreed. It was the one and only time he had a date with this girl. Kevin helped a friend.

Years later, between deployments, Kevin was home for a few months. One of his friends had opened a business in town, and he needed some help making ends meet one month. Kevin asked him how much money he needed, and then promptly wrote him a check. Much, much later, that same friend told me about that incident. He said, "You know that is a true friend when someone helps you with no expectation of anything in return." Does kindness define us as a person? Kevin wasn't a perfect person. But I don't think perfection defines us. I think our character defines us more than anything.

On September 21, 2013, Kevin's life changed completely, but who he was did not change. His circumstances and skills changed. His abilities changed. The thing that didn't change was his soul.

Chapter 6

Posted for friends and family: Group home Month 11

July 27, 2014

Today started with a good message at church. Kevin stood during the final song, "Amazing Grace." People who know his story were so inspired. This afternoon we went to the fitness center. His caregiver and Kevin get along very well. Kevin worked out hard for almost 45 minutes. He did 6 different exercises with three sets in each and lots of reps. He increased his weights with each set. It was wonderful to see him smile and push through the reps. We could see the sheer determination in his face. I asked him what he was smiling about. He said, "I'm working out." I was encouraging him to stretch out between sets. He told me, "Mom, I know what to do." Kevin continues to progress physically and mentally. As Albert Einstein once said, "In the middle of difficulty lies opportunity."

August 1, 2014

Ten months ago, I could only imagine the day that Kevin would walk into a restaurant, sit in a chair, and enjoy a burger and chips with very little help. It has been a great week with many steps up the mountain. Certainly, God is with us. Kevin has amazing strength. He continues to inspire me every day. He asked me earlier this week, "Why on Earth am I here?"

Kevin, you are here to show us the amazing strength of God's power.

August 3, 2014

Sunday–church followed by brunch and lots of smiles from the brothers. Kevin and Connor enjoyed some gentle teasing and laughter. Later today, Kevin enjoyed working out at the fitness center. I was impressed at how much his grip is improving and at the weight he can lift. He showed us that determination and perseverance as he pushed one more rep each time. I told him that even his eyes were smiling. He continues to make progress that is amazing. Vincent Van Gogh said, "If you hear a voice within you say, 'you cannot paint,' then by all means paint and that voice will be silenced."

Kevin is telling us each day, "I can…" And then he does.

August 6, 2014

It looks like Kevin will be getting his new bicycle sometime during the week of August 18. I worked hard to find something that Kevin can do, and I came up with the idea of trying a tandem bicycle. The traditional style won't work for us since he is blind and has hearing impairment. I wanted to find a side-by-side type of reclining bicycle so I could describe what he can't see while we ride. When I described my idea to the therapist, she couldn't imagine how this would work. I called my brother who owns a recumbent bicycle. He helped me find one that would work for Kevin. The engineer who designed this bicycle agreed to bring a prototype to show the rec therapist. It was a fit! We ordered it.

I got a call from the rec therapist at the VA, and she said she will be scheduling delivery and training for Kevin's staff. She has been such an advocate for Kevin, and she has successfully secured funding for the bike! The designer of the bike is in the photo along with Kevin and the rec therapist. I am grateful to the designer Jim (a vet himself) and to my brother Dan, who found Blackbird Bikes. As I have said before, truly there are angels wherever we look. Thank you for your ongoing prayers.

August 8, 2014

Kevin and his housemates have the Vikings game tonight. Fear not–Kevin remembers he is not a Vikings fan. I asked him if he wanted to watch the game. He said, "No." I asked why he didn't want to watch the game. "The Vikings aren't my team," he said. "I like the Packers." It was nice to hear that he remembers that. When I left tonight, he was cheering for Oakland. It is true, a Packers fan cheers for the Pack and anyone who is playing the Vikings. Kevin amazes me. I thank God for each day and for all the prayers that keep us going.

August 13, 2014

Kevin had a good day. He didn't have any appointments, so he spent the day working on physical and cognitive skills. He is getting more and more oriented to time, place, and his circumstances. He is making very good conversation. Tonight, we went to the fitness center and Kevin had an awesome upper body workout. He tried some different machines, and these required him to do some different movements. It was very disorienting at first and in true Kevin form, he pushed through the challenge and impressed everyone who saw it. At the end of the day, he was tired and satisfied with his day. I am thankful for every step and all who are with us in this journey up the mountain.

August 14, 2014

Kevin continues to move forward, and all the staff comment on his improving memory. He is a funny guy, and he makes people laugh. He usually has a comment that brings a smile. Tonight, the housemates went shopping. One of the staff asked Kevin if he needed anything. He responded immediately. "A steak..." So, tomorrow night we are going to grill steaks at my house. The summer is coming to an end. It is nearly 11 months since Kevin's accident. I know that God holds Kevin in His loving hands.

John 14:27–Peace I leave with you, my peace I give you. I do not give to you as the world gives. Do not let your hearts be troubled and do not be afraid.

August 15, 2014

Kevin and his brother enjoyed their steak dinner. They had a good conversation, and we all enjoyed the beautiful summer evening. Kevin enjoyed sitting on the deck and listening to the sounds of nature and the people hailing from the lake. After dinner, Kevin said he wanted to walk around. So, we went to the front walk and Kevin walked 30 feet to the driveway. He did a great job with a little support from his assistant. On the way back to the group home, he told me he was pleased with the evening.

At one point I asked him what he was thinking. He said, "I'm thinking about people." I asked, "What about people?" He said, "I'm wondering what the people I know are doing." Yes, Kevin is getting stronger in mind and body. We are following God's lead. I know there are good things in store for Kevin.

August 18, 2014

Kevin had a hard night with some tough dreams. He had a hard time getting to sleep and he was awake for a long time. Despite that, he still got up and went to the VA for his PT and OT appointments. Tonight, a friend of mine stopped by to see Kevin with me. He made a valiant effort and engaged in good conversation. At one point we asked him what he would say if he wrote one sentence in his book. His comment was, "Life is hard, but I am harder." I asked him what he would like to do if he could do one thing right now. He said, "I'd stand up and give you a hug. In fact, I think I'll do that right now." Guess what? He did with a little help from my friend and me, he stood and gave me the best hug. Then he told us he was tired and ready for bed. Rest well, sweet prince...

August 19, 2014

"Success is how high you bounce when you hit bottom." *I read that quote by George S. Patton and I see Kevin. His spirit shines every day no matter what. Tonight, he asked me about my day. I told him it has been a long hard month. We chatted, did some mental math and then I asked him if he wanted to sing. He said, "Sure." So, we sang our usual favorite songs. Kevin's beautiful tenor voice was loud and strong. At the end of the visit, I gave him a kiss and a hug.*

He asked me, "How are you doing now?" I told him I really enjoyed our time together. He said, "I'm glad I could help you feel better."

Hmmm... He wanted to help me. Thank you. Kevin's spirit shines strong. He continues to move forward with determination, persistence, faith, and strength.

August 21, 2014

I asked Kevin how his day went today. He said, "eventful." "What did you do?" I asked. "I got up and talked to a few people, and then we went out" (he had an appointment at the Wellness Center) "and then I came home." It was nice to hear a realistic description of his day. Then we went on a nice bike ride for about a half hour. We greeted a few of the neighbors and everyone was impressed with his bike! Kevin picked the turns (right or left) and he did a great job steering and pedaling. It was nice and we were both hot and a little tired when we got back to the house. Kevin enjoyed some time in the living room and then he headed off to get ready for bed. It was a successful day.

Kevin and his sister lived their first few years in the same town as their paternal grandparents and great-grandmothers. Their father had a large family, and his seven siblings lived near each other. Both Kevin and his sister had the good fortune to go to church with their extended family, and enjoy Sunday dinner of ham, turkey, or roast beef and potatoes with them. I would walk from our house through the quiet tree lined neighborhoods, first pushing them in the stroller and then walking with them as they grew. In the movie in my mind, I see Kevin working hard to keep up with his older sister. When we get to the park, I can see him pull me to the swings. He loved the swing–the wind in his face with his long blond hair and the movement. He was always smiling when he was swinging. I can hear his laughter still.

Kevin was the youngest child for thirteen years, before his brother was born. He worked hard to keep up with his sister, and they were good friends, most of the time. Kevin was a watcher; he watched others and then he attempted to repeat what he saw them do. I remember the day he wanted to try tennis. We lived across from an elementary school at the time, and his sister would go to the school and hit a tennis ball against the wall. I can hear the "bounce-hit, bounce-hit" of the ball as I watched from our deck. It was nice because the fence around the school yard generally kept the tennis ball from rolling out into the street. Kevin could watch her from our yard, too.

After about 20 minutes, Kevin begged me to let him cross the street to hit the tennis ball against the wall. With a racket that was slightly smaller than him, he ran up the step to the deck. "Please," he begged. "I want to play tennis." Finally, I succumbed and allowed him to go. I watched him get to the corner, look both ways, and dash across the street. I had asked him if he wanted me to go with him before he left. Of course, he didn't.

I watched from my spot on the deck as he dropped the ball and swung at it like he had observed his sister do. He swung and missed a few times before he hit the ball. The first time he hit it, the ball barely made it to the wall. He attempted to hit again, and he improved. Finally, he hit the ball to the wall, and it bounced back towards him. He ran hard to hit the ball as it returned, and he missed. Undeterred, he tried again, and again. About a half hour was all his little seven-year-old body could take, and he came back home. He was disappointed with himself. He wanted to be able to play "real tennis." I had to explain to him that he did a great job, for his very first time trying to hit a tennis ball. "It will take a lot of practice," I told him.

Kevin was always willing to try new things, even as a child. He wasn't afraid of hard work. He took swimming lessons and worked until he could swim across the pool without stopping. Each year he tried a different activity in the winter–gymnastics, wrestling, hockey, and basketball. He liked basketball best and played that in middle school. He sang in the church choir, and the school choir. He played baseball, football, and tennis. He ran in track and held the middle school record for running the hurdles for over 10 years. He had roles in the local summer theater company. Anything he decided to do, he gave it his very best effort.

He played baseball most summers. He wasn't a big kid, but he had big determination. He was at bat with two strikes. He fouled the ball, not once but many times. He kept fouling the ball, but he didn't strike out. Finally, his at bat ended when the pitcher threw a wild ball that hit Kevin. He advanced to the base with a smile on his face. He didn't strike out.

This is the determination he showed, even as a very young child. He showed this same determination in all that he did. Hard work, determination and grit defined his life.

Posted for friends and family: Group Home Month 12

August 23, 2014

It has been a busy Saturday. Kevin and I started the day with a coffee followed by a bike ride. We went for about 25 minutes and Kevin did a great job. Later today, we went to the fitness center and worked on upper body exercises. Kevin told me, "I didn't think we were going to work so hard today." It was worth it though. After our workout we had a nice steak dinner on my deck at my house. The weather was beautiful. Hawks and eagles joined us by circling overhead. We sang a whole variety of old songs and Kevin smiled the whole time. After dessert of rice crispy bars, Kevin was tired and well fed in body and soul.

Psalm 104:24–How many are your works, O Lord! In wisdom you made them all, the earth is full of your creations.

August 25, 2014

I dropped Kevin's brother off in Steinbach, Manitoba, Canada today. Kevin was awake after a restful Sunday, and he called several times during the day. Each time I told him what we were doing (taking his brother to his hockey team) but the third time tonight he finally was able to tell me his concerns. He called me at about 8:30 p.m. He asked the time, the day, and the year. Then he asked where I was. After I gave him the details, I told him I would be back in Buffalo by about 10 p.m. He asked, "So, you are coming back?"

I said, "Yes. Were you afraid I was staying in Canada with Connor?"

He told me, "Yes." I could hear his relief when I told him I will see him tomorrow. What a reminder that we all move forward in faith and trust. Thankfully, we know that we are not alone. God holds us even though we can't see Him.

August 26, 2014

Kevin went to his Tuesday appointment, and he was still tired tonight. He did get up for me after I told him I was going to tickle him. That made him smile. Tomorrow he has three appointments at the VA. I wish I could be with him. I know that God has a plan for Kevin and for all of us. I came upon one of my journal entries from January. On that dark snowy day, I wrote:

Do not be afraid. Just believe. I need to know, I tell myself. "No," God answers in that soft still voice, "you need to trust."

So, tonight I put my trust in God that Kevin will continue his progress. God's hand is over him. Kevin, you will never be where God is not.

Matthew 28:20–I am with you always even to the end of the age.

August 27, 2014

Kevin had a busy day with appointments at the VA in Minneapolis. He is doing very well by all accounts, yet he still has times when he is frustrated and agitated. I look at the past 11 months and I am amazed at all that has transpired. I continue to pray for Kevin's continuing progress. He needs our prayers as much now as he has ever needed them. I am so grateful that Kevin continues to have an army of prayer warriors at his side.

Psalm 18:2–The Lord is my rock, and my fortress, and my deliverer; my God, my rock, in whom I take refuge.

August 28, 2014

The Vikings play tonight so Kevin had to wear his Packers gear. Thanks to his aunt who sent him a new Packers shirt! It is great. Kevin was a little down tonight. I asked what he wanted to do, and his answer was simple: to go home. We talked about goals and his determination to teach those goals. We sang, played some pattern games and some word games. He felt a little better when I left.

I pray each day for Kevin's continuing progress.

Mark 14:35-36–Father, all things are possible unto you; remove this cup from me; yet not what I will, but what thou wilt.

August 29, 2014

Why is Kevin smiling? Because he just finished a good workout at the fitness center! When I arrived after work, Kevin was still rather blue. I wanted him to go to the gym. It took a little encouragement, but off we went. When I told Kevin it is Friday night, he responded with, "Yeah, and I don't know anyone in this town." Then he asked me to promise him that he isn't going insane. Hard things to hear... So, we got to the gym and started on an upper body workout. That brought out the smiles as each set was more weight. I was so impressed with Kevin's effort and his right-hand grip. He worked his way up to 100 pounds in the final set with each sequence. Finally, he finished his workout with a 30-foot walk. When we got back to the house, he felt satisfied, and he was still smiling.

Carry on, soldier. You will make it to the top of this mountain. You are loved by many, and you do have friends. You are not alone.

August 31, 2014

Today is the last day of August and Kevin is nearing the end of year one post rugby injury. His challenges are many and he continues to be an inspiration for people who know his story. He continues to show perseverance, grit, and incredible strength. Today at church, he asked to stand at every point in the service. He shows God's grace with each step.

Tonight, we went to the movie, "When the Game Stands Tall." He was able to use the secondary audio headset and this new feature was amazing. It is audio closed captioning for the visually impaired. The story is filled with great messages of faith and hope. Kevin listened intently. At one point, the team's coach shared Matthew 23:12 with his players and a particularly difficult parent. All we know is that Faith, Trust and Love will get us through. God has a purpose for him and for each one of us.

Matthew 23:12–For those who exalt themselves will be humbled, and those who humble themselves will be exalted.

September 2, 2014

It is interesting that Kevin considers memories "time traveling." He has used that term from the beginning as he emerged from his coma. Tonight, I asked him to tell me about "time travels." He shared memories of his childhood–some good and some not so good. He is gathering those memories and sorting them into place.

Now we are working on building new memories and holding all the pieces together. He is working so hard, and each step is often painfully slow. Yet, Kevin persists, and he trusts in God. He is so strong. I am blessed to have this amazing son. We are blessed to have your continuing prayers.

September 4, 2014

Kevin can make the most insightful comments. He had a good day by the reports. He had an appointment this afternoon, so he got back at around dinner time. I worked late again so he was just relaxing when I got there. The aide said Kevin asked him about the appointment and where they were going. After the aide told him they were going to the VA, Kevin's response was, "Oh great."

When I got there, I told him I just finished another long day. He commented, "Well, I had about 30 minutes of brain twisting activity today." That was probably true, and it was rather funny. We chatted for a while and Kevin said he needed to get ready for bed. This is a small thing; however, initiating for his needs is such a huge step in the world of traumatic brain injury. Little accomplishments add up over time and Kevin will keep moving up that mountain.

September 5, 2014

Kevin never ceases to amaze me. He has a great vocabulary. Tonight, we had dinner at the group home. Kevin enjoyed pizza. After that we went to his room and played a game of "The Last Word." We adapt it but Kevin was amazing. The first 20 cards were subject cards. Kevin had to give words or phrases that fit the subject. Parts of a house. He said, "backyard with a fence, deck, front door." Things you are afraid of–he said, "falling, dying." Then we switched to words that started with a letter–words that start with "I"–he said, "Independent, incredible." And we went on for about a dozen more letters. I was astonished at the words he came up with. He was tired by the end of our visit. I gave him a big hug and held on for a long time. This has been a long journey and it continues. I told him that he is smart, strong, and courageous. He continues to shine a light in this world. Kevin blesses us each, and every day.

September 9, 2014

We had a medical team meeting at the VA Hospital this morning. It was a hard day for Kevin, but he made it through. Kevin has been discouraged and depressed about his current state. It is truly understandable. He has lost his sight, some of his hearing, his tactile abilities on the right side of his body, and we suspect some of his sense of taste and smell. Despite it all he keeps persevering and fighting. He is an inspiration. What story will he tell? I think he told us: "Life is hard, but I am harder." Truly, his is a story of resilience and faith. Keep the prayers coming.

September 10, 2014

Kevin had a good day. I was frank with the staff at the meeting at the VA yesterday. Kevin needs goals and a reason to continue this journey. He has so much life ahead of him.

Today the care team moved forward with more focus and purpose. Kevin put on his shirt this morning. He worked on getting his shoes on. He walked the full 30 feet from his bedroom to the kitchen for breakfast. He completed his exercises, and he was ready to head to the fitness center tonight. We had a full 60-minute workout. One of the guys stopped by and told Kevin, "Hey, you lift more weight than I do." This guy was about 6'4" tall!

Kevin smiled and kept working. He was tired after that. We got Subway on the way back to the group home. Kevin was tired and satisfied with a day well done.

"People seldom see the halting and painful steps by which the most significant success is achieved." –Anne Sullivan (Helen Keller's teacher)

September 11, 2014

Kevin had another productive day. He worked on a lot of skills to increase his independence. He seemed quite a bit happier tonight. He was tired, though, and said he was going to head to bed. He really wasn't interested in watching Thursday night football. Of course, everyone had to remind him that the Packers lost their first game. He just smiled and said, "There are a lot of games left in the season."

September 14, 2014

It was a good Sunday. Kevin and I went to church. He had a sleepless night but still got up and made the 11:00 a.m. service. Lots of people are starting to greet him. A lovely couple introduced themselves after the service. The gentleman had a brain tumor removed when he was in his forties, and his wife spoke to Kevin's heart. She promised she would be a prayer warrior for him. Kevin is an inspiration. He is showing us that despite challenges we can continue to sing praises to God.

Psalm 146:9–the Lord watches over the sojourners.

September 15, 2014

Kevin asked some tough questions tonight. "How many years do I have to stay here? How long have I been here? Why am I here?" This weekend marks one year since the accident and Kevin is aware of so much. Yet, he is not where he wants to be either.

I picked up a book off my shelf tonight. There was a bookmarked page. So, I opened it. The book is titled simply, KEEP GOING: The Art of Perseverance, by Joseph M. Marshall III.

As I read the dog-eared page, I thought about how both Kevin and I have had to continue one step at a time. Determination keeps us moving even though the improvements are almost microscopic at times. Yet, each step provides us with the incentive to take the next. That is perseverance.

Kevin keeps doing that. Despite the dire predictions of many people, he gets up every single day and takes one step after another. He is following the path that God has set before him as slow and as painful as that is. I know that God's will surrounds him.

September 16, 2014

Another day of hard work. Kevin continues to forge ahead. It is hard work, both physically and mentally. He was especially tired tonight. Yesterday, he was awake from 7:00 a.m. until 1:00 a.m. He was awake by 8:00 a.m. this morning. He seems to be making more tiny connections each day. He can recall little things and that is good.

Each day I see people out walking their dogs, jogging, biking–all so effortlessly, it seems. I think of the complaints we have about our lives, and they seem so trivial. Kevin shows me every day that my aches and pains are nothing compared to what he has overcome just to walk 30 feet. What plan does God have for us? It is human nature to ask that question. It is the power of faith to live each day with the knowledge that His will be done.

September 18, 2014

Kevin is still having a tough time during the nights. He asks the night staff to stay with him. It is hard. This morning I told him he couldn't sleep all day–it was time to get up and keep moving. The staff looked at him with surprise as he said, "OK."

He proceeded to sit up, and so his day began. I told him we'd take a nice bike ride after work. When I got there tonight, Kevin was eating dinner. He did a fantastic job eating. He took his dishes to the sink as the aide pushed his wheelchair, and that was good too. Then we went for a nice long bike ride. His caregiver rode the bike with him, and I rode my bike next to them. He smiled a lot, pedaled hard, and met several kids in the neighborhood. One young lady chatted with him quite a bit. He had a nice conversation with her. It was a beautiful evening in so many ways.

September 19, 2014

It is a bittersweet night. A year ago, we had no idea what the next day would bring. Kevin and I had emailed, and voice messaged a few times. Connor was heading into his first hockey games of his senior year. We were planning on getting together for a family night on Saturday after Kevin's rugby game and Connor's hockey game. That was not to be, as it turned out.

My friend Bev and I went to see Kevin after work. He was still in bed. It was a hard day. He told me he didn't know what was wrong–he just didn't know where he was. So, I told him the events of the past year. He knows what a coma is. He understands the situation. We talked about how important it is to keep moving forward, to not give up. In the end, Kevin was able to articulate the three things he must do: get up; keep working; be nice to others. I continue to pray to God: Thy will be done.

I pray that the next twelve months are as fruitful as the past twelve months have been. Kevin continues to impress us. He is amazing.

September 21, 2014

Today, so many good things happened. Kevin and I went to church later than we planned as Kevin had another rough night. He did get up and get ready when I got there. He walked to the bathroom and to the kitchen. It brought me to tears. Yes, it is a slow process, and he still needs help, and he is walking! A year ago, we were praying for these steps. So many people greeted Kevin today. He is surrounded by prayers. He stood and sang and inspired us all yet again. This afternoon, we decided to take a break from working out. We spent two wonderful hours at Deer Lake

Orchard. First, we stopped at the farmyard. We fed the goats, sheep, and one hungry cow. Kevin fed her three or four apples. We visited the horse, who had been giving rides all afternoon. She took the photo opportunity, and we got a great picture. We sat by the fire as we waited for the wagon to take us through the grounds. Kevin enjoyed a beautiful apple from John (grandfather to the owner's children.) John talked to Kevin and thanked him for his service. He asked Kevin his age. I was so pleased when Kevin answered, "Thirty." That is the first time he has been so close to his age when someone asked. That was a great step. When we rode on the wagon ride, it was quite bumpy. I asked Kevin if it felt like riding in a Humvee. He said, "No, because if it was a Humvee, people would be shooting at us." Enlightening...

We finished our visit and took a nice apple back with us. I am so grateful that we could have a blessed day. We begin year two and only God knows where Kevin will be next September 21. Please keep prayers coming.

Kevin's grandfather, my dad, sent this letter.

Life is not always easy. Kevin does have a hard road to travel. It is easy to see how he can become depressed. We are all praying and cheering for him every day. I remember an old saying from my mother and your Grandmother Carlson for our family. "I will lay myself down to bleed awhile and rise and fight again." In our family, we don't quit no matter how difficult the road. Kevin is showing that trait and will continue to struggle, but in the end will overcome many of the current difficulties with his attitude of being hard and he is harder for all he has been through. God bless Kevin and keep up his spirit every day.

Sent with prayers for Kevin, Grandad.

Some say we are the products of our genetics, and others say we are the product of our environment. There is more to us than that. I think that who we are is part genetics, part environment, part our will, and part our spiritual connection.

Our family has a history with the military in the United States that goes back to the American Revolution. I remember my grandmothers, both my father's mother and my mother's mother, telling me about ancestors who had fought in the Revolutionary War and each of the wars following that. Our family also has a history of immigrants who left their homelands to come to the United States. The stories of our family members are filled with challenges and successes. My mother's brothers were in the Air Force, and so was my dad. They served during the Korean conflict. By the time the Vietnam War came, they had completed their service to their country. Kevin's father and his older brother enlisted in the Navy at the end of the Vietnam War. They also served their country. Kevin continued that long line of service to the United States. By the time he enlisted, the draft was gone, and he was a part of the all-volunteer military. He and his fellow service members were deployed multiple times over the following years.

When Kevin left for Camp Shelby, he was excited. His commanding officers assured the troops and family members that the Red Bulls would be the very best trained forces in Iraq. Camp Shelby Joint Forces Training Center is in the heart of Mississippi. Kevin and his fellow soldiers left Minnesota in the fall, not too many months after Hurricane Katrina struck the Gulf coast in late August, 2005. Kevin described the outcome even in Central Mississippi as devastating. Traveling around the base, he could see the ravages of that force of nature. The 134,000-acre camp had an area built to replicate the terrain that the soldiers would see in Iraq. As a student of the military and art of warfare, Kevin loved his time at Camp Shelby. He shared stories about how he learned to recognize and identify IEDs. Once he described that his assignment was to create an IED. He approached this task as a puzzle, and he was proud that he successfully finished that assignment. No task was too big, or too small for him to put forth 100% effort.

By the time he had been at Camp Shelby for close to six months, he was waiting with barely concealed excitement about the impending duty in Iraq. We flew into Biloxi, Mississippi and were surprised to see so many signs of Katrina: damaged traffic signs, garbage piled along the roads, and water marks to the top of the first floor of our hotel. This was nothing compared to what Kevin would see once he was boots on the ground in Iraq. While his sister, brother and his fiancée and I wanted to spend time with him, he wanted to be with his squad. We stayed in Jacksonville, Mississippi during this time and connected with many other family members whose soldiers were getting ready for this massive deployment. When the day arrived for the deployment ceremony, it was rainy and cold. The soldiers marched out for what seemed like an hour. Kevin and approximately 5000 other soldiers were deployed as part of the 1/34th Brigade Combat Team.

During what ended up being a 22-month deployment Kevin and his team members, as part of the 1st Brigade Combat Team, helped complete a total of 5,200 combat logistics patrols and secure 2.4 million convoy miles. They discovered 462 improvised explosive devices prior to detonation and captured over 400 suspected insurgents. They completed 137 reconstruction projects and helped start two Iraqi newspapers.

During this deployment, I read and listened to the news carefully. While I didn't know exactly where Kevin would be at any given time during the deployment, I knew where his base was located. I got up every morning at 5 a.m. and went to the local fitness center where I could work out and watch the news. It was at this time in February 2007 when I was expecting to learn of his imminent return to the United States that I heard the news that the 134th was being extended by the President as part of the "surge" strategy.

Kevin called me shortly after I heard that news. When I picked up the phone, I was expecting him to tell me that he would be staying in Iraq longer than expected. I said, "I heard on the news that you guys are being extended."

"What? When did you hear that?" he asked. He sounded surprised.

"I heard it on the news," I responded.

"What the fuck!" he responded. "I don't know anything about that."

He was upset and angry and the call ended quickly. I found out later that the news broke here in Minnesota before the troops at Kevin's level were informed. That breakdown in communication contributed to Kevin's growing frustration.

During the next five months, Kevin talked less, and seemed angrier when he talked with me. He didn't share much about his experiences, but he was involved in many situations. Kevin would call me to tell me he would be out of communication for a week or two at a time. I learned later that these times generally were connected to incidents. The deployment was grueling by now. Kevin's team traveled Iraq mostly during the night. Kevin worked at night and slept when he could during the days. He told me he went to bed with his gun by his side. He told me he wasn't sleeping, and he had a short fuse. He blamed it on the continuous intensity of the missions. He was ready to come home.

Chapter 7

Posted for friends and family: Starting Year 2

September 22, 2014

Happy Monday. Kevin had appointments at the VA Hospital this morning. He was tired when he got home. He had a productive day by all reports. I talked to him tonight on the phone. He wants to get home and he wishes it could happen right now. I tell him he is making little steps every day. One day I know he will be able to live independently. He has the same hopes and dreams he has always had. God willing, he will achieve those goals. Prayers hold him up.

September 24, 2014

I found one of Kevin's journals tonight. He wrote this in 2010 and it looks like he was writing about a deployment. Kevin has a strong desire to serve others. It is hard for him to find a way to do that in his current situation. He is gradually finding that part of himself again. That is so important. In his journal he quoted, "Every servant has his place, no matter how lowly or modest. To know it is his greatest comfort, to excel within his greatest solace, and his master's contentment is his greatest reward."

God bless Kevin as he continues his journey.

September 29, 2014

Kevin and I had a hard conversation tonight. He wants to come home. He is focused on that goal. He asked me what happened to him. I told him the story of the past year and how much he is loved by many. I told him he has come so far. He still wants to go back to school. We talked about how important it is to keep working his memory as well as his body. He must pray for strength. He told me, "I want this nightmare to end." My heart broke when he said that. It must feel like a nightmare and yet we know he is in God's hands. He continues each day, fighting hard each step of the way. Each day is a new day and I pray that Kevin feels the strength of his prayer warriors through each battle.

October 2, 2014

Kevin had appointments at the VA hospital today. He met with his doctor, and it was good. Kevin has made many steps since she saw him two months ago. She was pleased and impressed. He was able to answer most of her questions and he showed a bit of his humorous nature as well. Still, he must adjust to seeing the world through his other senses. He has strong visual memory, and he could tell us he sees many places he has been. Yet, he has no visual context for where he currently is. Tonight, he said he just wanted to see me. So, I moved in front of him and gave him a hug. He reached up with his hands and felt my face–my eyes, my hair, my mouth, and ears. He "saw" me with his hands. Tonight, I say this ancient prayer from Numbers 6:24-26.

The Lord bless thee and keep thee: the Lord make His face shine upon there and be gracious unto thee: the Lord lift up His countenance upon thee and give thee peace.

October 7, 2014
Kevin and his housemates went out for frozen yogurt last night. It was a fun night with lots of laughs. The staff told me Kevin laughed a lot and made quite a few humorous comments. They had frozen yogurt, too.

Kevin was quiet tonight, though. He did laugh when I told him I would have to tickle him if he couldn't smile. We are in a lull right now—still moving forward with a slow speed, and we'd all like to see things move more quickly. It is a good reminder that God's timeline may not be ours. We keep our faith, and we are grateful for each step forward, no matter how small. We are grateful for your prayers.

October 8, 2014
Wednesday: it was a beautiful moon this morning and the partial eclipse was amazing at sunrise. It reminds me of God's power. Only God can create this beauty. Kevin is a child of God. God knows every hair in his head. God knows his past, present and future. Today I pray for all the possibilities that God holds for Kevin and for all of us. Each day is a blessing and for that I am grateful. Kevin reminds me that love is the true meaning of life and trust in God is what matters most.

October 9, 2014
Kevin was painting this afternoon when I visited. He picked red for his paint. He told me he saw pictures in his mind. He painted a dog—one that protects people, he said. It was a Rottweiler, he told me. The dog's name was Connor, just like his brother. Then Kevin painted a sun. He

asked me if it was a beautiful day–it was, I said. I suggested that a bike ride might be in order. Kevin agreed. So, Kevin and his aide headed out for a ride before dinner. It was a good day.

October 11, 2014

We headed out at 11:30 a.m. this morning. The sky was a beautiful blue, and the sun was shining. Kevin, his caregiver, and I loaded up and headed into the city. We were headed to Faribault to catch a Bokspring rugby match. We had good conversation along the way but as we got closer Kevin said he was feeling sick. He was anxious and fearful. His mates were expecting him, so I told him we would just stop by for a few minutes and leave if he wanted to.

Kevin got to the pitch, and he was immediately welcomed by some of the players' wives. He began to relax, and he stayed for the whole game. After the pictures and some warm hugs, we headed to Owatonna to drive by some of his familiar places. It was good. On the way back to Buffalo, Kevin continued to try to make sense out of this past year. "When I wake up from this dream," he said, "where will I be?"

I had to explain that while it seems like a dream, this is real. I told him of all his successes so far and that he continues to set and reach his goals. When we got back to Buffalo, he was ready to begin his work by walking from his room through the house to the opposite end and his chair in the living room. And the story continues...

October 12, 2014

We had a good Sunday morning–church followed by breakfast at Perkins. The service was good. Kevin is greeted regularly by so many people. We are blessed. Later this afternoon, I visited Kevin. When I arrived, everyone was laughing and having a good time. We talked about the Vikings (they lost) and the Packers (they won.) There is a fun rivalry going. Some of the staff try to convince Kevin to cheer for the Vikings. He just smiles and says, "No."

Kevin wanted to push away from the table in his wheelchair. I told him to go ahead and move himself. I think he realized that it is okay to move on his own. So, for the next 20 minutes he was moving backward, forward, and all around the room. Alexa, his caregiver, told him she was going to set up an obstacle course. She said she was going to have him do the course in his chair and then walking. He smiled and gave a laugh. It was so nice to see him exploring and moving on his own. It was a wonderful afternoon.

October 17, 2014

Kevin has had quite a string of good days. Today he hit the wall. He was tired, physically, and mentally. He told me tonight that he is tired of talking. Nonetheless, he did engage with me. He drank the mocha that I brought from Starbucks. He played The Last Word. We did mental math, and we played some catch. So, despite everything it was a good day.

Tomorrow, Kevin and his housemates are going to the apple orchard. He will enjoy that. Before they go, I told him I'd bring him another coffee. He smiled. Rest well, my son.

October 18, 2014

Kevin and his housemates didn't get to the orchard today. They were short staffed. I stopped by this morning, and we enjoyed a cup of coffee: mocha for him and black for me. Kevin had a good day, though. He worked on walking, writing, and playing catch. I stopped by with my dog Daisy this afternoon. Kevin smiled a lot and he enjoyed petting Daisy.

Later, we went out to the patio and enjoyed listening to children playing in their yards. It was a beautiful day. I asked Kevin if he wanted to come help me clean the house. He said, "Ahhhhh... no." Everyone laughed. It was the first time he didn't want to come home with me. Some things never change. It made me smile, though. I love it when I can see Kevin laugh and smile. I am thankful.

October 22, 2014

I was able to join Kevin at his appointment at the VA this afternoon. He is 13 months into his recovery. The doctor assessed his status. Kevin still struggles with his memory. There are so many kinds of memory. His blindness does hinder him. Yet, he continues to show a strong and courageous spirit. He continues to work at rebuilding his pathways. He answered the questions accurately. He stuck with the meeting for an hour even through the difficult conversations. I start to wish... then I pray instead. I pray for God's continuing guidance. I pray that Kevin feels our love surround him and that God holds him in His hands.

October 26, 2014

I am grateful for our friends–people who watch and pray for Kevin. He was asking questions of the staff today: "Where am I and why am I here?" One of them told me that he told Kevin that he is working on his rehab like relearning how to walk. Kevin said, "I can do that." He proceeded to unbuckle his seatbelt and he put his hands on the arms of the wheelchair. He started to stand up. The staff jumped up in surprise. We know the message: with God all things are possible. Kevin shows us every day that God is at work through him. Prayers

October 29, 2014

Kevin had a good, busy, and productive day yesterday. The most astonishing thing to me is how much energy it takes him to have a great day. Today he was very tired. When I saw him tonight, he was tired and rather sad. I pulled out all my tricks and he finally laughed a bit. We played catch and he made a valiant effort to stay engaged. After about 15 minutes he asked, "What is the point of this?" I told him I just want to see him smile. A single tear slid down his check. He smiled. Life is hard sometimes. Yet, he keeps forging forward. Surely goodness and mercy will follow Kevin all the days of his life.

Prayers mean everything.

November 2, 2014

Each day I share affirmations with Kevin. I share the messages he gets from family and friends. Some days, like today, start out hard. Kevin didn't sleep well last night. He didn't want to face the day. Yet, I told him about all of you and how blessed he is to have so many people who pray for him and he got up. We went to church, and it was good.

This afternoon, we went to the fitness center and Kevin worked out hard. He smiled as he exerted himself. It was good. We went to my house and had chili for dinner while the sun set across the water and birds ate at the feeders. It was a good day. Through Kevin, God is sending us many messages. We are blessed.

.November 5, 2014

Some of our greatest lessons are learned through hardship. It is so hard to think that Kevin is into year two of his recovery. He gets frustrated and annoyed and yet he can speak and share his thoughts and feelings. It is slow, but he can now walk. He is slowly regaining bits of connected memories and he is now holding onto slips of new memories.

I am so grateful for each of these simple things. I am thankful for knowing that faith and love are all that really matter.

Jeremiah 33:3–Call to me and I will answer you and show you great and mighty things which you do not know.

We moved from Wisconsin to Minnesota when Kevin was 2 years old. We packed up our car and their kitten and drove the five hours from the little town where their paternal grandparents, great-grandmothers, aunts and uncles lived to southern Minnesota where my brother lived. Their dad got a job at Hormel after several years of intermittent employment including layoffs and strikes at factories in Wisconsin. The economy in Wisconsin, and in many parts of the country, was not doing well. Our little family was happy to be in a community where employment standards continued to be stable since World War II. This was the home of Spam, after all.

Kevin's sister entered kindergarten, and I was able to be home with my children for the first time. After walking his sister to school, only five blocks away, we would head home for the afternoon. Often, Kevin and I enjoyed walking the two blocks from our house to a small neighborhood grocery store where we would sometimes buy an ice cream treat. We walked another block to the local park where Kevin explored nature and the pond inhabited by ducks and some geese. Sometimes I would put him in the bike seat, and we would ride to the library and explore books. We would then walk to school to meet his sister for her walk home.

We enjoyed the local YMCA where I became a part-time fitness teacher and swimming instructor. Kevin loved being in the childcare at the YMCA. He enjoyed sitting in the lobby with me, watching people come and go. He enjoyed walking the track and watching tennis players from the balcony. Kevin and his sister often asked to spend rainy days and weekends at the YMCA.

Kevin enjoyed being active. He loved it and would laugh continuously when I would lie on my back, lift him up with my feet, hold his waist and he would pretend to fly like an airplane. He loved to "go fast" on the sledding hill down the street, and he learned to skate on the frozen pond that was the summer home to the ducks and geese.

We lived in a quiet, modest neighborhood that was the home to many of the employees, both laborers and management, who worked at Hormel, the largest industry in the community. Children gathered and played together and attended school and church together. But just one year later, our idyllic life was rocked.

Union members got a call to attend a meeting at the local high school auditorium in August 1985. The contract proposed by the company was rejected. This was a culmination of a series of events that began long before we arrived in town. My husband was part of a group of new employees. Our family was happy with the wages and stability that Hormel offered us. However, most of the workers felt betrayed by the company and the contract was rejected by a vote of 1,291 to 96. My husband was again on strike, now in Minnesota.

Our family moved into a world of turmoil. Approximately 1,500 people were in the union. We had a lot of company with many of our neighbors on strike as well. The union provided strike pay, but it barely paid for groceries. We no longer lived near my husband's family, so we didn't have that support. I went back to work, my husband disappeared into the world of the striking workers, and Kevin and his sister went to day care.

Things continued to spiral out of control in our community. Our family was like so many other families. My husband was a union worker, and my brother was in management. My daughter attended school church with children and grandchildren of union members and management. Teachers were divided and the school district told teachers they could not discuss the strike in the schools. My husband's parents drove the five hours each way to deliver food to us.

By February of 1986, we had run out of money, and we were at the end of an ultimatum from the company. Return to work by the end of February or the company would proceed by filling them with new hires.

The plant had reopened in January, and workers were invited back without losing any benefits, but the wage would be over 20% less than they had been making. Workers manned the picket lines, and those who crossed the line were labeled scabs. As the son of a strong union man, my husband refused to cross the picket line until we ran out of money. I went to our landlord and asked him to use our security deposit for our February rent, and I told my husband he needed to go back to work. My job selling radio advertising did not bring us enough money to live, or even move. We had no choice. He crossed the picket line.

The first night that he crossed the line, he met up with a few of the guys that he had worked with at 3 am at a truck stop restaurant. They decided that they would cross the line together. One of the guys, an avid hunter, brought his gun with him. I couldn't sleep, wondering what would happen. Cold weather and no money led many people to desperation.

At 4 am, I heard our garage door open, slam shut, and my husband ran into the house. He was shaking with fear. The guys were turned back at the picket line and guys with guns started following them. He hid in the bedroom for the rest of the day. When I walked out of the house in the morning, our front porch wall was spray painted with "SCAB."

Then governor Rudy Perpich sent the National Guard to guard the plant and access to the plant was limited. Kevin heard about the Army being in his town, and he begged me to take him to see the Army guys. It was an imposing sight to see hundreds of soldiers in white, with guns and shields surrounding the plant. In the movie in my head, I can see the clouds from their breath as they stood around the plant. With the plant being in the center of town, no matter how hard I tried, I couldn't protect my children from seeing that sight. I couldn't protect them from the chaos of the world.

By early spring, the national union leaders ordered the local union into surrender. The local union refused, and the national union put them into receivership and sent in national union trustees.

My husband went back to work, but his spirit and our marriage never really recovered. We divorced just 3 years later when Kevin was just 8 years old.

I taught my children that their opinions mattered. I asked them what they thought about their world. I wanted them to understand what they could about the world. Some people wondered why I asked my children their opinions. I wanted my children to know that they could think and understand things, even if the world looked like it was incomprehensible. I wanted my children to know that dissent and disagreement is part of life and that it can be resolved. What Kevin and his sister experienced during their very early years impacted their lives in different ways than it impacted our lives. Yet, we survived, and I think we ultimately became stronger in the end.

Kevin and his sister continued in the same schools and the same church. Some of the families left the town. Some of the families never again spoke to their former friends who crossed the picket lines. Some people, like us, took a breath and worked to survive, and to make the world a better place.

Chapter 8

Posted for friends and family: New residence: Changes again

November 11, 2014

Kevin celebrated Veterans' Day twice today. This morning, he and his caregiver Alexa went to the celebration at the Maple Lake school. He and the other Veterans were treated to lunch. This evening we went to Perkins, and he was treated with a Magnificent Seven meal for his service. He had a good day and was conversing about the day. He was happy to give the "peace sign" for a picture. I told him we are thankful for his service. He said, "I was happy to do it."

Isaiah 2:4–They will beat swords into plowshares...

November 12, 2014

November and an early snowfall bring colder weather. Kevin wanted to hibernate and sleep today. I saw escape as his motivation. So, we talked about doing things that will help him get to his goals. "What is your goal?" I asked.

"To go home," he answered.

"Will sleeping all day get you to that goal?" "No," he said with a sigh. "I'll get up in an hour."

"Pinky swear?" I said. And he reached his hand up and we hooked our fingers together. Later tonight I called, and we talked some more. He fulfilled his promise and had a good evening. Tomorrow we begin again.

November 18, 2014

Is Kevin serious about getting his skills back? That is a resounding "yes!" As he worked with his personal trainer today, he walked without the hemi walker (he had Paul with the wheelchair behind him and Andy holding into his gait belt.) He was standing tall, and he did it! Then he worked on the mat, doing sit-ups with great form. He did 30. I could recognize the man who used to pound out sit ups and pushups at a record pace. Another step towards his goals and another successful day.

November 20, 2014

I stopped by Kevin's house after work. Kevin was relaxed and enjoying conversation with the staff. He had a good day despite a sleepless night. I brought him a white mocha latte and he enjoyed it a lot! I still had some of my plain black coffee left, and I offered it to him. When he took a big drink, he made a face that clearly expressed total disgust. We all had to laugh. He laughed, too. We worked on identifying sounds in the kitchen. I asked him if he could smell the food. He said, "No, I can't smell things." That was the first time he told anyone that he couldn't smell very well. We have suspected that. He does seem to taste/smell the pungent things (like plain black coffee!) As with all other of his senses, it appears that his sense of smell has been compromised.

I thank God each day for each small step and for Kevin's gifts.

November 24, 2014

Kevin had a rough night. While these are not happening as frequently, they still happen. He is trying so hard to make some sense out of what still makes no sense. He doesn't express anger; he is sad and depressed. It broke my heart to hear him say, "I can't see you. I just want to see your face again." I assure him that he can tell me by my voice and that he can see me in his memories. I share all the progress he has made and how much he is loved.

Each day is a new day and the one thing we know for sure is that God's love is with us always. We are not alone. "Surely goodness and mercy will follow ...all the days of our lives."

November 25, 2014

Kevin came to my house tonight. We made pizza, watched Jeopardy, and had a good conversation. He was so relaxed. Joey, his caregiver, commented that it was so nice to see him so happy and engaged. We were at the house for about 2 and a half hours. Finally, Kevin said he was ready to go to bed. We headed back to the group home where Kevin stays. He doesn't consider it his home. He considers it the place where he sleeps. Kevin was tired but he put good effort into navigating the steps and the car.

We arrived at the house, and everyone greeted him. One of the staff asked him if he wanted to hear a knock-knock joke. Kevin started telling her a joke. He got to the punch line and said, "I forgot." He smiled and so did I. It was a very pleasant evening and one to cherish.

November 27, 2014

Kevin said that he is thankful that he is alive. Wow! What a statement.

It is amazing that a person can say that he is thankful that he is alive. On this Thanksgiving Day, I am grateful that I am alive. We are blessed that God is holding us in his hands. Blessings on this Thanksgiving Day.

November 29, 2014

William Stafford wrote a poem titled, "The Way It Is." In his poem, he talks about the thread that we hold that keeps us from getting lost by the distractions and the tragedies of life. It seems like we could be easily pulled off course. As I see Kevin living in his new normal, I see him stay on the course. No matter what happens and no matter how poor his memory, he knows he wants to be at home and to live a good life. He is a child of God. He is loved and redeemed.

Kevin, keep your faith and hold onto threads that make up our lives.

December 1, 2014

This is Kevin's first push-up in 14 months! He had a good workout session with Andy, his personal trainer, and Joey, his support person. We were all impressed with his strength and determination. He told me I could watch him work out, but I had to be quiet. That was good for a laugh from the guys. At the end of the session, we were chatting, and Kevin was tossing out comments. I said, "You look happy."

He responded, "I am. That's because I like being at this place." I am so grateful to everyone who has donated through this site and to help Kevin access things like the fitness center and the personal trainer. Thank you for your prayers and for your love. It is priceless.

December 10, 2014

Kevin had a good day yesterday but last night he came down with a cold. He was running a fever this afternoon. It is no fun feeling sick no matter how young or old we are. We are grateful for the warmer weather. We pray for those on the East and West coasts as they brace for nasty weather. Kevin is getting ready for Christmas. He helped decorate and has already got a few presents for his brother and nephew.

1 Peter 1:6-7–Though now for a little while you may have to suffer various trials, so that the genuineness of your faith, more precious than gold which though perishable is tested by fire, may redound to praise and glory and honor at the revelation of Jesus Christ.

December 14, 2014

Kevin struggled today. He was frightened and feeling alone. He was trying to make sense out of this crazy time.

He told me he was in a nightmare. He was running around trying to make people happy and a demon was chasing him. Finally, the demon caught him and is holding him in this dream. We talked about faith and trust in God and how that helps us banish all the demons. Only God knows the plan for our lives. All we can do is hold on with trust and faith and keep moving forward.

Psalm 23–The Lord is my shepherd; I shall not want...

December 22, 2014

Kevin had a rough night. It seems like Mondays are hard for him. We usually do several things on the weekends and staff think maybe that is why Mondays are harder. Kevin is accepting that he is blind. I asked him to draw a picture for me. He responded with a very matter of fact voice, "I can't because I can't see." I know that acceptance and recall are part of his recovery. Yet, my heart hurts to hear him say these words. Still, God is in charge, and I know His plan will unfold. One day, I pray that we will see that beautiful plan.

Psalm 88–O Lord, I call for help by day, I cry out in the night before thee. Let my prayer come before thee, incline thy ear to my cry!

December 25, 2014

Kevin had one request for Christmas morning: warm homemade banana bread. So, this morning when I woke up, I brewed my coffee and made a loaf of banana bread. Once it was baked, I wrapped it up and brought it to Kevin. He was in the living room, and all was quiet. I put the wrapped warm loaf in his hands and said, "Merry Christmas." Then I took it to the kitchen.

In surprise, Kevin asked, "Where are you going with that?" He wanted a slice. I cut off the end and took it to him with a glass of cold milk. It was wonderful to see his smile. What a difference a year makes.

December 27, 2014

We celebrated our family Christmas today. I really can't remember the last time all my children were together for Christmas. I'm pretty sure it was about ten years ago. This morning, my daughter Erica, my grandson Gunner, and I picked up Kevin at about 10 a.m. and headed to my house. Gunner delivered the presents and we opened them in our family routine–youngest to oldest. Kevin did a great job opening his presents. It took a lot of fine motor coordination and mental concentration. He did a great job and thanked us all. We finished with a lunch of quiche. Kevin was tired after a good three hours. He was ready for a nap and so were the rest of us!

It was a lovely Christmas celebration!

January 3, 2015

Saturday morning and Kevin has started one of his resolutions—to get a little "lighter." He didn't want a mocha latte this morning. Instead, I made a smoothie. It has been a long journey, these past 15 months. Kevin keeps trying to understand what has happened. It continues to amaze me that he shows so much courage and strength. Each day he gets up again and starts once more. He gets depressed and discouraged, and he keeps pushing through.

When I think of where he was just one year ago, today shows great growth. I pray each morning and each night for Kevin. Thank you for reading this and following Kevin's journey. That means so much to him and to our family.

January 4, 2015

We ventured out into the cold Minnesota morning and went to church. Kevin so enjoys singing at church. Even when we sing new songs, he catches on quickly. People are so welcoming and helpful. Today, a couple stopped and helped us get out of the car quickly. He is standing more frequently during the songs now. He can make it through two songs before he has to sit down. He puts his arm over my shoulder as he sings. Even though his challenges are many, Kevin still sings praises to God. He truly reflects God's goodness.

The day continued to be a very good one. Kevin enjoyed playing games and talking to his support and to me. It was a blessed day.

January 7, 2015

Kevin didn't sleep very well again last night. It was better, though. He is a trooper and he got up and moved. By all reports, he had a good day. He is the luckiest person, his support person told me. They were playing games and Kevin threw three Yahtzee scores in one game. He won several games in a row, and then won the next several card games. He enjoyed the games.

This was his final night at this house. He is moving to a new facility closer to Minneapolis tomorrow. This move will allow greater access to many services that will help Kevin's recovery. Kevin is looking forward to having more activities outside of the house. I thank God for Tadd's Lighthouse. It provided what we needed as Kevin was discharged from hospital care. We trust that this next move is just what God has planned for Kevin. Tomorrow is the beginning of the next chapter in Kevin's journey. The story continues and God is good.

Nothing is ever simple. When I received the ultimatum that I needed to find a residence for Kevin's move from the VA Hospital Polytrauma unit, I worked hard to secure something that I thought would be best for Kevin. After visiting many group homes, I knew that the location would be important so that I could be to him quickly and relatively easily. When I started looking, my goal was to find the place that best understood his challenges and goals. I started out looking for a place that could seamlessly pick up and continue his rehabilitation. I was quickly disillusioned as I discovered that the group homes I visited did not focus on rehabilitation. In general, the comments I received included things like, "We have a person-centered focus. We want our residents to be happy."

As I questioned further, I discovered that this apparently meant they wanted the residents to be quiet and not too much trouble. I told them, "Kevin is goal oriented. He is used to working hard and accomplishing his goals. Physical activity has always been his outlet for stress. He likes movies, sports, and conversation about political and world events. He wants to go home and have a job and a family." I asked, "How can we build this into his life at the group home?" The staff would look at me with a blank look that they used to hide their disbelief that this could happen.

If Kevin's residence was close to me, I would be able to help Kevin, and the staff, to reach his goals. By the second quarterly meeting with Kevin's large care team, I learned that his distance from the VA hospital where he was receiving his rehab therapies was a problem for both the residence and the VA. At first, the comments were about the hour-long drive each way that it took to get to the VA Hospital. "Too much windshield time for Kevin," commented one of the staff. "That's too many hours out of his day."

I suggested that perhaps the drive time could be used to engage him by playing word games, mental math, and conversation about world events. "No," was the answer. "He is in his wheelchair, in a van, and the driver and caregiver sit in front while he is secured in his chair behind them."

Kevin is blind and has hearing aids in both ears. This environment is not good for him. I could understand that. He is isolated in a van for two hours a day. There didn't seem to be any solution except to find a place in closer proximity to the VA Hospital so that he would have less drive time. I found out later that the members of the care team thought the drive to Kevin's residence, for them, was also too long. The care staff at the group home were unhappy with the amount of time they had to be in the car. I was the only one on the team that could see the benefit for Kevin to be living where I could see him quickly and easily as often as he needed it. The care team told me, "He needs to be able to function without you seeing him every day. He needs to accept his condition." One person even said, "With his brain injury, he probably doesn't even really know whether you are there or not."

I started looking for a new group home. The VA staff and the state-mandated care managers suggested the next home. "It is the best of the best," they told me. There was an opening in one of the homes about halfway between the VA and my home. I made an appointment and toured the house. I asked my list of questions, "How consistent is your staffing? How do you meet the needs of a person who is blind? What activities do you have for the residents? What type of social and work environments will my son have?" I was assured that this company was the best in the industry. Kevin would have good care. "You will need to make up your mind quickly," I was told. "Beds are not available for long. The residents in these homes stay there (until they die.)"

While the other residents in this home were a good 20-30 years older than Kevin, no one seemed to think this was an issue. All of them were in wheelchairs. Kevin could walk with assistance. Kevin had an acquired brain injury and the other individuals had different challenges. Kevin was blind. The other individuals could see.

I wasn't very comfortable with the move, but I felt that perhaps I was being selfish. The move would make my work life more difficult. I would be juggling work with a daily expedition into the city. I wouldn't be able to make multiple short visits anymore. I would need to factor in the commute to the residence and stay longer. If this was the very best for Kevin, I would make that work for him. The concession I requested was that he would be able to continue to attend church with me every Sunday in our town, as had become our routine. I was assured that would be possible.

I felt like we didn't have any option. If Kevin stayed where he was, it seemed like the agencies did not want to continue to provide the rehab services that Kevin needed. We would be on our own.

I started working with Kevin to prepare him for the transition to a new group home. I scripted a conversation for the aides who worked with him. Kevin had shown me that he needed things repeated consistently, to keep them in his memory. I talked about the positives to the move, and I assured him that I would still be there every day, even though I likely would not be able to be there as many times during the day. I talked about the neighborhood where the new house would be in the city. "Maybe we will be able to do more things like going to baseball, football, hockey and rugby games," I told him. "We can go to the zoo and the Mall of America because we will be a lot closer."

We celebrated Thanksgiving Day and Christmas together at my house. Because he had missed so many family holidays when he was in the military, I wanted to have all my children together at least one holiday a year. We had a lovely Christmas with both Kevin's sister and her family arriving from Kentucky and his brother coming home from Canada.

When they left, Kevin was packed up in a van and moved to the new residence. In the 28 months since he had received his Honorable Discharge papers for his military service, Kevin moved three times. In the 16 months since the rugby accident, this will be his fifth move.

Posted for friends and family: Thirty-third birthday month

January 9, 2015
*Kevin had a busy day today. He had a physical at the VA Medical Center in Minneapolis. It was a long appointment as it was an update for the new staff, a physical and some immunizations. Kevin was aware of his new location, and his caregiver said Kevin was the first person that he has worked with who was able to articulate some of his specific needs. This is the second indication in two days that Kevin may be making a big step with his memory. Yesterday, during a conversation with one of the new staff, Kevin was able to remember that his brother plays for Steinbach Pistons hockey. He came up with the team's name with no cues. I was surprised and happy to hear him say that. I pray that his memory continues to show improvements. I know this isn't a movie version of life; Kevin still has a long road ahead of him. Thank God for His goodness and you for all your pray*ers.

January 11, 2015
It was a great Sunday morning. The people at church were so happy to see Kevin. The new house staff brought him to Buffalo, and it was great. People at the church were praying that it would work. On top of that, it

gives the new staff yet another picture of Kevin and his abilities to interact within a larger group. He was so warmly welcomed and so was his support person.

As we usually do, we had a nice breakfast at Perkins. He was greeted by name when we were brought to the table. He had a good breakfast, and we enjoyed a good conversation.

John 14:27–I am leaving you with a gift–peace of mind and heart. And the peace I give is a gift the world cannot give.

January 12, 2015

Kevin and the new support team are getting used to each other. It is a challenge for all. Kevin called me this afternoon and wanted me to pick him up. I gave the support person some suggestions. I spoke with her tonight. She was impressed at how much Kevin can do. They had some conversations and played some games. Kevin had dinner, and the evening was going well. I pray for everyone. Through Jesus all things are possible. God is not finished with Kevin.

Matthew 7:7–Ask and it will be given to you; seek and you will find; knock and the door will be opened to you.

January 13, 2015

Short message tonight Kevin and I talked on the phone. He sounded tired. He is getting used to his new support team and they are learning about him. I pray that they see Kevin not in the terms of his injuries, rather in how he defines himself despite this accident. He continues his journey toward rehabilitation and recovery.

Finally, the words of Aristotle: "The quality of life is determined by its activities."

January 23, 2015

Kevin and I enjoyed a nice dinner tonight at a local cafe near the original indoor mall in Minnesota. We had good conversation and an excellent meal. Kevin rated his sandwich an "8" because he thought the bun was a little hard. Dessert, a chocolate and raspberry brownie, was an "8" also but the dinner overall was a "10." He is looking good. He had several appointments this week and getting out is making a difference. He has activities set up each day this weekend. Tomorrow he is meeting up for coffee with some rugby friends. Sunday is his birthday!

I know good things will come his way in 2015. I think of Helen Keller's words: "I long to accomplish a great and noble task, but it is my chief duty to accomplish small tasks as if they were great and noble."

January 27, 2015

There was a potluck dinner at Kevin's house. It was nice to meet more of the staff and some of the family members of Kevin's housemates. Kevin did a really good job with conversations. When you think about it, it is a complex task to eat without being able to see and to carry on a conversation with multiple people. I was so pleased that Kevin could track the conversation and enjoy the meal. He even smiled and laughed a little. After dinner, he was tired. He had a few appointments today. He was ready for some quiet time in his room. We sang a few songs and said a prayer and then it was time to head back home.

Proverbs 15:13–A glad heart makes a happy face.

January 30, 2015

A friend and I visited Kevin tonight. He was having a rough evening–he was asking a lot of questions. "What happened to me? Why am I here?

When can I go home?"

We talked about time.

Kevin described a lot of different uses of time. He identified time to work, time to learn, time to heal, time to party. Life has many moments, and the one truth is that God has a plan, and we follow Him.

Luke 12:23-31

For life is more than food and the body more than clothing. Consider the ravens: they don't have a storeroom or a barn, yet God feeds them. Aren't you worth much more than the birds? Can any of you add a cubit to his height by worrying? If then you're not able to do even a little thing, why worry about the rest? Consider how the wildflowers grow: They don't labor or spin thread. Yet I tell you, not even Solomon in all his splendor was adorned like one of these. If that's how God clothes the grass, which is in the field today and is thrown into the furnace tomorrow, how much more will He do for you–you of little faith? Don't keep striving for what you should eat and what you should drink, and don't be anxious. For the Gentile world eagerly seeks all these things, and your Father knows that you need them.

But seek His kingdom, and these things will be provided for you.

In 2003, Kevin received his first deployment papers to Kosovo. He was boots on ground and had experienced his first call to combat, and then he called me to tell me he was okay. That was in 2004, more than thirty years later. It was then I remembered that dream from my teenage years. I realized, the person in that dream was my future son. From that day on, I said a prayer of gratitude to God. I knew that my son would return from combat, and we would be able to hug each other on a street with the sun at his back. When he was on the tours of duty in Iraq, my friends would say, "How could you let him enlist? How can you bear it? Aren't you afraid that he will be hurt or killed?"

"Yes," I replied. "I pray every night that God will hold him in His hands. I trust that he will return safely. He is a child of God and I know that God will allow him to return."

Tracking time is such a human creation. Time passes. We all know that when we reflect on the memorable moments of our lives. Sometimes time flows quickly with disastrous consequences like a flooding river as it tears into house and land. Sometimes time is like water in a marsh. It sits. It doesn't seem to flow anywhere. It absorbs everything around it. It is thick with hidden life. "Everyone responds to a brain injury in their own time. What we know is that the skills that they have by the end of two years after the injury is probably where they will end up," the doctors tell me.

I wonder, "If that is true, why is Kevin's recovery defined by a calendar and clock created by other people? What if Kevin needs more time; time not defined by our clock?"

Posted for friends and family: Months 17-19

February 1, 2015

Kevin had a rough Saturday, and he was distressed Saturday night. He is confused about what has happened to him. We know this happens periodically as he makes some big steps, and then correlates his present with his past. Still, knowing doesn't make it any easier. Kevin made it to church, and he was quiet and seemed rather distant. He told me he didn't want to talk about anything. We went to our usual Sunday breakfast, and he was a little more willing to talk. He is feeling like the world is not a place that is good to him. At the end of the conversation, he was willing to go back and participate in an activity. I reminded him how many people see him as someone who is a role model and inspiration. Please continue to pray.

February 12, 2015

Tonight, Kevin and I shared God's miracles. When Kevin was brought by the medics to Regions Hospital after his accident, he was enrolled in a clinical trial to help improve outcomes for people who suffered traumatic brain injury. Tonight, the survivors and families of the trial participants gathered with the medics who brought them in, the doctors and the researchers who worked in this trial. The results were revealed. Sadly, this study results indicated the treatment was inconclusive. We learned that not one single human trial has demonstrated success in treating TBI. Every year the equivalent of the passengers of 175 class 747 airplanes die each year from traumatic brain injury. It is a sobering thought.

What we know is that each human is God's miracle. Life is precious and more fragile than we know. It is by the grace of God that we are here. Kevin and one of the medics who brought him to the hospital had dinner together tonight. He is one more angel in Kevin's life. Only God knows our path. Tonight, he shared a glimpse of that path, I think. Thank you for your continuing prayers. You really do not know the miracles that you share, but God does.

February 21, 2015

Kevin called me this afternoon and we had a good chat. He wants to come home so badly. I have been reading him the book: The Alchemist *by Paulo Coelho. We have been talking about our life's purpose. Kevin told me that his purpose is to show people happiness.*

March 2, 2015

Kevin finished the biplane he built for his nephew Gunner. It is red, white, and blue–All American! He offered this advice to him, "Give everything a try. Fight for what you believe in."

"What do you believe in?" I asked.

"I believe in Truth, Justice, Peace, Love, God, and Family," Kevin replied with conviction.

As always, Kevin, you are an inspiration. God holds you up.

March 4, 2015

It is a blessing that Kevin continues to become more aware, and it is also heartbreaking at times. Tonight, he called me and asked me why he can't come home. He asked me what happened to him and why he is blind. As I explained what happened at the rugby game, I could hear his fear. I reassured him that God loves him and has His plan prepared. We need to have faith and never give up.

Isaiah 40:30-31–Even youths shall faint and be weary, and young men shall fall exhausted; but they who wait for the Lord shall renew their strength; they shall mount up with wings like eagles; they shall run and not be weary; they shall walk and not faint.

March 15, 2015

"This injury does not define Kevin's life–God defines it."

Kevin amazed us today at church. After we were seated, I went to get Kevin and his support a cup of coffee. When I returned with the coffee he was walking. I looked at her and she said, "He wanted to walk around until church started." We moved and greeted some people and then he sat in a regular seat. It was a wonderful sermon and Kevin asked to go forward to the altar at the end. He sat on the stage area while we sang "Holy, Holy, Holy." The minister came forward and said a prayer for Kevin and for all of us.

March 21, 2015

As Kevin began to have increased awareness these past few weeks, he started to struggle with his new reality. He became very distressed, anxious, and angry about his blindness, his inability to walk without assistance and his lack of activity. He became so agitated he was unable to calm down. Because of this, he was admitted to the VA Hospital in Minneapolis on Wednesday. He is at the Polytrauma unit where he was a year ago. Many of the staff there worked with him before and that is good for him. He will be there until Tuesday it appears. They will be checking medications and his general wellbeing. He was very tired after the incident and has been calm and coherent. We know that God is in charge. Prayers appreciated.

It is so hard to get phone calls in the middle of the night. One night, after Kevin was out of high school, I woke up from a vivid dream at about midnight. In my dream, a policeman was knocking on my door to tell me there had been an accident and Kevin was in trouble. My eyes opened and my heart was racing. I took a breath and tried to rationalize the dream. I decided to go to his bedroom to check on him, only to find that he wasn't home. He had gone out that night with friends. Generally, he would be home by midnight, but he wasn't that night. I went into the family room and decided to read for a while until he came home. I couldn't sleep anyway. At about 3 a.m., he still wasn't home. He didn't have a cell phone at that time, and I didn't know where he was. I started getting worried, so I decided to see if I could figure out where he was by checking his computer. He often got together with friends for online gaming. I worked for a few hours, and I couldn't figure anything out. I couldn't decide if I was angry with him, or if I was just afraid for him. I wanted to yell at him when he got home for not telling me his plans. I wanted to hug him when he got home safely. I was frantic, and sleep was not an option.

Kevin finally arrived home at about 5:30 a.m. He was just fine but very surprised that I was awake and waiting for him. He was with friends playing games, and time got away from him. He was sorry for making me upset. I told him we would be getting him a cell phone that day and I expected he would call me to let me know when plans changed. He promised he would.

Just after Kevin got home, I received a phone call. It was my mother. My cousin, whose name is also Kevin, had called her. His daughter was in a car accident at about midnight that night. She was in intensive care in a trauma unit in the city. My cousin was there with her. Things were not looking good for her. My mom lives over 750 miles away, and she hoped I would be able to go to the hospital to be with them, and to give them support. In my job, I worked with families whose children have disabilities. My mom thought I might be able to give my cousin hope that things could be better, even if his daughter had injuries that would leave her severely disabled. The doctors were telling him that his daughter was not responsive, and it appeared that she would be paralyzed if she survived. When I walked into the hospital, my cousin said, "One day we are talking about where my daughter will go to college, and the next day we are wondering if she will ever be able to wake up and walk anywhere again." We talked about how important hope is for all of us, and we prayed.

It was a long journey, and it continues for my cousin and his daughter. She was paralyzed but is cognitively intact. Eventually, she learned to paint while holding a brush in her mouth, and she became a very good artist. She attended college classes. She is living in a handicapped accessible home. Her life changed completely, and it has been a long, difficult journey, and she is with us still.

Kevin would call me many times during the night. Sometimes it was to tell me he was OK, and sometimes it was to tell me that he was in trouble. Eighteen months after the rugby accident, he needed others to help him call me.

At 3:00 a.m. one morning in March 2015, Kevin's group home staff called me. Kevin had tried to get out of his bed by himself, and he had fallen. He was on the floor in his bedroom and didn't want anyone near him. He was yelling at the caregivers telling them he was going to kill them, and he was making quite a scene. He told them he wanted to talk to me. I said, "Let me talk to him."

"Kevin, what's going on?" I questioned.

"Mom, you have to come and pick me up," he yelled. "I'm ready to be picked up. I'm ready to get out of here and to come home. Come now."

"Kevin, it is 3:00 a.m. I can't come now. I will be there in the morning," I tried to explain. "Go back to bed. I'll be there when you wake up."

"Mom, if you aren't coming to get me, I will walk out of this place right now," he told me. "I'm going to kill these people. I don't care if I die. I need to Get. Out. Of. Here. Now."

I knew that he couldn't walk without assistance. In fact, he couldn't do much of anything without assistance. He was not going to kill anyone or himself. He didn't have the means to do that. He needed to calm down, though. I knew that the caregivers would call the police if he didn't calm down. "Kevin, nothing would make me happier than if you could walk out right now, but you know that you can't do that," I tried to rationalize with him. "Take a deep breath. I will get there as soon as I can."

There was a long pause. Then Kevin stated in a more subdued voice, "OK, then I'll crawl out of here." I told him to let the staff help him back to bed and I would be there in an hour. After some assurances and coaxing, he finally agreed. The group home made the arrangements to have him transferred back to the VA hospital. I got dressed and met them at the group home and went with them to the VA emergency room. He was assessed and admitted back to the Poly Trauma unit at the VA hospital. I prayed to God that He would release Kevin from this misery. "Please heal him," I prayed. "Please let me bring him home."

March 25, 2015

Kevin had a good night, but he woke up at 4 a.m. Still, it was a good day. We had a lot of conversations tonight. A lot of his questions still revolve around the question "Why?" We don't know why things happen. Still, we keep our faith in God. Kevin asked me to tell you all thank you for your prayers and concern. He wants you to know he is coming back, and he is doing well. He will be discharged tomorrow. I will pick him up and get him settled back at the group home. He keeps working and we keep praying for God's plan to continue to unfold.

March 28, 2015

Kevin called me at about 9 a.m. this morning. He wanted to do something. So, I headed to Plymouth and picked him up. We went to the fitness center and spent the morning working out. He did 2 miles on the bike followed by a variety of weight training exercises. After the workout, we enjoyed lunch at Perkins. We had good conversation and a few prayers. It is so hard to make sense of this new life. In fact, it doesn't make sense. Yet, Kevin continues to forge ahead. He is a child of God, and he is a believer. We continue to pray for strength and courage.

March 29, 2015

Kevin is making improvements in his cognitive functioning. It is truly amazing. I wish that all of you could be here with him to experience the steady changes. While it is painful at times, I do see the growth and I am thankful for God's grace. We see the mountains and we know that God made the mountains. What is the reason for this? We don't know. Only God knows the reason why Kevin and we are on this journey. We trust in Him and we keep moving forward.

2 Corinthians 12:9-10–

But he said to me, "My grace is sufficient for you, for my power is made perfect in weakness." Therefore, I will boast all the more gladly about my weaknesses, so that Christ's power may rest on me. That is why, for Christ's sake, I delight in weaknesses, in insults, in hardships, in persecutions, in difficulties. For when I am weak, then I am strong.

April 4, 2015

1 Peter 1:7–

"These trials will show that your faith is genuine. It is being refined by fire as fire tests and purifies gold–though your faith is far more precious than gold. So, when your faith remains strong through many trials, it will bring you much praise and glory and honor on the day when Jesus Christ is revealed to the whole world."

Through Him all things are possible. Let us never forget that Kevin is in His hands.

April 13, 2015

It has been a very difficult week. Kevin is becoming more and more lucid. His memory is still poor, but it continues to improve. However, the more he can figure out things the more depressed he gets. He has struggled with even getting out of bed. On Friday, he went to the doctor. He has been refusing to eat and take fluids. He was very dehydrated, and the doctor threatened to hospitalize him. Fortunately, he did take fluids and ate some food after that. So, he made it through the weekend. Sunday night was difficult, and he was deeply depressed. Please pray for Kevin. He is not alone, and God does have a plan. Please pray for Kevin so that he can see a future that is filled with promise.

April 16, 2015

Kevin had a good appointment with his personal trainer this afternoon. He accomplishes so much working with him. He knows how to get Kevin motivated. Today, he had Kevin jumping! They started with stomping. Then he asked Kevin to jump like he would in sports. It was not a smooth movement, but his feet left the ground. Then, the trainer had Kevin walk with a weighted vest. Again, it was amazing. Kevin used the punching bag, and he also used the climbing rope to pull himself up out of his chair. He started the session with a stoic expression and ended with a big smile on his face. Pray that good days continue and that we can all make it through this.

April 17, 2015

Kevin still has a hard time getting up in the morning. He did show perseverance, and by the time I saw him after work, he looked good. We met at Barnes & Noble and enjoyed conversation and coffee. Kevin's conversation is so interesting. He takes some time, but he always comes up with great comments. We talked about books, movies, and sports. We are blessed that he has this capability. He can communicate. Thank God for blessing him.

I don't know what God has planned for him. I do know that whatever He plans, it is for good. So many people keep him in their prayers. I am grateful.

April 21, 2015

Kevin had a strong day! Thank you for your prayers. He could remember his morning into the afternoon, and the afternoon into the evening. He is completing more tasks with fewer or no cues. I received a text message this afternoon. He asked when I would be able to come down to see him. I suggested that we go out to dinner tonight. I asked him to think about a place he would like to go. Later, I got a text suggesting pizza. When I picked him up, he was ready to go. We enjoyed a short 15-minute drive and a nice evening. His support person asked him to describe the dinner in one sentence. Kevin thought for a moment and said, "We had an exquisite dinner event tonight."

Nice! I have many prayers of thanksgiving on the way home.

April 26, 2015

Thank God for Sunday! It was nice to have Kevin and Connor at church today. I pray that I will have my family together again soon. In the meantime, we are blessed to have so many people holding us in prayer. Kevin was very conscious today. He had a bit of an edge to his voice, but he was strong and participated in all the songs. He is getting so much stronger, and he is determined to be more independent. I was amazed at how well he is getting in and out of a vehicle. He is doing a great job communicating his confusion. He knows that he wants more in his life and he continues to work toward that goal. We know that through God all things are possible. Continue in faith.

Chapter 9

Posted for friends and family: Months 18-19

April 28, 2015

Kevin had a great night out at the Twins game at Target Field. He was the recipient of a gift of two tickets by the dugout. So, he and his support person headed to the game. They had a great time and Kevin even scored a baseball that was hit foul into their seats. It was an enjoyable evening, and the Twins won the game.

Kevin has been blessed this week. There are many people who care about him from the person who paid for his Sunday dinner to the people who gave him the tickets to the many people who hold him in prayer. Thank you for keeping him in your hearts. It is true; despite all the troubles in this world, God is here.

April 30, 2015

It is hard when I can't report a good day. Kevin struggled today. He works so hard, and he makes many gains. Then he has a day where things seem so surreal. How can his life have changed so completely?

How can a person wake up almost two years later and have lost so much?

He will get through this challenge with God's help and many prayers. We need to keep our faith and trust God and know that His plan is beyond our understanding.

Psalm 23:4–Even though I walk through the shadow of death, I will fear no evil; for thou art with me; thy rod and thy staff, they comfort me.

May 6, 2015

Kevin continues to have good days and not so good days (don't we all.) He has times when it seems he is dealing well with this new life. He even smiles at times, and he enjoys simple things–the Twins baseball game, holding a dog or cat at the animal shelter, going for a bike ride. He enjoys working out at the gym and going to church. His life has changed in many ways, but God doesn't change.

Hebrews 6:17-18 So, when God desired to show more convincingly to the heirs of the promise the unchangeable character of his purpose, he guaranteed it with an oath, so that by two unchangeable things, in which it is impossible for God to lie, we who have fled for refuge might have strong encouragement to hold fast to the hope set before us.

May 17, 2015

Kevin has good days and days that are harder. He had several hard days this week and today was harder as well. On days like this he doesn't even want to get out of bed. He has a hard time understanding where he is and why he is there. His support person worked hard and never gave up on him. Kevin finally got up and he was able to go out for a while. One of the aides asked if I would let him bring his dog to visit for a while.

That cheered Kevin up. He made it through another day. As each day begins and closes, we still have much to be thankful for–friends and family and the grace of God.

May 24, 2015

It was a good message at church today; Kevin listened intently and so did the entire congregation. God is in control, and we need to trust and love each day with gratitude and with peace in our soul.

Kevin had a rough start to his day, and he made it to church anyway. He had a great workout at the fitness center. He ended with 70 pounds of weight on the bench press machine with his left arm. When given the option for less weight and fewer reps, he didn't take it. He worked hard and completed the task.

When I see him smile, I smile. We followed the workout with a Sunday meal–cheeseburgers and a mocha latte.

Yes, we need to live our lives with a smile.

June 1, 2015

Kevin started his volunteer job at Feline Rescue today. He is going to work for two hours on Mondays with opportunities to add days. I asked him how many days he wanted to work. He said, "Five or six." We all need a purpose in life. It is good to be of service. Kevin has that mission ingrained deeply in his soul.

June 4, 2015

Thursday. Freedom Farm and horses in the morning and a training session with fitness center in the afternoon. I am so thankful for the people who help Kevin with things physical. He is so much happier when he is doing physical things. He smiles more. He talks more.

Today, when his trainer asked him to walk toward my voice, I said, "That reminds me of when we used to play Marco Polo."

I asked Kevin if he remembered that game. "Yes," he said. "We played it in the pool when we were swimming." True indeed.

I know that one day, if God is willing, Kevin will push that wheelchair away. Each day he gets inches closer.

I found this statement in my journal last night, "We are called to be faithful even through the tears." Truly, we are travelers in this world, and we are blessed to have Angels and fellow travelers who join us in our walk.

June 7, 2015

What a lovely Sunday. We had a good church service followed by a good workout. We had a nice lunch and then we watched Kevin's brother's baseball game. The weather was beautiful. Kevin was very vocal, and he cheered on the team. In the 7th inning we all sang, "Take me out to the ball game." Kevin was amazing! He was right on target for the whole game. One of my friends said, "Every Sunday should go like today."

June 13, 2015

It was a gentle but steady rain this morning. It did not deter the small and powerful group of people who gathered on the lawn on the west side of the Minnesota capitol building. Today, this group paid tribute to the Minnesota military families by dedicating the new Minnesota Family tribute and honoring families of our past, present, and future service members. Special guests included Gold Star families. I felt honored to attend with Kevin and to be acknowledged as part of the foundation that he and his fellow service members built their values on. (It is a small group; fewer than 1% of the population that chooses to serve in the military.) It was touching that the steady gentle rain kept falling, and it seemed appropriate somehow.

The tribute is a field of glacier rocks gathered from across our state engraved with sentences from letters written to and from service members from Minnesota. The letters began 150 years ago with the 1st Minnesota and the Civil War and continue through to the current wars.

Reading the lines on the rocks tells the story of honor and service. A special table was built with a gold star as the base and the North Star on the top. The rain stopped when the program ended and the people attending moved across the grounds reflecting on the lives of service.

No, freedom is not free, and those who serve have scars that others may never see.

As he was growing up, Kevin always had pets. When he was born, his sister had a kitten named Muffin. She was a playful white kitten, who was a part of Kevin's entire life, even though she was technically his sister's cat. Cats tend to be independent creatures who really belong to no one, unless they have decided that they want to connect. Kevin was about 10 years old when Muffin became sick. She was 12 years old by then, and perhaps it was her age. Kevin and his sister wanted her to get better. They kept her warm and made sure she ate, as well as she could. Kevin was her caregiver her nurse for a few weeks.

As we approached Christmas vacation that year, I decided to take Kevin and his sister to the Science Museum of Minnesota in Saint Paul. We had about a 2 hour drive each way to get to the museum, and it was a "big" trip for us. We packed our sandwiches in a cooler, and our warm Minnesota winter coats. Before we left, Kevin and his sister said goodbye to Muffin who was cuddled in her cat bed.

After a wonderfully interesting day at the museum, we made our way back home. When we arrived, Kevin ran to check on Muffin. She had passed away when we were gone. Kevin was beside himself. "We should never have gone," he cried. "If we had been home, she never would have died." As a 10-year-old, it was hard for him to understand that his presence would likely not have changed the outcome for poor Muffin. That is a hard message to hear.

Muffin was gone, but we eventually had another kitten that we rescued from a farm. She was so small that she fit into the palm of my hand. The farmer thought she would likely not survive–she was too small, it was too cold, and the farmer couldn't identify her mother. I asked if we could have her and the farmer immediately agreed. She looked like a puff of smoke in Kevin's hand, so we named her Smokey. She was Kevin's cat.

Kevin loved Smokey and took the best care of her. Sadly, as the years passed, Smokey also became sick. Kevin was in high school by this time. As Smokey was declining, we took her to the local vet who determined her kidneys had failed. She was not going to survive. He recommended that we put her down. Kevin was devastated. He didn't want her to die. He wanted to save her. He brought up that Muffin died because he wasn't there to save her. As a young teenager, he couldn't believe that Smokey would die. We talked about euthanasia for animals and why that decision would be the best for poor Smokey. It was a hard decision, and Kevin cried many tears as he held Smokey until she closed her eyes for the final time.

A little later that year, Kevin's little brother wanted a pet. We again rescued kittens from a farm. The mother cat had been killed and her litter of four kittens had been left motherless at about 3 weeks old. My friend asked if we could take two of the kittens, rather than the one that we had planned to take. Kevin had his new kitten that he named Cleo, and his little brother had his kitten that he named Buzz (after Buzz Lightyear.) Kevin fed both kittens with an eye dropper, and they quickly began to thrive. Both of my boys loved their cats.

Some months later, Kevin was outside in the yard. He heard a noise that sounded like a mewling, but it was very faint and inconsistent. With extreme patience, Kevin listened and determined that the sound was coming from the foundation of our garage. There was a crack in it, and he discovered that the sound was coming from there. He eventually coaxed a very small, very black kitten to come out of the foundation. He named it Dante, as she came out of the depths of hell. He brought her back to health, and she lived with us for several months. When a friend was looking for a kitten, Dante seemed to be a good match. Kevin took her, now the picture of health, to her new home.

I remember a cold winter evening when Kevin was out of high school and living in an apartment with some friends. He called me, "Mom, I found a kitten in the garage. I think it is freezing. What should I do?"

I encouraged him to hold the kitten near his body and try to bring up its body temperature slowly. Once it started responding, he could try to give it a few drops of milk or water. “Let me know how it is going,” I said.

Later that night, Kevin called me. The sadness in his voice broke my heart. “Mom, the kitten died. I couldn’t save it,” he said.

“Honey,” I said. “I’m so sorry. You tried to help it. You did what you could.” He wrapped it up and dug through the frozen ground to bury it.

During his deployments, Kevin told me he really wanted to help build things up, rather than just destroy. During his tour in Kosovo, he was most proud of the work he did with youth in an impromptu soccer league. When he was in Iraq, he wished he could have been more involved with the rebuilding of roads and bridges. He wanted to be a part of improving the life of the people he was protecting. He asked me once, “Why do people serve in the military, and not want to rebuild the country?”

“I don’t know the answer to that,” I replied. “All I know is you are exactly the kind of person I want to defend me.”

Posted for friends and Family

June 16, 2015

Physical activity is so important to Kevin. Before his accident, he used physical activity to relieve stress, to combat boredom, and to enjoy life. I read some research recently that indicated that physical activity also promotes brain healing. Kevin is getting stronger each week. He was a machine at the fitness center on Sunday. He powered through over 30 arm curl reps. His determination is remarkable. I know his journey continues and God guides his steps.

June 17, 2015

There is something about the love that we share with other living, breathing creatures. Kevin has a good heart, and he shares it with others. Today, he met one of the fellow travelers on this journey. Her son had a TBI at about the same time Kevin had his accident. About a year and a half after her son's accident, her son passed. She wanted so much to meet Kevin and give him a hug as she can only hold her son in her memories. She asked Kevin if she could give him a hug. He reached out his arms and held her close. They talked and I watched them both smile and enjoy the conversation. We are all travelers and love can make all the difference.

Chapter 10

Posted for friends and family: Almost to the end of year two: post rugby accident

June 24, 2015

Kevin had a session with one of the vision rehabilitation therapists today. It was a good session as the therapist was able to see the grit and determination that Kevin has. Before his session, he was asking me about the accident. He knows he is blind. At one point I asked him if he had any thoughts about it. He responded, "Yes, but they aren't appropriate to say out loud." I told him that it was OK; he could whisper them to me. He had a few choice words to say!

His concern is about getting a job in law enforcement. A cop can't be blind. I said, "Let's take it one step at a time. God has a plan."

When he met with the therapist, he did everything she asked him to do. He showed her how he can take care of his daily needs–brushing his teeth, shaving and other tasks.

We talked about chess, and he named each piece correctly. He explained how to play that game. The therapist is going to bring a chess

set that is adapted for the blind in her next visit. At the end, I asked Kevin if he had a thought about why she was asking him to do these things. He thought for a few moments and said, "So I can learn how to deal with being blind." Then, she asked him if he ever played any musical instruments. He said he didn't. I shared that Kevin sings and I asked if he would like to sing a song for her. With no suggestions from me, he started singing "Amazing Grace." I wish my phone hadn't died so I could have recorded it. It was strong and loud and perfectly on pitch-beautiful.

His awareness continues to increase. I thank God for that. With Jesus leading us, we can get through this. God has a plan and I know that someday we will see it.

June 26, 2015

It was a very good day. After Kevin's appointment this afternoon, we went to Clifford E. French Park in Plymouth. We spent some time listening to the children play on the playground. Kevin said he always liked the slides the best. So, we decided to try one! Kevin walked up several ramps, five steps, and then he climbed into the slide tube. He wanted to go first. With me at the top and his support person at the bottom, Kevin let go and slid down. It was pure freedom for a few precious seconds. We continued exploring the playground, ending with the excavator at the sand area. Kevin told us he remembered that, too. We finished at the park just ahead of the rain and we headed to dinner. Connor joined us and the brothers had a lot of conversation with Kevin tossing out plenty of big brother advice. They were both smiling and laughing through the meal. At the end, we all agreed that it had been a great day. I asked Kevin, "Do you feel loved?" He answered with an emphatic, "Yes."

July 1, 2015

Tonight, Kevin and I went to a concert in the park. I am trying to give Kevin opportunities to re-experience things we have done in the past. When he was little, we had some fun concerts in the park around July 4th. It gives us something to talk about and I can share memories with him. I am careful not to use "Do you remember…" He feels bad if he doesn't remember. Instead, I share what I remember and then we talk about the event that we are now sharing. Kevin enjoyed the music and he listened to children laughing and people talking. He enjoyed some food, and he said hello to a few people he met. He got a chance to pet a few dogs. We listened to the airplanes flying in formation over the crowd and Kevin talked about the symbolism of the formations. It was a lovely evening.

Luke 12:22-3–

And he said to his disciple, "Therefore I tell you, do not be anxious about your life... for life is more than food, and your body more than clothing... Consider the lilies, how they grow, they neither toil nor spin; yet I tell you, even Solomon in all his glory was not arrayed like one of these... Seek his kingdom and these things will be yours."

July 9, 2015

Kevin ran a marathon (relatively speaking) today. He walked and was on his feet for a full thirty minutes. He was engaged and focused throughout the half hour. He could name muscle groups like biceps and triceps and quads and hamstrings. He was accurate each time. When he finished, his muscles were shaking, he was sweating, and he had a big smile on his face.

The race is not always for the swift.

July 19, 2015

Kevin and I enjoyed a good day starting with a good church service. The message was right on target. We had a great workout after church. Kevin did a lot of work on his abs. My background in coaching and physical education is sure helpful! He stood at "attention" and he laughed when I asked how long he had to stand in that position. He looked like the soldier that he is. After that we enjoyed a midafternoon breakfast. I love to see him smile.

We remember that through Christ all things are possible. Everything we do is for his glory.

July 23, 2015

It continues to be a busy week. Kevin had another doctor appointment at the VA. Kevin did a great job answering questions. He is getting closer when asked the year ("2013," he said.) He also did a nice job telling the doctor what he'd like to do (go camping; take a horse on a long ride to a campsite; go target shooting; go to Japan and Australia.) He also had good rationale for why he wanted to do these things. The doctor asked him why he wanted to travel to Japan. He said, "I want to study the culture of the Samurai." She asked if he was a good shot. He said he was "fair." After she asked what his scores were. When he said he was classified as a sharpshooter, she said, "That sounds better than fair to me."

At the end of the diagnosis, she determined that his recent malaise is probably due to boredom. So, I got on the phone and arranged for him to go to a paintball course. Again, another person stepped up. I am so grateful to the young man who answered the phone. I asked if they could accommodate his needs. We have an appointment for time at the paintball course!

I have worked with people my whole life. My grandmother and my mother were both teachers. I started teaching when I was in elementary school. During the summer months, I put together a "summer school" for the younger children. I started babysitting for others by the time I was in 5th grade. I put together handmade flyers and took these through the neighborhood the summer that I was in 6th grade. Each afternoon I had 6 children who came to our front porch for two hours of learning and craft activities. I charged fifty cents per child, each day and I'm sure the parents were happy to have a few hours each afternoon for themselves.

I gave piano lessons to younger children when I was in high school. My piano teacher brought about six of her students who were in high school together and taught us how to teach beginner students. We were the group that worked with the younger children. As the children gained skills they were transferred to the more advanced teachers. My fellow high school classmates and I learned from our teacher who was considered the master teacher in our town.

I briefly, for about two weeks, considered a medical career path when I was deciding on my college major. I loved to learn, I decided, but I really didn't want to deal with blood and sick people. I like the research part better than the actual medical aspect. I completed my Bachelor of Science program in education and became a high school teacher. I was assigned the students who had difficulties learning as my first assignment. I remember the dream I had before I started my very first teaching assignment. In my dream, I walked into my classroom. The room was empty of students. I went to my teacher desk and began to check out the items that had been left for me. I opened the first book. It was filled with totally blank pages. "How odd," I thought in my dream. Then I opened the next book, and it was filled with blank pages, too. I opened book after book, and all of them were filled with empty pages. I awoke, sweating and in a panic. From that point on, I knew that I could never be totally prepared for the future. I knew that I would have to use my research skills to find the answers that no one would be able to give me.

When Kevin began awakening from the coma, I kept asking doctors and therapists for the best ways to help Kevin. Generally, their answer was, "It is too soon to tell what he will be able to do. He has a serious brain injury. His brain is 'angry' and it needs time to heal."

I knew from my work with students of all abilities, including some very disabled children, that every person is capable of learning. Every person, no matter how disabled, needs to be able to learn. I had worked with some children who had lost portions of their brains to tumors, or injury. I knew that learning is finding the best way to reach the person. I hadn't been involved with anyone who was in a coma before, though. I hoped that the medical people would be able to provide research-based best practices to help individuals recover from brain injury.

I learned that the definition of "rehabilitation" that I was using did not seem to be the same definition that the medical field uses. I always considered the term "rehabilitation" to mean that a person would be restored to health or normal condition." Not so, I learned. In my son's case, he would never be restored to his usual condition. I was frequently told that rehabilitation would stop when progress was no longer evident.

In my career, I believed that progress was always possible. My teaching career taught me that what can be considered as very small step, can be huge progress for an individual. If Kevin had been a high school student when he sustained the hit in rugby, he would have received an education for the years he had remaining. Instead, as an adult, he would be discontinued from therapies when the therapists determined he was no longer making adequate progress. I used my teaching background to start building a program for Kevin so that he could build on his strengths and continue to build new pathways in his brain. I increased my research to look for materials, instructional strategies, and resources for individuals who were blind and had sustained a brain injury. I added "veterans" to my search.

What I learned was that very little instruction was described in the literature for individuals with brain injury. Most of the research addressed forms of accommodation that involved visual cues. In fact, when Kevin was at the second hospital for their coma stimulation program, the doctors recommended that I bring pictures, familiar objects, calendars, and books in Kevin's room so that these could trigger his brain as he began to awaken. At the time, we didn't know that he couldn't see these things.

When I discovered he couldn't see, I knew that visual

strategies would not help him. I started creating instructional strategies that relied more on touch and hearing. I researched instructional strategies for the blind. I learned that these strategies typically required a strong memory. Kevin's short-term memory skills were drastically changed. "Surely," I asked many times, "Kevin isn't the only person who has these issues, is he? He has some skills that we can tap into."

I began to try various strategies to help Kevin. The first time I asked him to write his name in January 2014, he surprised the staff. It was sloppy, and it sloped across the page, but it was clearly his name. We needed to figure out a way to help him orient and hold the paper. He was left-handed which was helpful as his right hand was impacted by the brain damage. I tried a variety of writing implements from pencils and pens to markers and paint brushes. He was able to write, but it took someone to work with him. As a teacher, I expected that. Unfortunately, the aides who worked with Kevin in the group homes didn't see this as something they were required to do. I shared that it takes 10,000 repetitions to really learn something well. Kevin was virtually relearning everything. It would take time.

In early 2014, I came across research from Boston University describing Chronic Traumatic Encephalopathy. The research was fascinating to me. The research matched what we saw with Kevin after his first Iraq deployment and following deployment. I asked if it was possible that Kevin's extreme physical and cognitive response to the rugby accident could be connected to his many exposures to IEDs when he was in combat. I was told that I should let that go.

Even though his record showed that he complained about blackouts, headaches, trouble sleeping, and a myriad of other symptoms, he had not sought medical treatment after the blasts. "The rugby accident makes it too difficult to prove," I was advised. "Let go of that idea." No matter what evidence I brought forward, I felt like I was getting nowhere. I kept working with what I knew and researching what I didn't know.

Kevin was making slow progress in some areas, but he would take three steps forward and two steps backward many weeks. Some weeks were even worse, and it would seem like he would lose most of the gains he had made. He was so frustrated, and so was I. However, neither one of us was going to give up. He had always demonstrated that he could overcome all odds and come out on top. I worked hard to make learning a game, or at least fun. I knew that most people learn better when they enjoy what they are doing. Kevin was good at working through problems with his mind. He liked math and art. Kevin enjoyed games and singing. He enjoyed setting and reaching goals. He loved movies and animals. He wanted to do things that helped others. I tried to build these things into every day.

July 25, 2015

Kevin had a good Friday. He had an appointment with the vision person. She was impressed with how quickly he learned how to use his new water bottle, TV remote, and talking watch. He can now check the time and date anytime he wants to. He was really interested in that. He also navigated his phone with the help of Siri. After a few practice runs, he was able to repeat the process. Still, his recall is poor, so he needs cues for the processes. Yet, this is one more step towards more independence.

He had a great time at the Twins game last night. The Twins beat the Yankees and it was fun for him to participate in that excitement. He stayed for the fireworks. This was a golden day, and we praise God for it.

July 26, 2015

On this day 25 years ago, the Americans with Disabilities Act was signed into law. Kevin and I spent the day at the Minnesota History Center celebrating this momentous event. We met a lot of people who have created new lives after surviving disabling accidents or illness and people who were born with disabilities. We listened to people who fought to get this law passed. We heard about the continuing challenges. We heard stories of grit and hard work. It was a good day.

As we were heading to St. Paul, Kevin and I chatted about family and friends. I asked him what advice he had for his nephew who is starting kindergarten this fall. Kevin said, "Don't give up and keep working hard. Don't believe them. Nothing is impossible."

We met an artist who lost her sight. She was in the Air Force before she lost her sight. She was a featured artist who made one of the posters commemorating the day. Interestingly, the writing on the picture was "I'm possible."

July 28, 2015

Kevin had a good workout today. I met him at the fitness center. He started out getting to the floor. His support person was a little nervous. She asked, "Have you done this before with him?" Her eyes showed her surprise as he then did 100 crunches. He also worked his pecs and quads and hamstrings. He even did the cobra yoga position. It was a good solid hour of floor work. At the end of that I had him walk to the cabinet to put his equipment away. I told him how proud I am of his persistence.

I thank God for his love, for all of you who continue praying for Kevin. We are blessed.

August 4, 2015

Kevin is working hard this week. He wants to make his right-hand function better and he keeps pushing himself. I think it started with paintball, then fishing, and brushing his horse. I have been impressed with his choice to use his right hand even though he could do a task more easily with his left hand. His persistence is shining. Tomorrow, we are going to participate in a Disabled American Veterans' Day at the park. Kevin is showing so much more awareness. Please keep praying. –God hears us.

August 5, 2015

We went to Veterans' Lake today and it was a great event. Veterans' Lake is a memorial set up by a family to honor all service members. It began with a donation of land by a family. Now, there is a fishing pond surrounded by beautiful gardens and memorials. Today, we fished, visited booths, chatted with other vets and their families. Kevin was honored as were all the veterans–this day was for them. There were many Boy Scouts who were volunteering along with many other volunteers. The booth with weapons was a hit with Kevin. He got a big smile as he named each one and described them in detail. The operator of the booth called him a "talking encyclopedia."

We ended with a lunch of the fish that had been caught, corn on the cob, salads and lots of homemade cookies and bars. Again, I am thankful to the people who are praying and providing Kevin with these opportunities. The ones who serve others show God's true love.

August 10, 2015

Kevin and I chatted on the deck this afternoon.

Me: Do you have any questions, concerns, or comments?

Kevin: Not any of the last things you said.

Me: Comments?

Kevin: No comments. Questions... what happened to me?

Me: I know you know what you have been told.

Kevin: Yeah, I got hit in the head–brain injury–playing rugby.

Me: Yes. It was a terrible accident. Some good things have happened, though.

Kevin: Like what?

Me: People all over this country pray for you every day. And, each day you are recovering more.

Kevin: Please tell them "Thank you" for me.

August 21, 2015

It took us a year to get this event to happen and today Kevin was able to experience kayaking. He was able to use so many skills that he has been practicing over the past year. I am so thankful for the prayers and for the diligence of his personal trainer, Andy, and all the people who have been supporting him including therapists, caregivers, friends, and family.

We arrived at the park early so that we could have some time to acclimate to a new place. We went on a trail, out on the dock, and then we just sat for a while under an old oak tree. We talked about acorns (one fell and bounced off Kevin's head) and how miraculous such a little thing can grow so big.

Kevin smiled his little half smile. I asked him what he was thinking. "Nothing," he said, "I'm just happy."

Then he proceeded to get into the kayak very easily. He took the paddle and off he went. It was amazing to think of all the miracles that have led us to this day. I know that God's plan is unfolding and only He knows where it leads. We just breathe each moment and have faith.

August 23, 2015

Yesterday, Kevin and I joined some Wounded Warriors and their family members in packaging food for "Feed My Starving Children." Kevin scooped the rice, and he did a good job. We quickly discovered we needed to adapt the station to accommodate him. He was tired after the two hours of constant scooping and dumping the rice. Our team didn't miss a beat.

One of our team knew Kevin from before the accident. It is always good to serve others. The group sent the packages off to children in Afghanistan with a prayer.

August 25, 2015

Kevin got a different wheelchair today. It is much lighter and easier for him to use without someone pushing him. While I pray that one day, he will no longer need a wheelchair, I am grateful that this chair will help him be more mobile.

We had a good day. Kevin continues to ask about what has happened over these past 23 months. He doesn't remember the accident at all. I can only imagine how hard it is for him. He is so strong, and he continues to work and have faith. I read a quote today:

I've always held on to my faith. Faith, hope, and love are the things that ground my life. No matter what happens, faith, hope and love continue.

It is my mission to help Kevin and other people because people must have hope to live.

August 28, 2015

It had been a tough two days. On Thursday, Kevin told his support person that he didn't feel well. They were en route to Freedom Farm for his horse therapy. By the time they arrived, about 20 minutes after that, Kevin was in an almost catatonic state. He was not responding to anyone. The staff called me, and I made my way to Waverly. After attempts by all of us, including Cassie his horse, we determined that this might be a medical issue. We made our way back to the Buffalo ER. After a battery of tests, the doctors determined that he had a toxic level of ammonia in his blood. They consulted with the CDC and determined that this was likely due to an issue with a medication. Unfortunately, the condition is very rare, and it took many hours to get him transferred to a hospital that had the required treatment medication in hand. So, following a trip by ambulance, Kevin was admitted to Mercy hospital late last night. The treatment was administered, and he responded well. He remains at the hospital tonight, and if all continues to go well, we hope he is discharged on Saturday.

Kevin was extremely lucid this afternoon and we had several long conversations. He is so insightful. He shared that he feels like he floats in and out of this place and an "Oz" world. He wanted to understand how he can see in his dreams but live in a dark world when he is awake.

With a normal ammonia level, his thoughts are much clearer. The ammonia must have been building up quite some time.

I am grateful that Kevin is surrounded by prayers each day and that we are provided with people who can help in times of great need.

September 1, 2015

Kevin is on a new medication that helps his body process ammonia. I keep learning about the human body. I certainly have a greater understanding of how each tiny piece of the body has a role. That metaphor in the Bible is very powerful.

Kevin asked me to bring him a Happy Meal today. He asked me if he still has his comic books (he does) and if he had a black lab named Rocket (we did.) He keeps pushing forward and he is looking very good. I am so thankful for each small step. Each step is progress.

September 10, 2015

Kevin seems to be doing better. We had lunch today and chatted about the new Apple products. We also talked about football. Kevin was engaged and contributed to the conversation. He is still on medications to help his body metabolize ammonia. He has appointments with his doctors next week. Pray that the doctors have God's guidance, and that Kevin has a guardian angel by his side.

Each day I seem to meet someone else who has a connection with a family member who is suffering a brain injury. All I know is that with God's help, we will move through this darkness into eternal light.

Psalm 23:4–

Even though I walk through the valley of the shadow of death, I will fear no evil; for thou art with me; thy rod and thy staff, they comfort me.

September 16, 2015

Kevin had a long and productive day at the VA in Minneapolis today. He had three appointments. However, the most enjoyable part was a special event with presenters of adaptive sports for veterans. He enjoyed conversations with other veterans, and we got some good leads for activities that Kevin can explore. He impressed the guys at the golf table as he immediately took the golf club with the right grip. He is also interested in adapted hockey (sled hockey) and exploring the St. Croix River.

He ended the day with a smile.

September 21, 2015

Say a prayer and sing of praise today. Kevin's life changed completely two years ago today. He continues to be a mirror reflecting God's power and the power of prayer. Thank God for each step of progress. Kevin's theme song is "Amazing Grace."

My life is consumed with so many tasks. I took early retirement in July, 2015. I spend hours researching and planning for activities that Kevin can do. I spend time working with him. I hope that the aides learn from my modeling, and I encourage them to use the strategies that I use when I am not there. I build a schedule for Kevin and ask them to follow it. I am so disappointed for Kevin when I return and find out that not a single person has followed the schedule. When I ask the supervisor about this, I get the response, "Kevin didn't want to do it." That doesn't sound like him at all. "You weren't here," I am told. "Maybe he will do things with you, because you are his mother." I doubt that is the only reason he does things. He has lived the past 10 years of his life without my presence and done very well.

I am his legal guardian and his conservator. The paperwork required for that is incredibly complex and confusing. Errors can trigger audits and loss of resources. It is stressful on top of worrying about Kevin as a person. Kevin was awarded 10% service connection for tinnitus, and he was classified as 100% disabled, but not service connected through the VA. As he is in a group home, he is also on Medicare and classified as disabled under Social Security. Every cent that is paid to anyone must be included in the accounting and strict timelines are required. I must provide well-being reports, and documentation to the court system, the county social service system, the state human services system, and the VA system. I wonder how other parents handle this work without falling apart under the stress. I see that many people don't survive. They become sick. Some die. Some ultimately give up and the residents who don't have anyone who is able to be with them day to day begin to languish in the system. The system provides food and shelter. I want Kevin to have a quality of life that goes beyond that, no matter how disabled he has become.

Kevin shows me glimmers of himself. I cherish each, and every shining moment that I see. He may not be able to recall much as it happens, but he does have thoughts and memories. He lives in this very moment. He doesn't live in the past, and he doesn't anticipate the future. He lives in the here and now. What is life? Life is what is happening right now. I want Kevin to have opportunities to live his life. I get the feeling from his caregivers that this is unrealistic, and too much to ask. I will not accept that answer.

At first the VA staff encouraged me to not apply for the VA disability. "It will just go to the state," they tell me. As Kevin was in a group home and unable to pay the full cost out of his own resources, he is only allowed about $80 per month in his account. Everything else, his social security disability check and his VA pension check is sent back to the state to help cover the cost of his care. The VA covers medical appointments and equipment costs, but the state covers the cost of his aides. Kevin's checks cover the cost of his room and board and his medical spend down. I cover the costs of his activities, his personal trainer, his fitness center membership, tickets to movies and games for him and his aide. Kevin attends equine therapy under a grant from Freedom Farm, and I am forever grateful to those who help me provide him opportunities outside of the group home. Without my subsidy and help from friends and family, he wouldn't be able to do any of these things. I discover that most people who live in group homes don't have people who are willing or able to subsidize their activities. The group home residents generally have one activity a month. I am so grateful that I had set up a trust that friends and family can use to help defray some of the cost of giving Kevin opportunities to engage in his world.

Other residents at the group home are asking why they can't go to church and do activities like Kevin does. Staff at the group home are starting to resist working with Kevin. Apparently, my expectations are too high. I expect him to be active and involved in as much as he can be. I am grateful that I can be with Kevin and provide activities for him. He is so much happier when he is involved in his world, as difficult and complex as that can be.

Chapter 11

Posted for friends and family: Starting year 3 post rugby accident

September 28, 2015

Kevin had a good morning at Feline Rescue. The cats were "cuddly." Animals are a great way to remind us of the value of God's world. Who doesn't appreciate kind words and a loving touch? Cats respond with a purr. Humans respond with a smile.

September 29, 2015

Kevin has good insight. "I'm blind," he stated.

"Yes," I responded.

"Is it permanent?" he questioned.

"We don't know for sure, but maybe," I responded.

"When I am dreaming, I see people's faces and places. When I am awake, I only see darkness," he observed. It brought tears to my eyes.

I challenge each one of us to imagine that world as Kevin experiences it. We would want rich descriptions and a focus on sound and touch to

enrich the world. We would want to truly have experiences in darkness.

October 10, 2015

Freedom Farm had an event for the individuals who participate. Kevin and the other veterans were a part of the event. Kevin truly enjoyed participating. Kevin was asked if he wanted to say anything as part of the program. He held the microphone and thanked everyone for attending the event. I was so proud of him. Later, when he was asked to be in a picture with the other veterans and the Rodeo royalty, he agreed but was rather stoic. I said, "Kevin, come on. You are in a picture with some beautiful ladies. Can't you smile?" Of course, he grinned so that his dimples showed.

The Freedom Farm Mission Statement

Freedom Farm enriches lives by partnering with the unique attributes of the horse to improve mobility, build confidence and encourage personal growth in children and adults with physical, mental, and emotional challenges.

October 12, 2015

On Sunday night, Kevin had another reaction to a high ammonia level. We went to the VA emergency room and Kevin was admitted to the hospital. He was given medications and he was better today. However, the doctors still do not know what is causing this. Please pray for wisdom for the medical team and for Kevin.

October 14, 2015

Kevin was discharged late this afternoon. The doctors ordered a titration off the Depakote. It will take two weeks, and then we will see if his ammonia level decreases to the normal range. Kevin was tired but happy to leave the hospital. We pray that he continues to have faith to work through the challenges.

"We can only appreciate the miracle of a sunrise if we have waited in the darkness." –Unknown

October 17, 2015

Kevin is continuing to taper off the Depakote. He had another brief episode again and spent the night at the VA under observation. He asked me if he was coming off any drugs. I told him that he was and asked him why he was asking. He said he was having some weird dreams. This has been a rough week, but Kevin is in God's hands.

Psalm 25:10–All the paths of the Lord are steadfast love and faithfulness...

October 20, 2015

Kevin took his last dose of Depakote tonight. We are all watching carefully. He seems to have more energy already. The human body is truly a miracle. Each one of us is unique and we all respond in similar but very different ways. Kevin has been through so much trauma in his life. I remember a conversation we had when he returned from Iraq in 2008. He told me he was so discouraged because the efforts of the armed services did not seem to be changing the course. He was discouraged by the death and fighting all around him.

I told him he is the kind of person I want to defend me–compassionate, kind, ethical.

So, what do we need in society? We need people who have moved through the darkness and survived. We need people who continue to persevere and who continue relentlessly, even though the end is nowhere in sight. That is the very best we can do.

I struggle with understanding what is going on with Kevin's condition. Each time he starts becoming unreasonable and erratic, the people who work with him say he has "behaviors." I don't think what he shows us is what I would call "behaviors." As part of my career in education, I worked exclusively with adolescents who were classified as Emotionally/Behaviorally Disordered. What I see with Kevin does not fit with what I know about that. Certainly, he was depressed, anxious, and showed symptoms of PTSD after his deployments and before the rugby accident. These symptoms wouldn't disappear because of the rugby accident. These symptoms are still present. Yet, the issues with metabolizing medications and the whole ammonia level just doesn't seem to make sense. That isn't behavioral. That is biological or neurological. I keep coming back to CTE. Would CTE affect how his metabolism works? Would it affect how different organs work? I ask the doctors, and I am met with silence or the response "These things happen sometimes with brain injury. We don't know why."

I keep appealing Kevin's service connection rating. Yes, he had a rugby accident. It just doesn't make sense that what he is experiencing is just the result of that rather unremarkable tackle. I feel that his service injuries from IEDs may play some role.

I keep asking, "What is going on? It has been two years since the rugby accident. I thought he was supposed to be stabilizing by now. I was told that at the two-year mark, he will likely not improve much, but he won't get worse. "He will have what he has," they tell me.

I get the feeling that people don't have an answer to my question, and they want me to stop asking. I feel like they don't know what to do, so they do nothing. I want them to help us figure this out. But who am I? I am just his mother. I am a teacher, not a doctor. Is it wrong to think that the doctors have the answers? They test his blood and check his response to light. They ask him to squeeze their hand. They ask him the day of the week, month, and year. They ask him where he is. Sometimes he can answer correctly. Sometimes he doesn't know. Sometimes he just guesses. He withdraws. He doesn't want to disappoint me and them.

One day one of the therapists asked me to join Kevin's session. Kevin wanted to tell me something. "Don't ask me if I remember things, mom," he stated. "I don't remember them, okay? I just don't. I don't want to disappoint you."

"You never disappoint me, Kevin," I tell him. My eyes are filled with tears. "You are the strongest, most courageous person I know. You never have disappointed me." I vowed to learn a better way to share my thoughts with Kevin. I started looking at strategies for working with Alzheimer's patients. I started telling him the stories of his life without asking him to remember. He could just listen.

October 2, 2015

Kevin went to Freedom Farm today. This is the first time they have seen him off the Depakote and all the people noticed a difference. One of the vets said his eyes looked different, one noticed a difference in his speech. Suzy, his coach, said he responded more quickly to her directions. I was impressed at his retention of the commands. He needed just a few cues to get started and then commanded his horse, Cassie, with confidence. He works so hard to do the littlest task (like reaching with his right hand to find Cassie's mane.) He must work at controlling his body, listening for cues, remembering the proper commands, and relaxing. He is tired and satisfied when the session is done.

Everyone commented that this was the best session yet.

Next week, the VA is bringing a group of 10 vets to observe Kevin and the two other vets who are there. Kevin is going to demonstrate how to brush his horse.

It was a very good day.

October 25, 2015

Kevin is looking very strong today. Many people at church commented about it. We had a good service and followed that with a workout. Kevin rode with me from church to the gym. It's always nice to have a little time just to ourselves. He is still confused about this whole situation. We talked about a lot of things–the accident and what that means for him now. We talked about his loss of vision and how his other senses must take over now. He was clear and logical. During his workout, he did a nice job problem-solving.

In the sermon this morning, our pastor asked us each to answer this question: "What would you like to have more of?"

Kevin told me his answer. "I'd like to have more understanding of life."

We know that we will not understand this life, but we have faith and trust in God.

Jeremiah 29:11–

" 'For I know the plans I have for you,' declares the Lord, 'plans to prosper you and not harm you, plans to give you a hope and a future.' "

November 4, 2015

Praise God! Kevin had an amazing session with his trainer today. He went up and down 24 steps and remained on his feet for 30 minutes. The second half of his session, he worked on the mat. He has not been on the floor on his stomach for two years. He was able to work on lifting his head and turning it from right to left. Then he rolled from his stomach to his back 20 times. He was able to figure it out without any cuing. He finished with 10 sitting to standing positions. Each step in this journey has come with lots of perseverance and grit on Kevin's part and with the grace of God.

Zephaniah 3:17–the Lord your God is with you, the Mighty Warrior who saves. He will take great delight in you...

November 15, 2015

Today, after church, we went for brunch at Perkins. The staff know us well, and they always find us a quiet table. Kevin's support person shared with me a conversation she had with Kevin a few weeks ago. Her brother just graduated as a Marine. She told me that she asked Kevin what he thought makes a good soldier. Kevin said, "A good soldier cares about the people in America, and he cares about people in the other country, too." She told me that his answer brought tears to her eyes. Yes, I want a soldier like Kevin defending us. Thank you for your service, Kevin. Whatever God has planned for you, it is sure to be amazing.

November 17, 2015

Kevin had a full day of appointments at the VA today. It was a long day, and we were all tired. Each day continues to have positives. We met a man who had served in Desert Storm and suffered a TBI. He talked to Kevin about his memory difficulties. He told Kevin it helps a lot when the people he loves understand that he often forgets what he just said. He told Kevin it helps to have something he loves to do. It is good to share with others.

Galatians 6:2–Share each other's troubles and problems, and so obey our Lord's command.

November 21, 2015

Kevin called this morning. He was very present in the moment. His short-term memory is still very poor, but he converses well at the moment. He called again, and he just wanted to tell me he missed me. We got together for a movie, but he was sad that he couldn't see the screen. I know that God is in control, and I pray for wisdom to know what to do for Kevin. He has a lot of activities next week. He will be at the Vikings vs. Packers game tomorrow. Thank you to the Wounded Warriors project who got the tickets for Kevin and his support person. Kevin will be in full Packer attire and his support person will be in Vikings gear. They have the game covered!

November 25, 2015

On this evening of Thanksgiving, I am saying a prayer of gratitude for every one of you who continues to pray for Kevin. I am grateful that he continues to make slow and steady progress. When people ask me how he is, I tell them he exceeds the medical professionals' expectations. He is truly in God's hands.

At our church service tonight, we heard the Gospel message from Luke 12:22-32–

"Therefore, I tell you, do not be anxious about your life, what you shall eat, nor about your body, what you shall put on. For life is more than food, and the body more than clothing... Consider the lilies, how they grow; they neither toil nor spin; yet I tell you even Solomon in all his glory was not arrayed like one of these... O men of little faith... your Father knows what you need... Seek His kingdom and these things shall be yours as well."

What a Thanksgiving message. May God bless you.

November 27, 2015

Kevin and I enjoyed a good Thanksgiving Day and a nice Friday. Kevin enjoyed the traditional turkey dinner at Trenton House at noon. We chatted after dinner and loaded up our vehicle for an overnight stay in Minneapolis. It was quiet at the hotel, but we did enjoy sitting in the lounge, watching the football game, and conversing. Kevin loved sleeping in a king-sized bed. He rolled around and he was sleeping crossways in the morning. We got up and had a nice workout at the fitness center. We had a large breakfast followed by a trip to the Mall of America. We spent the most time at the bookstore checking out new audiobooks. It was a good day.

November 20, 2015

It has been a busy Thanksgiving weekend. We had a relaxing stay at The Grand Hotel in Minneapolis (Kevin really enjoyed sleeping/rolling around in his king size bed.) We worked out, had a great breakfast, and visited the Mall of America. Later this weekend we enjoyed A Christmas Carol *at the Guthrie. This was a performance that had audio description for the blind. Kevin knows the story and that was a big plus. The show was over 2 hours long, and he was attentive and engaged the whole time. On the medical side, Kevin is tapering off the final seizure medication. The good news is that he is more aware of his situation and that is also a challenge. He has so much to deal with. He feels like he has lost 3 years–and he is right about that. Pray that he can discern God's plan for him. Thank you for your continuing prayers and support for Kevin and our family.*

Our family has always enjoyed watching movies together. We love a good story. When Kevin was deployed, one of things that he brought with him was a 6-inch binder filled with his favorite movies. When Kevin was living on his own, he told me he often spent Saturday or Sunday afternoon at the movie theater where he would watch two and sometimes three movies in a row. He loved to be the guy who went to the opening night, especially for the movies that had a midnight showing. He would rent movies at the local video/DVD store, and the service counter knew him by name.

Kevin grew up watching Robin Williams. He seldom laughed more than a dry chuckle, but occasionally he would give a good belly laugh at Robin Williams. He also liked Robin Williams dramas like Dead Poets society. Kevin enjoyed watching many movies more than once. He liked a variety of genres. I could always count on him to go to what he called "mom movies." These were the more obscure, artsy movies that generally only lasted for one week in our small-town theater. In 1998, we went to the Robin Williams' movie, *What Dreams May Come.* The visuals of this movie were amazing for the time. The movie itself was outside of the typical movie for that actor. Robin Williams' character was willing to go to the depths of hell to be with his wife. He was never willing to give up saving his wife. Kevin was a romantic. He believed in love and family. One of the memorable quotes from that movie struck a chord with Kevin: "He's a guy that men want to be around; he has integrity." Kevin lived his life like that.

Kevin was sometimes a driver in the convoys in Iraq. When we took trips when Kevin and his sister were younger, they would navigate using the paper maps. I am hopelessly "directionally dyslexic" as they call me. We often had adventures that came from a wrong turn, or a turn too early or too late. Kevin was a better navigator than I was, and his sister could repeat a complicated route years after traveling it just once. I asked Kevin if he liked driving in the convoy. He responded, "Sure, someone else is generally navigating!" We often laughed at our side trips. We also had a saying, "If you know where you want to end up, you are never really lost." Kevin always seemed to have an idea of where he wanted to end up.

After Kevin left the military, he disappeared from family gatherings and trips. I invited him to Thanksgiving dinner, just a few months after his Honorable Discharge. He declined. “What are you going to do?” I asked him.

“I’m going to a concert and staying at a nice hotel in downtown Minneapolis–a really nice hotel. I’m going to have a great steak dinner, and I’m going to enjoy the show,” he answered.

“Who is going with you?” I questioned.

“No one,” he replied. Kevin was independent, and able to make his own decisions. I thought he needed time away from all the chaos of the service, his evacuation and hospitalization out of combat, and his divorce. I hoped that perhaps it would help him to spend some time doing something nice for himself. I told him that I hoped he had a great time. The next year he was barely emerging from the coma, and he couldn’t even eat the traditional Thanksgiving dinner. The following year, he was in the group home for Thanksgiving, and I joined him there for the more institutional version of Thanksgiving. For the two years following the accident, Kevin had never had a chance to splurge on himself by spending the night in a hotel and by having a restaurant steak dinner. He had not been able to attend a concert or theater production. I was working hard to find activities that Kevin could enjoy given his current state. I planned a Thanksgiving excursion to the city.

I had come to expect that I would meet resistance from the people who were a part of Kevin’s team. I had to request approval from each of the agencies. I had to provide a rationale. I had to arrange for additional payment for the support staff. I had to find support staff who were willing to take the trip into the city with Kevin and with me. I had to ensure that the hotel rooms were really handicapped accessible. After weeks of planning, arrangements were made but I was only able to negotiate a one-night stay.

I started talking with Kevin about the hotel and restaurant a few weeks before the excursion. He was excited. I told him he would have his own room with a king-size bed. He was excited about the bed. He had been sleeping in a hospital bed since the rugby accident. The restaurant would be in the hotel. He could have room service if he wanted to. Of course, he wanted a steak dinner, even though it would be Thanksgiving.

We packed up all of Kevin's supplies and equipment and loaded into the vehicle, the support person, Kevin, and I, and we made a short 20-minute drive into the city on that cold and windy Thanksgiving night. It was Kevin's first outing that would last longer than a few hours. The support person was apprehensive that he would be able to handle the noise, the people, and the unfamiliar environment. I assured her that Kevin has handled a lot in his life. "He'll have a good time," I assured her.

The first thing he wanted to do once we got into his room, after I pushed him around the space and described the furnishings, the view, and the layout, was to sit in the leather lounge chair. He wanted an orange soda. I transferred him into the chair, and I could immediately see him relax. We put the game on the TV, and he looked like the past two years had never happened. He just sat in the chair, listened to the game, and sipped his orange soda. Kevin wanted to take a nap on the big bed. We helped him climb into the bed where he proceeded to stretch out his arms and legs, and then he rolled over to one side and closed his eyes with a smile on his face. The little things mean so much.

Later we enjoyed dinner in the restaurant. Kevin had a steak dinner, just as he requested. He went to bed tired and satisfied. The next morning, we woke up and went to the fitness center and pool area located in the hotel. Kevin worked out and then he went into the pool. After a shower and getting dressed, we had a light breakfast of juice, coffee, and pastries before heading to the Mall of America, a place Kevin loves.

This was his first time at the mall since before the rugby accident. His favorite places have always been LEGOLAND, the bookstore, and the amusement park. On Black Friday, we wanted to get to the mall before it got too busy, but when we arrived closer to noon, it was already filled with people. As the aide pushed his wheelchair, I described the stores that we passed and the people walking by us. We came to a store where a few of the Vikings Cheerleaders were promoting a fundraiser for the MN Vikings Foundation. They were selling calendars.

"Kevin," I said, "the Minnesota Vikings Cheerleaders are here. Too bad the Green Bay Packers Cheerleaders aren't here. I don't suppose you want to talk with them."

"Heck yes," he answered. "Of course, I want to have a chance to talk with the ladies." That made the cheerleaders smile. Kevin wanted to get his brother, who is a Vikings fan, a calendar for Christmas. After that Kevin and the cheerleaders posed for a picture. Kevin was smiling from ear to ear.

It was an untraditional Thanksgiving dinner, but a satisfying one. We returned to the group home. He reached up and hugged me.

"Thank you, Mom," he said.

Chapter 12

Posted for friends and family: New beginnings

December 6, 2015

Kevin had a busy week with physical therapy wrapped up for the time being. The therapist felt positive about him. Kevin completed pool therapy and he will be getting a standing frame so that he can safely stand without a staff person providing hands-on support. In the meantime, it is critical that he stand and walk frequently so that his bones and muscles continue to maintain strength. It seems like a small thing, but it is very challenging to make this happen. So, please pray for strength for me to continue to advocate for Kevin; pray for Kevin so that he stays confident and positive; and pray for the group home that they have compassionate and competent staff.

December 8, 2015

Kevin has been feeling very sad and depressed lately. I asked him if he'd like to do something today and he suggested a trip to the Mall of America. Kevin enjoyed a little shopping. He picked out a dress shirt and sweater. I described each option and he checked out the feel of the fabrics. He picked a shirt with a light blue and black plaid. He also selected a black V-neck sweater. He ran the card through the reader when we checked out. He felt good about his selections and overseeing his shopping. We also stopped at an old-fashioned candy store where he selected a variety of M&Ms and a few other candies. Finally, we stopped at Marbles the Brain Store where Kevin explored some games. This store has a great mission. Play is good for the brain, and the store provides hands-on experiences where the products in the store are out for play. We spent about 45 minutes playing and I got some good ideas. Kevin enjoyed it. We headed home, tired and a little happier.

I am reminded never to take smiles for granted. I thank God for smiles.

December 16, 2015

Kevin had a trip to the VA this morning for a blood draw. The drive was quite unusual as they experienced snow, rain, and wind. We are heading towards a possible record "latest date the lakes freeze"–only in Minnesota.

I worked hard to cheer Kevin up. By the third Christmas carol that I sang, he joined in with a smile. I asked him what he was smiling about, and he diplomatically replied, "Nothing; I'm not saying." Yes, I know I'm not the best singer. We finished with a delightful rendition of "Silent Night."

Kevin does like to sing, and he does it well. It made my day to see him smile, even for a little while. As Tiny Tim said, "God bless us every one."

December 17, 2015

Merry Christmas from Kevin. I am sharing his thoughts as we talked about sending out a Christmas message to all of you. As we celebrate Christmas and a new year, He offered this advice, "Be wise and open-minded to what others have to say. Listen to your kids because they are smart. Tell your family you love them. Be careful and be safe. Say your prayers."

I pray for God's shield of protection for Kevin. We know that Kevin is in His hands.

December 24, 2015

Kevin really enjoyed the Christmas Eve service tonight. He looked so peacefully happy. He sang the carols with a strong clear voice. He was listening to the sermon intently. He held his candle high. During the final song, "Silent Night," he sang beautifully. It was wonderful to see him so happy and at peace. Merry Christmas.

December 27, 2015

What a nice time we are having. Kevin is at Breezy Point with me, his sister Erica, her spouse Dusty, and their son Gunner. Connor, my other son, will join us for a day this week before he heads back to Canada where he is playing hockey with the Steinbach Pistons. Yesterday after we arrived Kevin played Legos with his nephew Gunner. It was so fun to watch them interact in some battle for a fictitious city. Kevin had a response for every superpower attack that Gunner's character made. They smiled and laughed. It was so nice to see. Then we played cribbage. I told Kevin what was in his hand, and he picked the card to play. He also did the math for the points. We had homemade pizza for dinner and Kevin went to bed a tired and happy man.

We enjoyed pancakes for breakfast and Kevin did some of his daily therapies. We went to the pool this afternoon. We are watching football tonight. I am so grateful to have the opportunity to bring my family together this Christmas. Kevin has not had time with his beloved sister in a year, and to be able to be together for several days and nights is a true blessing.

Thank God for the gift of true friends and family.

December 29, 2015

Kevin enjoyed spending the past few days and nights with his sister Erica and her family and his brother Connor. We had a great time enjoying meals and activities together. We had fun playing together. We enjoyed singing a few songs and we shared Christmas gifts with each other. I think back to Christmas 2013 when Kevin was just beginning to emerge from the coma to this Christmas. God's hand is on him, and it is a miracle to see his progress. I pray for each step forward no matter how small, and I watch to see what God has planned for all of us. What we know for sure is that this world is not our home. Someday all sorrow and pain will vanish in His presence.

January 5, 2016

It has been a quiet week for Kevin with the break between Christmas and New Year's. After his trip to the resort, which he enjoyed immensely, he had a week of quiet. He has never been one for a lot of inactivity.

His sister Erica and her family and I went to Canada to catch a few of their brother's hockey games before they headed back to Kentucky. So, we stopped to visit on the way to the airport today. Kevin perked up and he enjoyed playing math and word games with his sister and her son. Then he had a good time with boxing. Kevin was smiling while he broke into a sweat. It is so important for Kevin to have lots of mental and physical stimulation. As always, he voiced his desire to go home.

I pray each day that he will be able to go home here on Earth. God has a plan, and we continue to listen and move forward in faith.

"Tide"
(Written by Joy Carlson, 1994)
I wade into already cloudy waters with conviction,
Stumble against rocks and forge on.
Sand gives way beneath my feet–
The current takes the rest.
I cannot struggle against this tide
The fight is only in my mind;
The force is stronger
It is my power.

Sometimes I feel exhausted from the weight of fighting for Kevin. Yes, he has significant challenges. He can no longer do the things that he used to do. He can no longer take photographs or go on his daily runs. He is totally dependent on those around him for mobility, for getting his meals, for his personal care needs. He can't see the TV or read a book. He needs cues to start a task. He processes language and information ever so slowly. Yet, he is my son. He is a human being, and he deserves to have some semblance of a life. He needs to be actively engaged in the world around him. He needs to have human interaction. He needs to feel loved. He needs to know that he is not forgotten. He needs to have hope for the future. I will do everything in my power to advocate for him, and to help him find meaning in his new life. He is my son.

After the successful Thanksgiving outing, I began planning a Christmas outing. I cherish spending time with all my children, and holidays are an important time to do that. My daughter and her family live in Kentucky and my youngest son is living in Canada. Kevin and I are in Minnesota. It is no small feat to coordinate a holiday so that we can be together. Two Christmas seasons ago, Kevin was just emerging from the coma. That Christmas Day in 2013, I was with Kevin, but he wasn't with me. He was "time traveling" and he was in a combat zone. He didn't recognize me. He thought I was someone sent by the enemy to trick him. I left him that Christmas Day in despair. In my brain, I understood, but my heart was breaking.

Christmas 2014, Kevin was living close to me. My daughter and her family traveled to Minnesota, and we spent that day together. We took Kevin on a day trip to Wisconsin to spend a few hours with their dad's side of the family. Kevin was a trooper. I have cherished pictures of those events sitting on my fireplace mantel.

Christmas 2015, a good friend donated a week at a resort to us. In November, I started the planning necessary to bring my children all together. I thought I understood the process to get Kevin released from the group home after setting up our Thanksgiving overnight trip. Traveling several hours away and taking more than 24 hours was a much more complicated and expensive process. Because Kevin needs so many hours of dedicated support for nearly everything he does, I need to petition each organization to agree that he can be out of the group home for several days. I need to secure and pay for the support person as well. It costs several thousand dollars. I thank God that my family stepped up to help with the financial costs. In the end, I was able to have Kevin join us for three days and two nights at the resort.

Traveling in Minnesota in the winter is always unpredictable. It had snowed the night before we left, and we needed to wait until the roads were plowed so we got a late start. As we travelled north and west, the snow began to blow. We arrived at the resort to a fresh 6 inches of white snow. Despite the weather, Kevin was excited to get out of the car. We pushed his wheelchair through the heavy snow and arrived at the ramp to the townhouse. There was a six-inch rise to get onto the ramp. Kevin's five-year-old nephew quickly ran ahead and began to shovel the snow off the ramp. Snow continued to fall on all of us, and Kevin smiled as the snowflakes brushed his cheeks and nose.

We unloaded our bags from the vehicles, and Kevin and his nephew settled into the living room beside the fireplace while we unpacked food and clothing and settled into the bedrooms. "Hey uncle Kevin," his nephew said. "Do you want to play Legos?"

Kevin responded, "Sure." After unpacking the Legos, they started playing superheroes. His nephew had two rockets that he had made from Legos, and he gave one to Kevin. Then they started playing a galactic war.

"Swoosh," Kevin said as he flew his rocket. "Watch out. I'm going to shoot you with my laser."

"I'm going to escape through a black hole," said his nephew.

"I'm going to use my superpowers to find you," said Kevin. And on the story went.

We all sat down and watched them enjoy this unfolding story. Kevin and his nephew were smiling and laughing as the story became more elaborate.

We decorated the living room with the Christmas decorations we brought and unloaded the games and presents. It was the start of a wonderful two-day holiday.

During our two days we went to the pool, played card games, made Christmas crafts, watched Star Wars movies, and cooked and ate family meals. Each night we went to bed tired and content. Kevin sometimes just sat and listened. Sometimes he offered his thoughts. I enjoyed seeing the satisfied smile on his face. I look at the pictures and I can feel the love that we all shared that Christmas.

Posted for friends and family: Kevin's 34th year

January 18, 2016

The weather has been so cold that the group home rules have kept Kevin inside on the weekends. It has been hard to miss church and all the people who look forward to saying hello to Kevin. Fortunately, the weather is supposed to warm up this week. I brought Kevin lunch today. We had a good time talking and singing a few songs. He is certainly communicating his understanding of his challenges. Today he observed that the TBI has impacted his memory and his vision. He continues to want to go home. He talked about having a place where he could have a black lab.

Kevin's birthday is January 25–just one week away. He requested a birthday cake–chocolate cake with chocolate frosting and vanilla ice cream. He thought 34 candles were a bit much. Two would be fine.

I pray that 2016 continues to hold good things for Kevin!

January 22, 2016

Kevin received the standing frame this week. When he is using the frame, he is safely supported while he stands. We take so much movement for granted, and we simply "do" without giving thought to what must happen in order to move.

Kevin has been primarily wheelchair bound or in bed for the past two and a half years. His long bones must bear his weight and his muscles must continue to activate in many positions or he will eventually lose the ability to walk and move without the wheelchair. So, while I am grateful for this tool, I am sad that he has come to the point where he needs to use it.

I pray every day for Kevin. I pray that he continues to trust in God's plan. I pray for peace and calm even though this world is filled with chaos and danger. There are good people and angels here and I am thankful for each one.

Please take a moment or two this weekend to say a prayer in honor of Kevin's 34th birthday.

January 25, 2016

Kevin enjoyed a steak dinner today for his birthday. We had great service and the food was wonderful. It was a pleasure to enjoy this birthday meal

with Kevin. We thank God for all the blessings He provides. I know that His plan is still unfolding. This year will be good.
We were blessed when Kevin was born 34 years ago as we are blessed every day.

Isaiah 40:31–"but they who wait for the Lord shall renew their strength, they shall mount up with wings like eagles."

January 30, 2016
Happy Saturday! I brought Kevin breakfast this morning along with his favorite white chocolate mocha. He enjoyed his breakfast sandwich and hash browns. We called Erica and had a nice chat. Kevin walked to the sink and then to his bedroom after breakfast so he could finish his stretching and exercises. He was motivated so he could go to the Mall of America this afternoon. It was a nice morning!

The big news is that Kevin will be flying to the Hines Vision rehab program on February 16. We have been working on this for almost two years and it is finally happening. He will be there until March 5. Praise God for this and for Kevin's continuing progress.

February 11, 2016
Kevin has been keeping busy while I was out of the country. From the reports I got, and the texts he sent, it was another good week. We are getting ready for the trip to Chicago. Kevin will be flying for the first time since 2012. He'll have a support person with him, and I will be driving. Pray that it will be a helpful and positive experience where Kevin will be able to learn more ways to see the world through his other senses.

Kevin has his annual meeting at the group home. It is hard to believe he has been at this location for a year already.

I prepared for the meeting by reviewing Kevin's goals with him and reviewing his progress towards those goals. The meeting will have people from the VA, from the county, his contacted case manager, the group home staff, and a few of his therapists. I shared my thoughts with the group home before the meeting in a letter.

Kevin continues to tell me that he wants to go home. He wants to live "the American Life." What does that mean? How will he achieve that goal? Kevin wants to have a job. He wants to enjoy movies, friends, sports, and physical activity. He wants to stay up past 9 p.m. and he wants to sleep late some mornings. He wants to have a pet. He wants to live in a small house with a yard. He doesn't want to live with me–just near me. Of course, he doesn't want to live with his mother. What 34-year-old man who has seen the world wants that?

These things seem to be so normal, and for Kevin so impossibly unlikely to happen. The group home staff share that Kevin has more outings than any other resident in their large corporation. He takes up more of their time than any other resident they have ever had. He has more rehabilitation appointments than any other resident they have. They can't fit his daily exercises into their schedule. I am happy that he will be heading to the Blind Rehabilitation program this month. I am hopeful that will help generate some strategies for dealing with his blindness.

I learn that Kevin cannot be out of our state for more than 30 days without losing all his connections for his services. I can't believe that this is our process. The program for blind rehabilitation generally takes a minimum of six weeks. We negotiate that he will be able to participate for a two-and-a-half-week assessment instead of the full rehabilitation program. I am going to go with him as his support person. The blind rehabilitation program will not provide a support person. I will stay a few blocks away from the hospital and arrive by 6 a.m. every morning to push his wheelchair from the hospital floor to the rehabilitation unit. I will help him with his meals, using the toilet, and in whatever other way I can. If I can't do these things, he will not be able to attend. I get ready to go. I am so grateful that I am "retired" from my career job. I am grateful that I have enough money to do this. I am his caregiver, but no one, not the VA nor the county services, offer to pay for my time and work. I do this because my son needs me. I am his mother, his advocate, his teacher, his care coordinator, his coach, his friend, and his care giver. On most days, I am the only one who still considers him a person, despite the devastating effects of brain injury, who has something of value to add to the world. We are both very lonely in this big world, but we have each other, and we have our faith in God.

February 16, 2016

Kevin is settling in at the Hines VA tonight and I am staying at the Fisher House just a block away from the VA. Kevin handled the flight well, and the pilot even gave him "wings." As a little boy, maybe about 7 years old, he heard the news of a plane crash. That year, we went to Florida and Kevin was very fearful that our plane would crash. The pilot and flight attendants were very kind and reassuring. When we landed, the pilot came out and asked Kevin how he liked the flight. Kevin answered, "It was great. We didn't even crash once." The pilot chuckled and gave him his first "wings." I don't know if Kevin remembers that story, but I am grateful for his flight crew and pilot this time, just as I was so many years ago.

I pray that Kevin's time in Chicago is all that God has planned it to be.

February 18, 2016

It was a good day for Kevin at the Blind Rehab program. Despite the confirmation that he does not have any functional vision, he went on to exceed expectations once again.

Does he have a long road ahead of him? "Yes" and many times again, "yes." However, his team was excited to see him learning and smiling. He even had a few moments where he chuckled out loud. Tonight, he asked to have dinner in the dining hall with the other guys. He enjoyed listening to their stories and smiled through dinner. They applauded him for his service and told him he is a true hero.

For all the veterans who, like Kevin, are struggling with so many issues, I offer these verses:

Psalm 73:23–I am with you.

Zephaniah 3:17–the Lord, your God is in your midst, a warrior who gives you victory.

February 20, 2016

Happy Saturday! It was a balmy 60 degrees in Chicago today, so Kevin and I ventured out to explore the VA complex. We met some interesting people and had some conversations. The Fisher House had live music and pizza this afternoon, so we participated. As you can see, Kevin enjoyed the pizza. The group was delightful. Kevin liked it and he even stood up and we swayed to one song. He told the performers they did a great job.

We decided to bring a pizza to the guys on the floor where Kevin sleeps. I picked it up and Kevin, one of the nurses, and I walked through the unit and passed out pieces of pizza. The last person is the youngest one on the floor–he is a 20 something guy who also has a TBI. While he can't eat pizza yet, we gave his family some pizza. Kevin and this young man had a conversation that brought tears to our mothers' eyes. Kevin was smiling when he got ready for bed. He was happy to give something to others.

All is well with his soul.

February 23, 2016

Kevin continues to work hard at Blind School, as we fondly call it. He is learning to use a device called a "Clorino." When the device is placed on an object, it can accurately detect color. It is about the size of a small cell phone, and it can be used on fabric and paper among other things. He is also working on orientation and mobility. Right now, that basically means using his other senses to determine where he is in space. He is "brain tired" and physically tired at the end of a full 7 hours.

After classes today, he took a nap. When he awoke, he told me he had a weird dream. He was floating "in and out of his body" and traveling in time. He couldn't control what was happening, and he just couldn't seem to get back into his body.

He is dealing with the aftermath of the accident and trying as hard as he can to make sense of it. We talked about finding his purpose and God's plan. I am grateful that faith and trust in God hold us through these difficult times.

February 25, 2016

Today is my birthday, and the fourth day in a row of classes at the blind school. Kevin is a good soldier who works hard to meet the expectations. It is hard work, mentally and physically. Each effort does not go without notice. Fortunately, he has the opportunity for a rest before lunch. He had another dream today–again he was in and out of his body. It felt like the twilight zone, he said. He couldn't get back into his body. I think he is dealing with the reality that the body he knew is so broken compared to what it was before the accident. Thank God that he can use his dreams to help him deal with this human body.

By the end of the day, Kevin was getting frustrated. He knows what he needs to do but he can't make his muscles respond as quickly and accurately as he wants them to. He can't find the words he wants to say, and he can't recall the events he is told he has experienced.

After his afternoon nap, he woke with a renewed commitment, and he wanted to get up and join the other vets for dinner. Before dinner, he chose to listen to a Comedy Central cartoon show. Suddenly Kevin had the biggest belly laugh. I was too slow to catch it in a photo, but it was the first time since the accident that I have heard him laugh so authentically. It was the very best gift he could have given to me. Thanks be to God for this blessing.

1 Thessalonians 5:16-18–Rejoice always, pray constantly, give thanks in all circumstances; for this is the will of God in Christ Jesus for you.

March 5, 2016

Kevin is back in Minnesota. We spent a few hours this morning demonstrating some of the things he has learned. The Hines Blind Rehab program is one of the best and I am so thankful that Kevin could participate. The staff who saw him today were surprised at his successes. Thank you for your prayers.

When Kevin is settled at the group home, I find out that we will be having another meeting in a few weeks. The group home has reviewed what I presented for Kevin's programming. They told me that I need to find another place for him. They can't meet his needs. His contracted case manager is a different person. His therapy services are discontinued. Again, I am told, "We can't keep giving him services forever."

What am I going to do? Where is Kevin going to be able to get what he needs to live his life? He is a human being who has hopes and dreams. He is a person who suffered a tragic fate. "He is so young," I say. "He is only 34 years old. He could live another 30 years or more. What are his options? Can I take him home?"

I get the same answer that I have heard from the beginning, "We will not send him home with you. You are not equipped to meet his needs."

"What are our options?" I ask yet one more time.

Chapter 13

Posted for friends and family: Transitioning again

March 17, 2016

Walk by faith not sight. Please keep Kevin in your prayers. God has His plan in place. Kevin has had a hard time since he returned to the group home. He wants to live independently and that is not possible.

Jesus has empowered us to live beyond our abilities and strength. If we look at our abilities and energy and the challenges we face, it seems impossible. Yet, when we walk with Jesus, it is His strength that carries us. Through Jesus all things are possible.

2 Corinthians 5:7–For we live by faith, not by sight.

April 7, 2016

Kevin has been doing very well with recalling newer memories. He is surprising a lot of people by remembering things like where he stayed in Chicago–Hines, the year, and commands for his horse, Cassie. I know these are tiny things for many people, but each time he can recall something is worthy of a celebration.

April 13, 2016

Please add a few extra prayers for Kevin. He is feeling like things are never going to get better for him. We know that he has come very far already. With each little step he makes, he inspires me. Pray that he does not fall into despair, doubt, and discouragement.

Matthew 19:26–Jesus looked at them and said, "With man this is impossible, but with God all things are possible."

April 16, 2016

Thanks to the Star of the East Masons who continue to surround Kevin with their brotherhood. We were able to celebrate with them at their dinner. It was a wonderful evening. Thank you, Masons. I can see how much you all care about Kevin.

I try to communicate how important it is for Kevin to continue to work his body physically and mentally. Brain injury best practices, and my own experience, indicates that "if you don't use it, you will lose it." Kevin has always responded to challenges. He has always been the one who will prove that he can do what others think he can't. That is his personality. He rises to challenges. The support staff who work with him don't seem to understand that. They seem to see him as this very disabled person who is incapable of doing almost everything. They don't know him like I know him. They seem to think I don't know what I am talking about. Their frame of reference is too small, I think. I try to show them by working with Kevin, rather than tell them what to do. Many of the caregivers check their phones or disappear from the room when I arrive. I am working with Kevin, so it appears that they think they don't have to be there. He is "covered." I try to explain that Kevin needs them to do things with him. He can't see things. They tell him not to move. They tell him to wait until they are near him. They are afraid he will fall.

When Kevin is standing with me, I will ask him, "How long can you stand here?" He is still in the military mindset. "As long as you tell me to," he responds. He follows orders. Unfortunately, his body and his mind are betraying him. He wants to do what people ask him to do.

"Everyone has five senses," I explain. "We all use our senses to understand what is going on around us. Kevin can't see at all. He has hearing loss, but he hears better than he sees. His sense of touch is impaired, but it is better than his vision and possibly better than his hearing. His sense of smell is impaired, and I think his sense of taste is impaired as well. Certainly, it appears that his circuits in his brain are operating so much slower than they used to. We need to give him a lot more time than most people need to process what we are asking him to do." His support staff become impatient.

I focus on his senses of touch and hearing. "Announce yourself when you enter his room," I suggest. "Tell him your name, and use the lyrics of a specific song that he can associate with your voice and your name. Remember that he doesn't really know you in any context except this moment. He doesn't know what you look like, or how you dress. He will only ever know your voice." I see the eye rolls from his support staff even as they quickly turn away. I know they think this is silly. They don't believe that this will work, so they don't even try.

"He won't take his medications," the group home administrator tells me. "He spits the pills out. He is non-compliant, and we can't have that."

"He needs to know his medications by name, and their purpose. He can be skeptical. He doesn't like drugs, and he doesn't know you." I tell them. "If he knows what he is supposed to take and the purpose of the medication, he will probably be more willing to take it."

At first, they want to just tell him what he is taking and the purpose of the medication. They tell me that he still won't take the medication.

"We need to give him some control," I tell them. "Can we mark the medication bottles with a tactile cue so that he knows the source of the medication?" I help one of his therapists build a set of cue cards using a variety of tactile symbols–something that is three dimensional. We attach these to an index card with the official name of the medication and a description of the purpose of the medication. I model using the cards with Kevin, and he starts to learn to associate the tactile symbol with the medication. "It might take him a few times to learn this," I tell them. "He will learn the names, and the purposes of the medication with repetition. I suggest that you do this each time you give him his medications. Once he knows what you are asking him to take, and why he is supposed to take them, he will be more likely to comply."

The therapist agrees with the plan, and she also models the strategy for the support staff. It takes time. The support staff would rather just pass the medications and move onto the next thing. I try to visit Kevin during the medication times as often as I can. I never once see the support staff implementing the strategy. I am so frustrated I could cry.

The support staff and the therapist are surprised when Kevin begins to identify the medications by their official name and describes their purpose. It has taken a month of work and I am so proud of his efforts. I know he has learned this with very little help from his support staff. It shows me and the therapists that he is capable of learning new information. It doesn't surprise me. It does surprise the support team. Still, they tell me, "He is just memorizing things and using your cues."

I am coaching him, but I am not telling him what to say. That is learning. He is learning new information. That give us both hope.

I write a message to friends and family almost every day. Our family is spread out across the United States and even into Canada, where Kevin's brother is playing hockey. All my brothers, my sister and my parents have Kevin on the prayer lists at their churches. Hope is the thing that makes human life tolerable. I hope that things will get better. I don't want the prayer warriors across the country to give up hope for Kevin. I want to be sure that Kevin continues to have hope. I pray many times during the day and at night for Kevin. I trust in God and His promises.

We have another meeting. The group home

administrator is armed with data. "Kevin is requiring more services and time than any other client," he tells me. "He is our most intensive resident. We need to cut back our services. He is two years past the rugby accident, and we aren't a rehabilitation facility. We are not going to continue all of these rehabilitation activities." The other agencies concur.

"Kevin is showing that he can learn," I say. I am told that I will need to look for another facility. I bring out the contract and ask how they can dismiss him. He hasn't done anything that would warrant dismissal. They aren't happy about that. "Can I take him home?" I ask.

No one has an answer and the meeting ends. I get a call from the VA requesting that I come in for a meeting. "We would like to recommend Kevin for a VA pilot program," the representative tells me.

"What is it?" I ask.

"It is the Assisted Living Traumatic Brain Injury Pilot Program that was authorized by the federal government a few years ago to try to figure out the best ways to assist our veterans in gaining more independence after a TBI." She explained the program to me.

"Frankly," she said, "most individuals who have similar characteristics as your son are not eligible to attend. They are incapable of learning."

"Everyone is capable of learning," I responded. "I have worked my whole professional career with that as one of my core beliefs. It is up to us to find the right channels to facilitate the learning." I am horrified that people who have injuries like Kevin's are left to languish. They aren't living life. They simply exist. I will not allow that to happen to Kevin.

"Let's get started," I say.

The ALTBI program has pilot sites across the United States, but there aren't any sites in our state. Kevin will need to leave our state. I already know that this will be a challenge. The pilot program ends in October 2017, so he will not be there past that date. "How will that work?" I ask.

"The group home will discharge him, and his VA services will be transferred to the state with the program. The VA pilot program will cover the costs of the program. First, we will need to submit the application. Then he will be evaluated by a team from the pilot program. He will be at the program for a minimum of three months. The last step will be determining the pilot program location.

Within a week, the assessment team completed their evaluation, and we started the next steps. I planned for a visit to the nearest pilot program location. I met with the administrators and reviewed the program mission, vision, and goals. I looked at the residence, which was a college dormitory that had been repurposed and adapted for individuals with physical disabilities. I talked with the support staff. I observed the rehabilitation site where Kevin would receive up to six hours per day of therapies.

Despite the distance, it looked like it would be a good fit. The administrator assured me that they had worked with many people with similar challenges, and that they have the best rehabilitation program for brain injured individuals. He showed me the outcome data that indicated most residents left the program with a higher level of independence than when they arrived.

"You can trust we will take exceptional care of your son," he assured me. I am so grateful that I could retire and spend the past year with Kevin. When he goes to the ALTBI pilot program, I won't be able to get there more than a few times a month.

Kevin would fly on a commercial airline to the facility. He would travel with one of the support team members. After that, he would no longer be affiliated with the group home. I will be a support person for the flight. We will check all his equipment for transport. The program would send a van for him and all of us would make the 90-mile drive from the airport to the next stop on his journey.

Before he was discharged, I asked the group home if they would consider accepting him when he returned. They politely declined. I will be spending the next few months looking for Kevin's next home so that he will be ready when he returns.

I start looking for houses in my community that could easily be made handicapped accessible. He wants to come home. I want him home, too. I found a new home within a few weeks where both of us could live. It would be perfect for Kevin. The house had been modified from a one family home to a home with a walkout basement unit and upstairs unit. When Kevin comes home, he can have his own apartment in the lower level with his own entrance. I can either walk down the stairs for easy access or use the outside entrance. Support staff would have a garage and separate entrance. I started getting ready to move to our new home.

April 20, 2016

Kevin braved the cool, rainy weather and watched the Twins play the Brewers. It was a good game. To Kevin's delight a Wisconsin team beat the Minnesota team. Thank you for your many prayers. It looks like Kevin will be heading to an Assisted Living TBI VA pilot program possibly as soon as the middle of May. The program specializes in neuro restorative practices.

We know with God all things are possible. Prayers are so powerful.

April 28, 2016

Things are happening for Kevin. He was referred to and accepted into a VA pilot program for rehabilitation of veterans with TBI. This is a national pilot program. There are various sites across the USA. Kevin will be going to southern Illinois for a minimum of six months. I will be sharing more information as it unfolds. Praises!

May 11, 2016

Things are moving along, and Kevin is getting ready for his move to the VA Assisted Living TBI pilot program. He wants to continue making progress towards doing more things for himself. He told me he would love to drive a car again someday. Who knows? With the technological advances that may happen.

Matthew 19:26–With God all things are possible.

May 12, 2016

Kevin is saying "until we meet again" to many people this week. He was at horse therapy today with his veteran buddies and Susie and the other staff at Freedom Farm. They presented him with a cowboy hat. They are looking forward to hearing about his progress at the ALTBI pilot program. He had a great ride, and he looks great wearing his new hat.

May 15, 2016

One last church service followed by our usual breakfast. I will miss doing that every Sunday. Of course, Kevin and Connor had to arm wrestle while waiting for our food. The next journey begins early tomorrow morning. Stay tuned.

God has plans for good things.

May 17, 2016

Day 1 at the ALTBI pilot program. Kevin had a full day with therapies and groups. I was able to observe a few of the sessions in the afternoon. Kevin told me it was a good day. He was tired and ready for a nap by the time he left at 3 p.m. They are also a teaching facility and Kevin may be a part of research projects through the University. Many of the people who have worked there have gone on to have their research published. Thank you for your prayers and thank God for this opportunity for Kevin.

Chapter 14

Posted for friends and family: Pilot Program

May 31, 2016

Kevin has been at the pilot program for two weeks and he looks really good. He is working hard Monday through Friday, and it appears that he is doing well. The weekends are still hard. He isn't as busy but I am working with his team to help them find things that are interesting for him to do. Please keep the prayers going!

Mark 10:27–All things are possible with God.

June 8, 2016

Kevin has been at the pilot program site for almost one month. It has been a tough week–Kevin has been working hard and he is tired. It is the longest time he has been away from family and friends since the accident. I talked to him tonight, and he seemed OK. He has been more edgy with others, according to his staff. I am praying for Kevin as he perseveres through this challenge and that he reflects all the love and prayers we are sending to him across the miles.

June 19, 2016

What a blessing to be with my daughter Erica and her family and Kevin at the pilot program site. Brother and sister still give each other hugs. We went to the church across the parking lot from Kevin's residence. After the service we chatted with the Episcopalian priest. We were all surprised that she had lived very near where I live now. She was a chaplain in the Army and at the same VA hospital where Kevin had spent so many months after the rugby accident. Another member of the congregation works in the behavioral program at the VA located just a few miles from the pilot program site. It sounds like the congregation will surround Kevin with prayers and encourage him each Sunday. God's plans continue to unfold.

Kevin has his evaluation meeting tomorrow and Erica and I are attending. We all appreciate your continuing prayers.

Kevin looks good and I am looking forward to creating his plan for developing more independence.

June 25, 2016

Kevin had a hard time this week after we left. He called frequently. He wasn't asking to come home. Rather, he wanted to know where I was and when I'd be coming back. His life can be frightening–not being able to see, having limited movement, and being dependent on others to assist him. We connected him with the Episcopalian church a mere 100 feet from his residence. Pray that the congregation will surround him and keep him close. The minister is from Saint Paul, MN and was a chaplain in the Army. She understands.

Isaiah 41:10–Fear not for I am with you. Do not be dismayed. I am your God. I will strengthen you; I will help you; I will uphold you with my victorious right hand.

After I got Kevin settled into his room, I asked the pilot program administrator whether it would be helpful for me to make the trip weekly, bi-weekly, or monthly. He indicated that most people don't visit very often. He said, "We find that the participants sometimes depend on family members too much. We want them to become independent. I suggest monthly would be the best."

It is hard for me to trust that Kevin will get what he needs. However, the program was selected by the military, and it was described as the "best of the best." That is what I want for Kevin. I will do everything that I can to make sure he has the best quality of life possible.

Before I leave, I ask the residential staff to let Kevin call me any time he wants to. He has his phone. I request that they continue to work with him on using it independently. He has always used the voice activated system. That's not new to him. He just needs to have the phone always charged and available to him, so that he can use it if he wants it. The support staff at his new residence says, "We don't like to have personal phones in the rooms. Someone might steal them, or they might be broken." I am surprised by that. It is Kevin's phone, and it is his connection to his family and friends. I tell them I want Kevin to have his phone available. Kevin has so little available from his previous life except for his family contacts.

I leave and return home, anxiously awaiting the next month when I would drive the 10 plus hours to see my son and hear the proposed plan for his continuing rehabilitation.

Kevin and I connect by phone a few times during the

month. At first, he is enthusiastic about the program. After the first weekend, he is less enthusiastic. I call the care coordinator and ask her what they are doing to engage him. She explains that the staffing is changing—many of the support team have left because the university is now on summer break. She assures me that this will be resolved quickly. Kevin is supposed to have someone assigned to work directly with him. She assures me that he will have that.

"I would like to know who the support person is," I request. "I can give that person a lot of information and suggestions about how to work best with Kevin. I can also tell Kevin about that person if I know who it is. I have found that it helps him trust people if I can talk to him about the person who is with him."

After all, I explain, he can't see the person and he doesn't know anything about that person. He can be distrustful when he is unsure of what is going on. He has anxiety, depression, PTSD–all symptoms that existed before the rugby accident. These things didn't disappear after the accident.

"He's very complicated," I say. "I can help you and help him get the best results possible."

I want to call in daily to talk with Kevin and to get a report on how things are going. The care coordinator assures me that everything is going well.

"Give us time to get to know him," she says. "We will have a meeting in 30 days. At that point we will review evaluations from the various therapists and the residential staff." I learned that the goal is to collectively build a treatment plan. The VA representative will be at this meeting as well. As a veteran, and part of the pilot program, the VA has a person who is assigned to be part of Kevin's team. That person will sign off on all the reports.

As a part of the pilot program, all of Kevin's reports refer to him as a number rather than a name. He was in the military, so this doesn't totally surprise me, but it makes me uncomfortable and sad. Kevin is a human being, and he is my son. He is so much more than a number on a report.

My daughter and her family are only about 6 hours away from Kevin now. She agrees to come to the meeting. We make plans to have a weekend with Kevin and with each other. "Let's take Kevin out to dinner, bowling, to a baseball game or something fun," I suggested. He enjoys being with his nephew and my daughter and her family. Of course, we will be present for the meeting. We also want to observe some of the therapy sessions. This will be a work visit, and a time for us as a family.

I have almost always been a working mother–often by necessity. I have always wanted to have a close-knit family. Consequently, I have made many conscious choices to plan my time so that I can do both. When my children were little and I was working, I made the decision that I would commit myself to them when I wasn't at work. When I was at work, I would commit myself to my work. I always had my children carry a book to read or something to do if I was supposed to pick them up. As they got older and could walk or ride their bikes home, they were given that option. By then, they were very accustomed to pulling out something to do in case they had to wait for me.

When Kevin was deployed, he told me that he was quite adept at the military "hurry up and wait" philosophy. Knowing that he had a more difficult time reading than his siblings, I asked him, "What do you do when you are in the waiting mode?" I was surprised when he told me he read books. "Real books not audio books?" I inquired.

"Mom," he said. I could imagine him thinking, Come on. I can read."

Kevin told me that there were lots of times when he couldn't use electronics during deployments. He could always read a book. He told me that he carried at least one with him whenever he was deployed. He told me he had some in my locker, too."

"What do you read?" I asked him.

"Science fiction, dystopian stories, history, mysteries, and gaming books," he responded. "You know. The usual."

Now he really can't read anything. He is blind. I think of how hard he worked to be able to read, and I am so very sad. I tell the pilot program the kinds of literature he likes. I work with the vision therapists to find tools that he can use so that literature is accessible for him. Sadly, he needs someone to assist him as the catalogues for books are written, not audio.

Kevin's short-term memory is impaired, and he needs cues and reminders. He needs to have short segments and then discussion about when he heard so that he can integrate his thoughts. He needs to have assistance to learn how to use the tools that he needs to function, and he needs lots of repetition. I try to tell the people who work with Kevin about what he has done in the past and what works for him. They don't want to listen to me. "We will observe and develop our own assessment," the care coordinator tells me.

"How will that work?" I ask.

"We will develop the treatment plan together. You will have input into that plan," the care coordinator responds.

My daughter and I attended the 30-day meeting. I was expecting to receive a report that I could review prior to the meeting, but nothing arrived either by regular mail or by email. We sat in the waiting area for the team to gather. As we waited, we observed other residents enter the building, as well as some of the staff.

Residents represented all ages, both male and female. Some were clearly in their late teens, and some were Kevin's age. Some were older. The population was primarily male, but there were some females. Some of the residents were in wheelchairs, and they arrived in a group separate from those who could move on their own. Those in wheelchairs arrived later than those who could walk on their own. They were divided into groups that rotated through their schedules.

The receptionist sat behind a glass window. Eventually, she came out of the room and asked us who we were, and what we needed. "We are Kevin Ash's family," I responded. "We are here for his 30-day meeting."

"Let me see what I can find out," she said. She returned 15 minutes later. "They are running behind with another meeting. I'll let you know when they are ready." We sat. We waited, wondering what would happen at the meeting.

Finally, we were ushered to a back room where a team was convened to meet with us. The facilitator of the meeting started describing how Kevin had responded during her sessions with him. I listened and took notes. When she was finished, the next person reported on her sessions with Kevin.

"Is it possible for me to have a copy of your reports," I ask. The team looked up silently. Finally, the care coordinator asked, "You don't have a copy?"

"No. We didn't receive anything yet," I said. "I would like to have the copies as we continue."

"I'm sorry," the coordinator said. "We will get you copies later. We can't stop the meeting, or we will not be able to continue schedule. We only have 30 minutes allowed for this meeting."

"What about his treatment plan? When will we develop that?" I asked.

"We will send you that along with the assessment document," the coordinator informed me.

The meeting ended shortly after that. I asked to have the care coordinator meet with me, but she only had a few minutes available. I was disappointed but not deterred. I started writing my notes with my daughter, and I sent those to the team following the meeting.

Posted for friends and family: Pilot Program–Month 2

July 2, 2016

Kevin had a better week. We talked a few times. He received his document reader. This is a computer that will read any print text (documents, typed letters, etc.) He is working hard so that he can gain more independence with the challenges that he faces. It sounds like he will be going to a barbecue and fireworks on July 4th. I know he appreciates all the prayers and comments people share with him. He wishes all his family, friends, and prayer warriors who continue to hold him in their prayers.

July 23, 2016

My daughter, grandson, and I spent a few days with Kevin at the Pilot Program. He is working hard, and it is hard work! We took some time to relax at the minor league baseball game. The game was excellent and the event for the night was "Christmas in July." It was a fun event, and we had a very enjoyable time. Now, it is time to get some rest, enjoy Sunday church and work on Monday.

August 7, 2016

I'm sorry to say that Kevin is very depressed right now. Please surround him with a few extra prayers this week.

I talked with Kevin today. He hasn't been able to go to church for quite a few weeks. Pray that this will also resolve soon. Pray for his case manager who had a family emergency this past week. She will be on leave for a while. Pray for the direct care staff–they need prayers too.

It took several weeks and quite a few phone calls to get the assessment report and Kevin's treatment plan. I don't understand why that was such a difficult request. I understand about family emergencies, probably more than anyone wants to think about. I understand how challenging paperwork can be. This is my son, and I am his guardian. I am charged with advocating on his behalf. I feel like the VA is failing in their promise to provide for him what he needs.

When Kevin was accepted into the ALTBI pilot program, I met with our local VA people. As part of one of our conversations, the staff member asked where I was going to live when I went with Kevin. “I’m not moving with him,” I responded. I was surprised she thought that. “Why did you think I was going to move? I can’t afford to have two residences in two different states. I don’t know how long Kevin will be there. It could be three months to a year. I will visit as often as I can.”

“Oh,” she said. “I just figured you would be there with him. You are so involved in his care.”

“I will still be very involved,” I responded. The conversation ended.

It is hard having Kevin so far away. I feel like I gave the program the opportunity to get to know him without a lot of input from me. I feel like that is not serving Kevin’s best interests. Once I receive the reports, I discover many errors in the details. His official number is written inconsistently. He is described as “paralyzed” and “deaf.” He is described as unable to talk. Not one of these descriptions is true. He can move, although it takes great effort on his part. He can hear, although he needs hearing aids. He can talk when he feels like he has something to say. He has a brain injury. I have been with him from the very beginning. I know him. I study everything I can find so that I can provide him with the best possible outcomes despite his current condition.

His treatment plan indicates that he will have only 3 hours

of rehabilitation per day. They describe him as too depressed to participate. I write to the VA coordinator and express my concerns. She tells me that she really doesn't have anything to do with the program. The VA contracts with them and they are paid to handle everything. I asked her how I would go about communicating my concerns with the Assisted Living TBI Pilot Program administrators. I tell her that I am happy to speak with whomever I need to. "If this is a pilot program, aren't we trying to develop a model that improves outcomes for our veterans?" I ask. These are national people, she tells me. She will share my concerns and get back to me.

I am discouraged but I can't give up hope. Kevin needs to know that his future is hopeful. He needs to know he is loved. I am committed to giving him what he needs.

Chapter 15

Posted for friends and family:

August 28, 2016

Thank God for the Rector of St. Andrew's Episcopal church. We met her when we were there in June. She has been instrumental in helping plan a visit to Kevin, from the people of the congregation. The first person visited him today. She has two therapy dogs and Kevin petted them the whole visit. He told her he wanted the dogs to visit again. So, the plan is that they will begin visiting him every Sunday. We have also secured a volunteer to take him to church beginning next Sunday. The Rector and the congregation are a gift from God.

September 2, 2016

Kevin had a haircut last night. He asked the staff to "take a picture and send it to my mom." He's looking good and the visitors this week seem to have helped a lot. Thank you! Thank you all for your continuing prayers.

September 5, 2016

Prayers were answered yesterday. Kevin made it to church. It has taken three months and he finally got there. Thank you for all the prayers. Kevin had several visitors this past week, and the Rector was instrumental in making that happen. God is good and we keep praying for Kevin.

September 20, 2016

Tomorrow is the third anniversary of Kevin's rugby accident. As I think back over the past three years, I see all the miracles and the angels who have been sent Kevin's way. Still, it has been a long, rough, and rocky road. I pray for each small step forward and that each slip back won't last too long. I am so grateful for your many prayers. As time passes, please continue to keep Kevin in your prayers. God holds him in His hands as He holds us all.

September 26, 2016

Harriet Beecher Stowe is quoted as saying, "Never give up, for that is the place and time that the tide will turn."

Kevin needs our prayers and support as often as we can send them. It has been slow and frustrating these past few months, but I feel the tide is turning. He has friends from St. Andrew's Episcopal church in Carbondale, and our prayers continue from afar.

Blessings, my fellow prayer warriors.

October 11, 2016

I am so thankful for the Rector and her congregation at St. Andrew's church. She has helped bring Kevin visitors who are helping him feel loved and valued. We need your prayers still–Kevin is struggling as he realizes that this new life is his life. I believe in God's power, and I have faith and trust in Him. I know that there will be something good that comes out of this terrible accident.

October 20, 2016

Kevin had a productive day. He worked on moving from a sitting position to a standing position. He also went to choir practice at the church, and he had a good talk with the Rector. At one point he teared up. She told him it is OK to be sad sometimes. We all pray for Kevin, and we love him very much.

When Kevin was in high school, he already started showing his love for service. He took a class called "Youth Service Leadership" twice because he loved it so much. In this class, he worked within the community with various groups. He especially loved working with the elderly. He brought his laptop computer with him each day and taught senior citizens how to use email, Facebook, and navigate the Internet. When the semester ended, they wanted him to continue. He signed up for the class again. When he graduated from high school, the senior citizens gave him a small plaque honoring his service. He loved the feeling he got when he helped others.

It breaks my heart to see how hard it is to help others see that Kevin still has value as a human being. Kevin has lived in this current brain injured, physically impaired, and sensory impaired state for three years now. The people who work with him never knew him as anything different than what they see now. I try to help them see Kevin as I know him. I can't get them to understand. Kevin's world is getting smaller and smaller and smaller. He is more imprisoned than the most hardened convict. He is disappearing a little more each day.

When Kevin was on his first deployment, he was a young man with dreams and hopes. He was setting off on the adventure of his life. He loved the military and he loved serving his country. He felt that he had something of value to offer. He wanted to make a difference in this world.

Kevin traveled the world with the military. In his travels he saw the beauty as well as the destruction, and terror that humans create. At the beginning, he was positive and optimistic about his impact.

During his second deployment, Kevin saw things that I can only imagine. He talked less and less about what he saw and experienced. I found a poem that he wrote mid-way through that long deployment.

Inspired by pain and anger,
I continue to force my body to drive on.
The madness inside me drowns the voices all around me.
Gripped by war, I continue to live on.
Why am I full of this thing inside me?
What is it?
This darkness, this hole that cannot take shape.
I cannot fight its ever-changing shape
As it starts to surround me, drinking the light around it.
But even so my feet will not move.

I will not run!
They stay planted in the blood-stained ground
Like that of aged oak trees standing against the test of time.

I could tell that something was different when he returned from that second deployment. He stayed with me, and he wanted to live in my basement.

"It doesn't have any windows," I said. "It isn't a legal room."

"Mom, I'm fine," he replied. "I like the dark. I like the quiet."

The first time I heard him screaming in the night, my heart raced. I dashed down the two flights of stairs to find him amid a night terror. "INCOMING!" he was screaming. "GET DOWN, GET DOWN!" He didn't remember it at all when I asked him about it in the morning. At least that's what he told me.

He wouldn't drive for the first few months after he returned. "I'm not supposed to drive or drink alcohol for a few months after we get back," he told me. I could understand why. He was so vigilant when he was riding with me. One windy day when I was driving him, he practically jumped out of his skin when a piece of paper blew across the road.

We went to a movie one afternoon. It was a war movie, set in the middle east. In one scene, a body was hanging from a bridge. Kevin told me later that he saw many executed bodies when he was there. As the convoys covered Iraq, he would often ride in the lead vehicle or the last vehicle. He told me of the times that a body would be in the middle of the road. Someone would have to remove it. If it was at the beginning of the convoy, the body would often be moved by someone by the time the last vehicle passed the spot. Someone was always watching them. The enemy was all around them, and often it was as if it was a ghost.

Kevin was surrounded by war. He was surrounded by the real thing, not a game. The things he saw were things we can only imagine from the Hollywood movies we see. Now his memories are bombing him like the IED blasts that he experienced. It is killing his spirit. His reality is breaking my heart.

Now, Kevin can't see, and he can't move without a person helping him. He is blind. He can't eat or relieve himself without someone helping him. He can't walk outside or go to the coffee shop unless someone helps him. He can't watch a movie. He can't turn on the TV. He can't recall something that happened a few hours ago, but he relives parts of his life as clearly as if they were happening right now. His world gets smaller and smaller.

In the movie in my mind, I see him sitting in a room with these images playing over and over in his mind. I see the support staff looking at him and thinking he is incapable of doing anything. Shut the door and his mind travels through the nightmares over, and over again.

Chapter 16

Posted for friends and family: Peace be with you

November 3, 2016

It has been a tough week. I got a phone call on Tuesday morning from the nurse in Illinois. Kevin fell and hit his head twice. Erica headed from Kentucky and Mother Kate answered my call and went to the ER. Thank God that he doesn't appear to have a concussion. He has some scrapes and bruises on his face.

I made some arrangements and flew out early Wednesday morning. Erica and I checked on Kevin and had numerous meetings about the incident and Kevin's health and well-being.

We are watching things closely, even though we are far away. We keep praying...

Colossians 4:2–Don't be weary in prayer; keep at it; watch for God's answers and remember to be thankful when they come.

November 18, 2016

Please pray that the doctors can figure out what is going on with Kevin. He has had two different infections in three weeks and was sent to the ER for the third time in as many weeks. This time he has issues with his intestines. He is very thin–he has lost about 35 pounds. Send him your love.

Philippians 4:6–Don't worry about anything; instead pray about everything; tell God your needs and don't forget to thank Him for His answers.

November 30, 2016

We need your prayers. Things are not going well for Kevin. He continues to lose weight and now weighs less than 140 pounds. He has an appointment at the VA hospital on December 9 to see if a new set of eyes can figure out what is going on. In the meantime, please pray that Kevin can get through this challenge. Surround him in love and prayers.

December 9, 2016

Prayers for Kevin, as things were not looking good last week. After last weekend he had lost another 5 pounds and things had deteriorated even more. We had him taken to the VA emergency room on Tuesday. He was admitted and is being stabilized. He will be transferred by military flight or by helicopter back to the VA Polytrauma floor where he started on Monday. He will likely be there for the next 2 to 4 weeks. After that, I am not sure what will happen next. I am at the hospital now with my daughter through the weekend.

He is in God's hands, and we all need prayers.

December 12, 2016

Kevin arrived at the VA late this afternoon. His doctor and I were able to have a good discussion. He is on the Polytrauma floor again so many of the nurses and staff are the same ones who worked with him three years ago. Please pray for Kevin and the doctors, nurses, and staff. It is so hard to see Kevin going back to where he was three years ago.

All we can do is have faith and know that God holds him in His hands.

December 16, 2016

I wish I could report that the doctors had discovered the cause of Kevin's symptoms. However, the doctors don't know the cause. Kevin has been a trooper–he has been in therapy or tests for the past three days. He still can't swallow without pain. He perseveres and tries to please his caregivers by trying to chew and swallow his food. He tries to do everything that is asked of him, but his body is weak, and he is fatigued. Please keep him in your prayers.

Philippians 4:6-7–Pray about everything; tell God your needs and don't forget to thank him for his answers. If you do this you will experience God's peace, which is far more wonderful than the human mind can understand. His peace will keep your thoughts and your hearts quiet and at rest as you trust in Christ Jesus.

December 18, 2016

Kevin's grandparents were able to visit him today. We sang Christmas songs. Kevin whispered all the words. He fatigued quickly, but he made a valiant effort. He opened his Christmas present from them–a warm new robe and enjoyed a peppermint candy cane. Keep prayers coming. Thank you to all his prayer warriors.

On the evening of Friday, December 23, I receive an email from Kevin's doctor. In it, I have the results of the assessments. The scar tissue in his brain is growing, and impacting on his brain, including the brain stem. His brain is dying. His brain is one third smaller than it used to be. He will not survive.

I am angry. I am alone. It is the holiday. None of the regular doctors will be back until after the holiday. I am shaking with anger. "How can this be happening? What is happening? Why is this happening?" I cry my questions in my prayers to God.

I go back to the hospital in the morning. The staff ask me where I want him to go. He can't stay on the rehab floor because there will not be any more rehabilitation. "Can't he go to the hospice unit here?" I ask. We make the journey through the hospital to tour the palliative care unit. I submit the paperwork to request a bed. I wait.

I sing Christmas carols to Kevin. I wait. Deep in my mind, I remember the funeral for the stepdaughter of a co-worker. She had died tragically after a short 25 years of a life of trials. Her mother spoke at her daughter's funeral. I remember thinking, "I would never be able to be as strong as she is. I can't imagine losing a child."

December 24, 2016

May God's love shine upon you this Christmas Eve and Christmas Day. It has been a long journey for Kevin. He has been undergoing many tests these past two weeks. He will be taking another path next week as he will be moved to the VA Palliative Care Unit at the hospital on Tuesday, December 27. I know that God is sheltering him in His arms and that one-day Kevin will go home at last. He will be perfect, and his broken body will be healed.

Prayers

The days and nights are so quiet now. Kevin no longer has nurses prodding him and poking him. Yes, they check on him, but it is a time of watching for them. They are waiting for the time that he will leave this world behind him.

It is so very quiet, except when I hear my son whisper, "Mom, what is happening to me?" I think to myself of all that has transpired since that fateful day in September before our lives changed so drastically.

So many things are happening. Why are they happening? I think back just a few months when I learn that Kevin is failing quickly. The ALTBI program staff would tell me that he won't get out of bed. He kicks the walls. He yells out. Then he is silent. They told me to take him home. I wanted to take him home. How can I do that? If I remove him from the program, I am told that he would longer be their responsibility. They won't assist me in finding an alternative place to allow me to make the arrangements to get him home. I told them that what I see is failure neurologically or biologically. "Aren't there any tests we can run to find out what is going on," I begged them.

I remember that they agreed that he will be transferred to a higher-level VA hospital a few hours away. I agreed to the appointment, and I worked on plan to get Kevin home. I worked with my contacts in my town and began the search for a bed somewhere or competent care givers that I can hire to assist Kevin at my house. I talked with my landlord about building a ramp and making the house more handicapped accessible. I am so grateful that I had the time to devote to this important work.

After a phone call with the ALTBI director, we agree that he will be transported to the VA hospital in which he started in 2013 when he is medically stable to travel. He has bed sores. He won't talk much. He doesn't eat. He weighs under 120 pounds now. They want to insert a feeding tube. My daughter and I pray and cry when we see him. We try all our tricks to engage him, and he gives us a sad smile.

We feed him milkshakes and popsicles. After we investigate the options with a feeding tube, I agree with my family. He will have a DNR/DNI in place. He will not have a feeding tube. The doctor meets with me and asks me if I understand that decision. I cry and cry. No mother should have to make this decision. It would take a court of law to remove the feeding tube if it were placed. I know that he doesn't want to live in a world that has no hope for the future.

It breaks my heart that Kevin has worked so hard and still he is failing. I know he has a brain injury. I know he faces many challenges. I cry as I think about all the struggles he faces every day. A lot of them are struggles because those who work with him don't understand what he needs, or they can't give him what he needs.

I recall my thoughts when we were planning for his release from the VA Hospital. I think about how the group home environment is not an environment that allows my son to live as he was able to live when he was not disabled. I learned that the environment is controlled by staffing requirements, work shifts, and programmatic rules. While regulations may be necessary, the resulting environment is clearly an institution. Putting the house in a residential area does not make the house a home. I learn from my observations that people with disabilities, like my son, are being held hostage through the current system that does not provide or any other viable option other than the group home long term care facility or "adult foster care facility."

In the silence of this, his final deployment, hospice care, I watch him, and I remember his life on Earth. I want to engrave his life in my mind.

My son, Kevin, graduated in 2001 and he started his career in the Minnesota Army National Guard in 2002. He took the core values to heart, and he served in three active-duty tours over the course of the following ten years and was honorably discharged in 2012. I saw his youthful idealism gradually erode into a stoic demeanor. He spent many holidays and birthdays in combat zones. Each time he returned from a tour of duty, he told me that his experiences would never be totally understood by anyone who has not served in combat. He told me that, as a soldier, he knew that no matter what happened, his countrymen would support him.

The memories of his life after his rugby accident play like a movie in my mind. Kevin lived in what the state of Minnesota calls a group home long term care facility or an "adult foster care facility" due to a catastrophic brain injury and loss of oxygen to his brain from an accidental injury he sustained in 2013. He is blind and he has brain injury that is manifested in very limited short-term memory, cognitive impairment, and right-side weakness. Despite these challenges, Kevin is very aware that his life has changed dramatically. He knows that he is in a place that is not his home. Kevin has good language skills, and he communicates clearly and frequently that he wants to go home.

I hold on to the memories of those days when he asked me to go home. I replay his final voice message on my phone just to hear his voice, "Hey, Mom. I'm calling you back."

Even now, Kevin knows that I am his guardian. On a bad day, he blames me for his current housing arrangement. He wants to be with his friends and family. He wants to choose his bedtime. He wants to live with people he knows. He wants to get a job, finish a 4-year degree, and find someone with whom he can have a lifelong relationship and maybe even have children. Still, he worries about me. He always thought he would take care of me when I needed him.

To bring Kevin into hospice care is a heartbreaking decision. The memories of the past 3 years run through my mind like a movie. I know the ending and I can't change it. I wish he could share more time with me.

Now in the hospice unit, Kevin has become more withdrawn and quieter. I ask him what I could do to make him smile. He whispers, "Nothing," then says, three times, louder with each repetition, "Get me out of here." My heart tears apart. The effort that these cost him are visible.

I hear the night nurse walking down the hall. I hear the quiet sounds of another family crying in the hallway. I know that another veteran has just passed from this world. Kevin's time left on this Earth is short. I want to remember the good things and I think back to a time when Kevin initiated the process to stand. That was a beautiful day. I asked him if he wanted to get out of the wheelchair. He said that he did. I helped him stand. The support staff came into the room and told him that it was time to use the toilet. As he was standing, the support person started to tell him to sit down in the wheelchair. I told her that he could walk to the bathroom. Because I was there, the person assisted him in walking the 12 feet to the bathroom. At one of his meals this week, the support person tried to guide his hand to some food on the plate without asking him if he needed help. I was there, and heard Kevin tell the person, "I can eat by myself." He wanted to be independent to the end.

Kevin loved going to movies. I remember when one of his support staff was talking and noticed that the theater started shows at 6 am. "Why would anyone go to a movie at 6 am," he said. I responded that Kevin used to work third shift and he would go to a 6 a.m. movie after work on occasion.

I think about the times since the accident that we were

able to go to a movie. He listens to the secondary descriptive audio. I remember the time he reached for my hand, and he held it throughout the movie. I wondered what it would be like to have no affectionate personal contact day after day. He has people who watch for his safety, and care for his physical needs, but unless I am with him (or another family member) he does not have the normal emotional and affectionate physical contact that the rest of us enjoy and need. About two hours into the movie, he pulled the headset off, leaned over and said, "Mom, I want to go home. Please, mom, I want to go home." When we left the theater, I hugged him, and told him I was leaving. He asked, "Why can't I go with you?" I wish that I had the opportunity for him to live at his own home. Even though I had to tell him that he was sleeping at the group home, I always thought that I would see him "tomorrow."

The hospice doctor checks on him every day. He is mostly silent. We now know that we must start talking about the final part of his journey.

My mind still struggles to wrap about what has happened to Kevin and to our lives. Just a few short weeks ago, he had to travel by air ambulance back to the very same VA Hospital where he started. He has many of the same staff that he had in the beginning of this journey. They are saddened by this turn of events. I ask for all tests possible.

It is so quiet on the hospice floor, but my mind keeps searching for memories. Kevin looks so much like he did when he first came to the VA hospital just two months after the rugby accident, and almost exactly three years ago.

In the movie in my mind, I replay each of the times that he achieved what none of his medical staff thought he could do. I see him singing "Amazing Grace" for the doctors and for his family. I see him standing and singing the songs in church. I see him singing into the phone on his grandma's birthday "You are my Sunshine." I see him laughing as he sings "Old MacDonald had a Farm." He says, "And on the farm he had a snake…" And he laughs.

I see him at the rehabilitation program meeting new staff. When I ask him if he wants to tell them anything before, they leave. He breaks out in song, "The sun will come out tomorrow."

I see him working out at the fitness center with his trainer. I hear him answer the question, "How far do you want to walk today?"

He answers, "As far as I have to."

In the movie in my mind, I see him with hope.

Now I see him as a shell of the boy, a shell of the man he came to be, and it breaks my heart more than I can bear.

"You need to make arrangements for his funeral," my daughter tells me. "I don't think he is going to make it through this time." I don't want to do that. I don't want to think about it, but I must.

My daughter and her spouse help me research and we pick a funeral home near the hospital. I make an appointment and meet with the funeral director. I tell Kevin's story again. He looks at me with compassion. Kevin will be cremated. We look at the urns and I take pictures to send to my parents and family. I want to have everything prepared and paid for now. I hope that we will not need to use it for a long, long time, but I know that my hope can't make that happen.

Kevin doesn't say much anymore. He listens for me. I can see sadness in his blind blue eyes. He holds my hand. He whispers, "I love you, Mom."

My heart breaks when I recall the day that we had to decide that Kevin would be moved to the palliative care unit. It was on December 27 when the regular staff returned from the Christmas holiday. It will be his last step in the journey on this earth. My daughter and I stay near him. "He doesn't need all of these medications," I tell the doctor, "Let him be at peace, and let him be present. Please don't drug him into unconsciousness." The doctor agrees to remove the medications. Kevin calls to me often. Nights are the worst. He wants assurance. I am with him, and I sing to him. I tell him that he is a child of God. I tell him he is smart and brave and loved. I tell him he is handsome, strong, and courageous. I tell him he will be going home. They want to give him a prescription for morphine. When he cries out for me, the staff and the other patients are disturbed.

"How long will this last? He is wasting away. Surely, this can't go on much longer."

I give them permission for morphine. He sleeps.
The doctor doesn't say much. The chaplain comes often and tells me that all will be well. I tell family and friends that it is time for them to see Kevin one last time. Many come to hold his hand one more time. It is unbearably hard to see him disappear before our eyes.

January 11, 2017

Time is short for Kevin, and we know he is in God's hands. He continues to fight the good fight. One day he will be free of all the pain of this world and his body will be perfect–the lame will walk, and the blind will see. I will keep you posted. Thank you for your prayers.

2 Timothy 4:7-8–I have fought the good fight, I have finished the race, I have kept the faith. Now there is in store for me the crown of righteousness, which the Lord, the righteous Judge, will award to me on that day–and not only to me, but also to all who have longed for His appearing.

In the movie in my mind, I replay the message that he shared with his sister before he was evacuated from combat in his final tour of duty. "I love you. I love Mom and I love my dad and I love my brother. Tell them that. I want you to remember that always," he tells her. "One day I am going to head out and I will not come back. I want to disappear from this world." That was the beginning of this long farewell.

His brother comes home from college. His father stays with him at night. We will be with him to the end of this time on Earth. He whispers to me, "Mom, where am I?"

"You're in your bedroom," I tell him. "We are all with you. Your dad is here. Your sister is here. Your brother is here. We love you. You are not alone." He closes his eyes, and yet still he lives.

I find friends who come to sing for him. They sing for hours. I pray that he will go with songs surrounding him. A cousin brings her puppy who snuggles next to him. The puppy kisses his cheek. He still breathes.

The nurses check for the signs. Still, he lives. I make arrangements for donating his organs. It is unbelievable. He is dying in hospice. His organs can't be accepted for transplant. I am so angry that not even his dying wish will be satisfied. In death he will not be able to serve one last time.

I remember the brain research project at Boston University that is studying Chronic Traumatic Encephalopathy in athletes. I ask him if he wants to donate his brain. He gives me a nod as he tries to squeeze my hand. I ask to have it donated after his death. "Where would we do that?" I am asked.

"I don't know how to do it," I say. "I just know it from articles I have read. It is through Boston University." I am grateful when one of the social workers tells me she will take my request to her superiors, and someone will let me know. The next day, the paperwork is started. I am called into the office and begin yet more paperwork. Arrangements are made to harvest his brain, his eyes, his spinal cord, and his spinal cord upon his death. It will be transported to Boston University within 24 hours. I ask what feels like 100 times, "How can we make sure that everything is ready? I don't want any mistakes with this." I will make sure his dying wish is fulfilled.

It has been over two weeks and he is still holding on. I try to be calm and peaceful with him, but it is a façade. I am sobbing in my heart. "He deserves peace," I tell myself.
The nurse calls us to his bedside. "He looks like this will be

his last day," she says. Still, he breathes. The doctor and the nurses shake their heads. "He is so young and strong," they say. His heart is so strong."

"Yes," I think to myself one more time. "You are strong and brave and determined. You are courageous and kind. You are smart and handsome. You are a child of God. You are not alone."

Three more days pass and still he lives. Then, I tell my daughter that I can't go on anymore. She tells me to go and try to sleep. She will call me if anything changes. Reluctantly, I head out to where we are staying at the Fisher House. It is hard to walk in and out of this house. All the people who are staying there have family at the hospital. They are so filled with hope. They are filled with the promise that things will get better. We were once at that place, too. My daughter tells me, "It is so hard to be there, Mom," she says. "I see the hope in their eyes. I don't want them to lose that hope. And yet, Kevin is dying. He will leave this place in death." I quietly move to our room. I call my daughter and she assures me that she will call me if things change.

I fall into a deep sleep. I am awakened by my phone. "Come back now," my daughter says. I gather my things and travel the short few blocks back to the hospice unit. It is midnight and it is cold. The snow is blowing. It is like the day that he was born 35 years ago this month.

I arrive at the hospital. Kevin's dad, sister, and brother are there, along with one dear friend. The night nurse is standing watch at the door. His breathing is labored and shallow. But still he breathes. I crawl onto the bed with him.

I hold him in my arms. I whisper into his ear. "We are all with you. It is okay. Your family is here. You are loved. You will only be alone for a moment. It is okay. You are going home. You are loved." I start singing "Hush little baby, don't say a word. Momma's going to buy you a mockingbird." I whisper Psalm 23. "Though I walk through the valley of the shadow of death, thou art with me." Still, he breathes.

Finally, I whisper in the quietest of voices, "Kevin, it is okay. All you have to do is Just. Stop. Breathing. It will just be a moment. Your grandparents and all of those who have gone before you will be there. You will be in the arms of Jesus." He lets out his breath. His breathing stops. He has said his final goodbye just 10 days before his 35th birthday and 21 days after he entered hospice.

The nurses cover his face with bags of ice. They want us to leave the room. They must get him ready to harvest his brain. I won't leave. I watch as they prepare him to travel on his last journey, to the morgue. It is now 1:30 am. A call goes out and hospital staff line the hallway for this last journey. His body is covered with a Blue Star flag. We surround the gurney as we walk silently through the hallway. Some of the staff are soldiers. They salute him as he passes by. He is gone as the elevator door closes.

January 15, 2017

Kevin Ash was a warrior until the end. He passed away January 15 at 12:50 a.m. CST. He will continue to serve, as his brain is being donated to the Concussion Legacy Foundation Brain Bank at Boston University where he will represent high school athletes, veterans, and rugby players in this important research.

John 14:27–Peace I leave with you; my peace I give you. Do not let your hearts be troubled and do not let them be afraid.

The funeral is beautiful. It is filled with friends and family. Some of the soldiers who were in his squad are present. Some of his rugby team are present. He has touched so many lives. The Masonic Temple performs the Scottish sacred rites. The bagpipes play "Amazing Grace." We show his story in pictures and in the awards that he earned in combat. Some of his support staff and hospital staff join us.

His urn is buried with military honors 6 months later at the Fort Snelling National Cemetery in Minneapolis. That is a hot July summer day. A friend of a friend arranges for a fly over. I cry yet more tears.

Even now, I know he is still with me. Sometimes, deep in the night, I sense his presence. He tells me he loves me and that all is OK. In my dreams he is strong and perfect. He is glowing. He is healthy and happy. He is free at last.

Some quotes help me understand. A friend shared with me that her uncle once said, "You are born into death and die into life." C.S. Lewis said, "There are far better things ahead than what we leave behind." Dietrich Bonhoeffer reminded us that "God does not give us everything we want, but He does fulfill His promises leading us along the best and straightest paths to Himself."

I find myself walking down the hospital hallway once again. It is dark outside, and the hallway lights are dim. The quiet is punctuated by my footsteps. They seem to say, "I. Want. To. See. My Son." My pace picks up as I near the door. I push the door open with a swoosh and I burst into the room. It is late at night and the nurse at the desk looks up.

"You can see him anytime you want," he says as he points to another door. My heart beats through my chest as I open the door and see an emaciated figure on the bed, highlighted by the hospital bed light. "That is not my son," I say out loud. I start to turn and feel a tap on my shoulder. I spin around and see him–my son. He has his John Bong stick in his left hand. He is strong and healthy. He is glowing. He reaches out and wraps his arms around me. He says, "I love you, Mom." I hold him close, and we stand together. I say, "Kevin, how are you doing?" He leans and whispers in my ear, "I'm doing fine." He has always answered with that–I'm doing fine.

I hold him and he hugs me. "But how are you really doing, Kevin," I whisper in his ear. He holds me just a little tighter and waits until he whispers back, "Mom, I'm doing great." My heart soars and I feel tears in my eyes. As the tears spill onto his chest. I hold on like I never will let go. I know this is a dream, and I don't want it to end. I want to hold this memory forever.

When I wake up, I open my eyes and look at the dark room. I get up and make breakfast. I know that he is doing great, and that I can see him in my dreams. I know that we will be together again one day.

This life on Earth is but a moment in time. Kevin taught me that this very moment is the moment in which we live. All things on this Earth will pass away. We must do what we can in our life for good. We must trust God.

Epilogue

On July 6 in the year of his death, I was notified that Kevin had been diagnosed with CTE Level 2 that was connected to his many IED blast exposures in combat. His brain had been injured and had started to deteriorate over the next six years. The one blow from the rugby accident did damage, but it didn't cause the CTE to develop. I was assured by Dr. Ann McKee from Boston University that Kevin's brain will contribute to many others as they study the miracle that makes us humans who live, love, hope and dream. It is Kevin's legacy that one day no one else will have to suffer in silence through the unknown while disappearing from this Earth.

January 2018–CBS 60 Minutes did a feature story on veterans who suffered brain injuries in Iraq. Kevin was featured in the story.

September 26, 2018–KARE 11 TV station in Minnesota produced a story sharing the story of veterans and CTE. This story was awarded an Emmy in 2019.